CHANGING BODIES, CHANGING MEANINGS

CHANGING BODIES, CHANGING MEANINGS

Studies on the human body in antiquity

Edited by Dominic Montserrat

London and New York

First published 1998
by Routledge
11 New Fetter Lane, London EC4P 4EE

Simultaneously published in the USA and Canada
by Routledge
29 West 35th Street, New York, NY 10001

Typeset in Garamond by
Ponting–Green Publishing Services, Chesham, Buckinghamshire

Printed and bound in Great Britain by
Biddles, Guildford and King's Lynn

British Library Cataloguing in Publication Data
A catalogue record for this book is available from
the British Library

Library of Congress Cataloguing in Publication Data
Changing bodies, changing meanings: studies on the human body in
antiquity / edited by Dominic Montserrat.
p.   cm.
Includes bibliographical references and index.
1. Body, Human, in literature. 2. Body, Human–History–Social
aspects. 3. Literature, Ancient–History and criticism.
I. Montserrat, Dominic, 1964
PN56.B62C48   1997
809'.9336–dc21   97–2928

ISBN 0–415–13584–2

CONTENTS

Part III Modifying the early Christian body

Part IV The ancient body's trajectory through time

PLATES

ix

FIGURES

NOTES ON
CONTRIBUTORS

Angus Bowie is Lobel Fellow in Classics at The Queen's College, Oxford, and author of *The Poetic Dialect of Sappho and Alcaeus* (New York 1981) and *Aristophanes: myth, ritual and comedy* (Cambridge 1993).

Gillian Clark is a Senior Lecturer in Classics at the University of Liverpool. She works on the interrelation of 'pagan' and Christian culture in late antiquity.

Richard Hawley is Lecturer in Classics at Royal Holloway, University of London. His doctoral thesis was on gender in Attic drama. Publications include: contributions to *The Bloomsbury Guide to Women's Literature*; articles on women philosophers, Athenaeus, Aspasia, Greek declamation, and he was also co-editor of *Women in Antiquity: new assessments* (London 1995). He is currently finishing *Greek Drama: a sourcebook* and *Greek Drama: an introduction* (both for Routledge). Since 1988 he has co-organised the Oxford 'Women in Antiquity' seminar series.

Lynn Meskell studied for her PhD in archaeology at King's College, Cambridge and is now Junior Research Fellow at New College, Oxford. Her current interests are the application of feminism and queer theory to archaeology, the sociopolitical implications of the discipline, and Mediterranean and Egyptian archaeologies. She has written widely on debates surrounding sex, gender and the body in antiquity, and is currently editing *Archaeology Matters* for Routledge.

Dominic Montserrat is Lecturer in Classics and Ancient History at the University of Warwick. He is the author of *Sex and Society in Graeco–Roman Egypt* (London 1996) and co-editor of *From Constantine to Julian: pagan and Byzantine views* (London 1995). He has contributed many articles to journals and is currently researching a book about the presentation of Egypt in English popular fiction between 1860 and 1940.

Penelope Murray is Lecturer in Classics at the University of Warwick. She is particularly interested in ancient poetics, and her publications include *Genius: the history of an idea* (Oxford 1989) and *Plato on Poetry* (Cambridge 1996). She is currently working on a book on the Muses.

Jane Stevenson was educated at Cambridge. She went on to be a research fellow of Pembroke College, and then Lecturer in Late Antique History at the University of Sheffield. In 1995, she became a Warwick Research Fellow in the Humanities.

Nicholas Vlahogiannis has taught Ancient History in the Department of History, University of Melbourne, where he also completed his doctorate. In 1992–4 he was a Visiting Fellow in the Centre for Hellenic Studies, King's College, London.

Terry Wilfong is currently Assistant Curator at the Kelsey Museum of Archaeology, University of Michigan, and editor of *Bulletin of the American Society of Papyrologists*. He received a PhD in Egyptology from the University of Chicago in 1994, and has lectured and published extensively on ancient, Graeco-Roman and Late Antique Egypt.

ACKNOWLEDGEMENTS

This book is the product of many minds and bodies, all of whom deserve acknowledgement, recognition and thanks. My first debt goes to all the contributors to the *Anthropometamorphosis* conference and their patience as this project developed, and in particular to Angus Bowie, who stepped in with a contribution to fill a vacant slot literally at the last minute. Then there are those speakers who, for various reasons, were unable to submit their contributions to this volume: Alan Griffiths, Matthew Leigh and Eleni Vassilika. Also, there are all the participants who made the conference such a stimulating couple of days, especially Desbina Christodoulou, Matthew Fox, Lin Foxhall, Mary Harlow, Eirann Marshall and Alison Sharrock. I thank the British Academy and the University of Warwick's Humanities Research Centre for providing generous financial support, and I owe a major debt of gratitude to the staff of the centre, Peter Mack and Marian Franklin, for making the logistical arrangements for the conference run so smoothly. My co-workers in the Classics Department at Warwick University were always interested in and supportive of this project. I would like to thank particularly Michael Whitby, who kindly made the engravings in his magnificent 1632 copy of Ovid's *Metamorphoses* available for illustrations, and Mark Vermes, who did much of the initial proofreading of articles and conversion of computer discs. Friends from different Departments of Warwick University and other institutions were also very helpful and enthusiastic, especially Sue Wiseman, Bridget Bennett, Kate Chedgzoy and Maria Wyke, who read various parts of the manuscript. Angela and James, my parents, also read the final manuscript and spotted many mistakes and inconsistencies: many, many thanks to them. Sue Hogarth deserves thanks for inspiring part of my own contribution, and also for providing the photograph of the mummy in the Niagara Falls Museum. At Routledge, I would like to thank Richard Stoneman, for having faith in the project, and his efficient editorial assistants: Vicky Peters, Ruth Schafer and Coco Stevenson. Finally, this book is for M. D.: *ut fulvum spectatur in ignibus aurum, tempore sic duro est inspicienda fides* (Ovid).

ILLUSTRATION ACKNOWLEDGEMENTS

The editor and publisher also wish to thank the following for permission to reproduce copyright material. Every effort has been made to contact copyright holders and we apologise for any inadvertent omissions.

The Egypt Exploration Society, London, for Plates 7.1 and 7.2; Sue Hogarth and Fred Farnham for Plate 9.1; the Petrie Museum of Egyptian Archaeology, University College London for Plate 9.2; Michael Whitby for the frontispiece and Plate 5.1.

ABBREVIATIONS

Abbreviations of the works of ancient authors in the text and footnotes generally follow those used in *A Greek-English Lexicon*, ed. H. G. Liddell and R. Scott (9th edition, revised by H. S. Jones, Oxford 1940) and *The Oxford Latin Dictionary*, ed. P. G. W. Glare (Oxford 1982): it is hoped that any divergences are self-explanatory. The following are the abbreviations used in references to journals, series or collections of ancient sources:

AAASH	*Acta Antiqua Academiae Scientiarum Hungaricae*
AB	*Analecta Bollandiana*
AJP	*American Journal of Philology*
ARC	*Archaeological Review from Cambridge*
BAR	*Biblical Archaeology Review*
BASP	*Bulletin of the American Society of Papyrologists*
BICS	*Bulletin of the Institute of Classical Studies of the University of London*
BMCR	*Bryn Mawr Classical Review*
CAJ	*Cambridge Archaeological Journal*
CQ	*Classical Quarterly*
CR	*Classical Review*
CSCO	*Corpus Scriptorum Christianorum Orientalium*, Louvain
CSEL	*Corpus Scriptorum Ecclesiasticorum Latinorum*, Vienna, 1866–
DE	*Discussions in Egyptology*
Diels-Kranz	Diels, H. (ed.) revised by W. Kranz, *Die Fragmente der Vorsokratiken*, Berlin, 1961
FGrH	Jacoby, F. (ed.) *Die Fragmente der griechischen Historiker*, Leiden, 1923–58

FHG	Müller, C. (ed.) *Fragmenta historicorum graecorum*, Paris, 1870
HSCP	*Harvard Studies in Classical Philology*
JAA	*Journal of Anthropological Archaeology*
JAC	*Jahrbuch für Antike und Christentum*
JEA	*Journal of Egyptian Archaeology*
JECS	*Journal of Early Christian Studies*
JHS	*Journal of Hellenic Studies*
JMA	*Journal of Mediterranean Archaeology*
JRA	*Journal of Roman Archaeology*
JRS	*Journal of Roman Studies*
MDIA	*Mitteilungen des Deutschen Instituts für ägyptische Altertumskunde in Kairo*
PCPhS	*Proceedings of the Cambridge Philological Society*
PG	*Patrologia Graeca*
PL	*Patrologia Latina*
PP	*Past and Present*
RB	*Revue Bénédictine*
RE	*Pauly's Real-Encyclopädie der classischen Altertumswissenschaft, herausgegeben von Georg Wissowa*, Stuttgart, 1892–1957
ROC	*Revue de l'Orient Chrétien*

1

INTRODUCTION

Dominic Montserrat

Man Transform'd, or The Artificiall Changeling; A view of the people of the Whole World or, a short survey of their Policies, Dispositions, Naturall Deportments, Complexions, Ancient and Moderne Customes, Manners, Habits and Fashions. A Worke every where adorned with Philosophicall, Morall and Historicall Observations on the Occasions of their Mutations and Changes throughout all Ages.

The seventeenth-century physician John Bulwer's book, better known by its neologistic classical title *Anthropometamorphosis*, 'humanity-changing', provided the inspiration for a conference held in the Classics Department at Warwick University in April 1994. The papers delivered there are the nucleus of this collection. The idea unifying the contributions was to adopt a form of Bulwer's methodology, and approach the body in the ancient world through a single aspect: different types of modification, which was to be defined in the broadest sense. The conference itself was a response to the growing awareness of the problematic status of the human body, particularly the ancient body, as an historiographical category. In some ways, the study of the ancient body is developing along lines comparable with early studies of ancient women: indeed, much scholarship on the body in antiquity has a direct link with the study of sex and gender, though by and large it has avoided the same methodological pitfalls.[1] Recent studies on the ancient body are withdrawing from the idea of 'the body' as an undifferentiated, nomothetic category (as 'women' were considered) and are beginning to examine the diversity and complexity of attitudes, practices and contexts. Concentrating on ideas surrounding *change, modification* and *transition* seemed to be an interesting way of exploring the plurality of the ancient body. Speakers were asked to think about

1

how the different ways in which the body altered could be a means of conveying ideologies – of status and control, of gender and ethnicity, of nature and culture. Sometimes in antiquity, body modification constituted a social norm, such as among Herodotus' tattooed Thracians; when modification was not normative, what was being delineated by opposition? Was body modification the constraint of a natural structure to a societal norm? Do ancient forms of modification have anything to contribute to the debate on whether the most fundamental structures of the group are anchored in the most basic experiences of the body?

Having said that, the work of an obscure doctor writing in England under the Commonwealth might seem a strange point of departure for a collection of essays on the changing body in antiquity. Because of the splendid woodcut illustrations in the 1654 edition of *Anthropometamorphosis*, Bulwer is most often encountered in popular books on the history of bodily 'aberration', implying that his project was the same kind of ethnographic antiquarianism. In such books, Bulwer's modified bodies mutate once again, into quaint props in an exotic, otherly environment.[2] But Bulwer was doing something very different. *Anthropometamorphosis* was one of the first early modern works of what might now be termed comparative cultural anthropology, and an early study of the body as social metaphor. As the epigraph to the title page of the 1654 edition shows, Bulwer presents a pluralist world composed of diverse societies, which are in turn composed of living, functioning individual bodies – bodies which change according to societal pressures or geographical conditions. Bulwer was also aware of the links between the fragmented, mutable, *social* bodies he described and his own time and place: the changing body politic of an England which had executed its King and was experimenting with a new form of government.

Anthropometamorphosis was not the first book by Bulwer to place the changed or divergent human body at its centre. As a physician, Bulwer was a pioneer in audiology, with a special interest in teaching the deaf to lip-read and speak, or to communicate by using sign-language. Previously, he had published *Chirologia: or the Naturall Language of the Hand* (1644) and *Philocophus; or the Deafe and Dumbe Man's Friend. Exhibiting the Philosophicall Verity of that subtle Art, which may inable one with an observant Eie, to hear what any man speaks by the moving of his Lips ... apparently proving that a Man borne Deafe and Dumbe may be taught to Heare the sound of words with his Eie, and thence learn to speake with his*

Tongue (1648).[3] The latter book is movingly dedicated to two deaf aristocrats, Sir Edward Gostwicke and his younger brother William, as well as to 'all other intelligent and ingenious gentlemen, who as yet can neither hear nor speake'. For Bulwer, the modified or aberrant body is a means for people to communicate across boundaries: his bodies speak. And while he is suspicious of the blasphemy implicit in body modification – why should man want to alter what God has made perfect? – he still treats these bodies with empathy. In fact, Bulwer saw the ancient world as being superior to his own times in this respect. Commenting on the physical changes wrought by midwives or nurses on the new-born, he says that they

> abolish that figure which is preternatural & introduce into the head the shape desired. Afterwards (as *Pansa* saith) all the body is to be extended & remitted, and every part reminded of its office. And these crimes both of commission and omission, committed by Midwives & Nurses so frequently in these times against the tender bodies of Infants, appear more notorious if we reflect upon the carefull practise of ancient times in this matter of high concernment.

It is important to note Bulwer's empathy with the strange or changing bodies he describes, because this is one of the central themes that emerged in the papers presented at the conference which appear in this volume.

Anthropometamorphosis is a very topical subject. Those of us living in Europe in the late 1990s are confronted with modified bodies in all kinds of contexts. Extensively tattooed and body-pierced individuals are visible on the street or in the lecture theatre. TV guides now routinely contain advertisements for clinics offering breast implants, liposuction and other forms of cosmetic adaptation. Change of the human body is being taken to the limits of technology, though one might argue that this is not a wholly modern phenomenon. An Egyptian mummy, for example, is a sort of cyborg in that it represents the maximum technological effort available to transform the body at that time and place. Permanent modifications such as abortion, dentistry and cosmetic surgery were also available to the ancients. Yet with growing sophistication, the manifestations of our ability to modify the body become more extreme. Contemporary body artists like Orlan and Stelarc experiment with different somatic boundaries. They attempt to transcend the (corpo)real by grafting coral 'horns' onto the forehead or the largest physically sustainable

nose onto the face. At the same time they raise questions about ownership and control of the body as biotechnology develops. Will it be possible for individuals in the future to go beyond the parameters of their genetic codes and determine the shape of their bodies via their own, chosen DNA sequences?

On one level, Bulwer's *Anthropometamorphosis* might be used by the body artists and sociologists who see the (modern) body as the cultural product *ne plus ultra*.[4] The sociologists argue that pervasive images of the modified body, of the kind I have outlined above, reflect the separation of the body from the political and economic strictures of society. These socio-cultural changes have been connected with the end of feudalism dependent on élite land ownership, the rise of industrial capitalism, and the emergence of a post-modern world based on control of communications and sign-systems where traditional links between property, the body and sexuality have become blurred. Self-identity is now more strongly invested in the corporeal self, and now more value is added to the body through the processes of commodification and enhancement. For sociologists like Bryan Turner and Anthony Giddens, the modified human body is a product of high modernity, and as such is a locus for theorisation about structures and movements that go far beyond the limits of the individual body. To put it another way, many post-modern treatments of the human body, and of the modified body in particular, are not about the body at all. They have little connection with the emotional and experiential reality of inhabiting a body, whether changed or unchanged. Bodies observed and theorised are bodies cast adrift from their human occupants.

For the ancient world, this approach is not entirely adequate. Nor is a Foucauldian archaeology of the body, with its tendency to place less emphasis on individuality and human intentionality than on (male) strategies of control over the body. Modern responses to the ancient body which do not take cognisance of such notions can too easily degenerate into ethnographic lists of bodily practices and prodigies, or present the ancient human body as a passive spectacle or museum artefact.[5] Many ancient bodies have been treated in this way, such as the remains of those who fell victim to the eruption of Vesuvius. Their bodies are not only acorporeal (constructed from plaster blown into the matrix left in the hardened volcanic ash after the body decayed), but also ancient and otherly. As such they are not invested with the emotive realities of their lives – and of their deaths from asphyxiation. Literary treatments of the destruction of Pompeii

4

have taken the bodies as their starting point, such as Théophile Gautier's novel *Arria Marcella*. The plot hinges on a scene at Pompeii where the protagonist, Octavian, views a glass case containing a mass of solidified volcanic ash on which the outline of a dead woman's body is imprinted. In Octavian's mind, the dead Roman woman becomes transfigured into a member of an ideal harem of ancient beauties, including Cleopatra, Semiramis and Aspasia, all because of the curve of her body preserved by the eruption. The Pompeian body, then, becomes re-animated by a fetishistic attention to its preserved parts.[6] Egyptian mummies are another example of the same phenomenon. The body is a husk, a prop in a drama, a *tabula rasa* on which fantasies of the ancient world are projected. I quote Susan Kus' critique of the American exhibition of Pharaoh Ramses II's mummy (the italics are my own):

> the artifactual accoutrements were in place to re-create a historical drama but the sensual and the emotional were not – there was no 'smell of death' and for me Ramses is neither god, hero nor father ... [w]e talk about desire for power, about awe before the gods and before kings, about magic as the audacious confrontation of human and natural forces, and about ideological notions of purity and danger being tied to psychological processes. *The physical and the emotional are part of our social theoretical discussions as much as are cold, calculated motives and logics.*[7]

To instate the physical and emotional as part of the discourse on the ancient body, I would certainly not advocate an essentialising empathy which creates false links between people across spatio-temporal boundaries. The extent to which one may empathise with the ancient world in any cognitive way is highly problematic, a difficulty which several of the chapters here address. But Bulwer, with his interest in the lived and varied experience of the body, and his desire to make the changed or aberrant body into a means of speaking, is perhaps uniquely applicable to the sources used by classicists, archaeologists and ancient historians. Through such an approach it may be possible to see reflections of individual, embodied selves in all their variability. The contributors to this book show how studying the ancient body in states of modification and transition can reveal glimpses of these reflections. So Gillian Clark points to the corporeal anguish suffered by Christian martyrs, and Lynn Meskell

to how the funeral assemblages of infants hint at emotional reactions to child death in a Bronze Age community. The ancient body can be a reminder of both our closeness to, and our distance from, our ancestors.

In order to consider all these ideas, a group of speakers with a wide range of ancient world interests was invited to the conference. It was felt important that contributions represent divergent historical contexts and periods outside the traditional definition of 'classical' culture: hence there were papers which dealt with Bronze Age Egypt and Africa in Late Antiquity. The source material was analysed using very different theoretical perspectives, ranging from Lacanian psychoanalysis to post-processual archaeology. Yet out of this diversity came a cohesion, which is reflected in the arrangement of this book.

In the first two chapters, discussions of ideal and aberrant bodies set the scene for the more general construction of somatotypes in the ancient world. Nicholas Vlahogiannis and Richard Hawley both address links between culturally specific notions of physical beauty and manifestations of power in the ancient world. Taking aberrant bodies as his starting point, Vlahogiannis shows how disabling also usually meant disempowerment, but points out that disabled people were not automatically marginalised, and that social integration was still a possibility even in non-élite groups. Obviously, this may depend on all kinds of emotional and familial scenarios that are now irrecoverable. Most relevant here are ancient burials of handicapped children from ordinary, non-élite families.[8] What were the concatenations of personal circumstances that led parents to bring them up, perhaps in the face of societal abhorrence? A handicapped child might have been the sole survivor of many births, or the late only child of a middle-aged couple. These burials poignantly illustrate the inappropriateness of making generalisations about the ancient world, and the importance of acknowledging human intentionality and personal response to particular sets of circumstances within a given culture. Hawley provides a corollary to Vlahogiannis' data, demonstrating that in fifth-century BCE Athens the discourse of physical beauty was something malleable, which could be manipulated to enforce social distinctions of importance to maintaining the Athenian state. The modified bodies of prostitutes are an important focus here. Beauty, commodified via cosmetic aids, is one of the ways in which disreputable *hetairai* can be differentiated from respectable *gûnai*. The texts suggest that bodily alteration can be utilised to index

6

and monitor acceptable sexual protocols – even though, as Hawley suggests, this ideology may not have operated in reality.

These chapters are followed by two case studies on the changing body using sources from very different parts of the ancient world: the Latin high literature of Augustan Rome, and the hagiographies of Late Antiquity. Using a Lacanian perspective, Angus Bowie argues that the human body lies at the centre of the narrative of the *Aeneid*. Bodies in the *Aeneid* are a metaphor for decoding the text itself: the readers' desire to explore Virgil's bodies parallels their desire to master the text's symbolic system. Bowie concentrates on the somatic experience of Dido, both of her own body and the bodies of those she desires or desired in the past: Aeneas, Ascanius and Sychaeus. Here Virgil pays much attention to the incorporeal body, often a body that has undergone a transition, such as that of the dead Sychaeus who appears to Dido in an insubstantial, unbodily form as an *imago*. The Latin word *imago* is replete with nuances of physical change: a ghost, an ancestor-figure, a reversed image cut into a gemstone, even the pupate state of an insect. Dido's bodily desire is doomed to frustration in her relationships with Aeneas and Ascanius, when what seems to be possession turns out to be as illusory as an *imago*. Apart from suggesting new ways of reading the *Aeneid* through the medium of the body, Bowie's chapter raises many questions about bodily experience in antiquity, especially about experiencing the body as an integer, an idea discussed later in the book by Terry Wilfong. Developing from this, the status of humanity within the changing body forms the theme of Penelope Murray's treatment of Ovid's *Metamorphoses*. Murray points out how Ovid places the mental suffering of Io after she is transformed into a cow at the centre of the story. Ovid even plays around with her name as a sort of mnemonic for her altered state: *Io* is one of the standard exclamations of desperation in Greek tragedy. The dehumanised Io thus becomes reduced to a cry of pain and grief. Like the man who turns into a beetle in Kafka's *Die Verwandtlung*, Io finds out the hard way that human identity is bound up with the way in which others see us, and that one's external appearance, especially when it changes, does not necessarily correlate to how one feels oneself to be.

In the next two chapters, Gillian Clark and Terry Wilfong consider perhaps the best known modified bodies from the ancient world – Christian martyrs. Early Christian body practices, particularly those

of the martyrs and ascetics, exemplify important shifts of thought about the human body, both as a vehicle for the soul and as a lived entity. The mutilation of the martyr's body renders it more perfect, a conduit for the spirit which brings the heavenly down to earth. While the rhetoric of martyrdom was often sexual, the martyr's body would remain inviolate as it was plundered and penetrated. Clark addresses the complex relationships between medicine and religious cult, and martyrdom and changing bodies. She examines how the body of the martyr, through mutilation and the shedding of blood, became imbued with a spiritual power that was communicable via relics. Wilfong uses the rich (and often neglected) corpus of Coptic texts as his starting point, juxtaposing literary accounts with documents to reconstruct a holistic picture of the body in the changing social milieux of Late Antique Egypt. He demonstrates how the Coptic language sources often present the human body as a series of parts rather than a whole unit. This 'textual fragmentation' raises questions about how the total body was inhabited and experienced. What idea did people have of how they looked *as a body* in a world without photography and only small, indistinct mirrors, a world where one could only see one's body in parts?

The last three chapters analyse the *Nachlass* of the ancient body and different ways in which subsequent cultures have received the bodies of their ancestors. Lynn Meskell examines how the body has become *the* bone of contention in the debate between opposing theoretical camps. From an archaeologist's viewpoint, she argues for the ultimate inadequacy of adopting such inflexible positions in dealing with the ancient body. The growing willingness of archaeology to consider ideas from other social sciences offers new avenues for accessing individuals in the past, via the embodied individual. My own chapter concentrates on Egyptian mummies, the changed body of antiquity *par excellence*. The trajectory of mummies through time in some ways mirrors that of the victims of Vesuvius: they are fetishised to recreate an ancient world which is totally sexual. An important part of this sexualisation is the creation of biographies around the bodies. Finally, Jane Stevenson provides a coda with her analysis of the uses of 'Greek' nudity in Victorian culture. Her witty and allusive chapter is a reminder that although modern studies of sexuality, the body and gender in the ancient world often treat their themes in terms of dark forces of power and oppression, the ancient discourse is often comic, ironic and playful. Modern discourse on the ancient body should be serious, but it need not always be solemn.

NOTES

1 These stages of scholarship on ancient women and their relevance to the body are most clearly delineated by King 1995.
2 See e.g. Fiedler [1978] 1993: 156 (miscited as 'John Buliver'); Brain 1979: 14.
3 Bulwer also wrote two medical treatises on correcting tongue and ear disorders surgically, *Glossiatrus: Tractatus de removendis Loquelae impedimentis* and *Otiatrus: Tractatus de removendis Auditionis impedimentis*.
4 There is an extensive bibliography: see Braidotti 1989; Butler 1990a, 1990b; De Lauretis 1986 *passim*; Dutton 1995; Foucault 1977, 1978, 1985, 1986; Giddens 1984, 1992 *passim*; Grosz 1994; Laqueur 1990; Moore 1994; Seidler 1989; Shilling 1993.
5 On these points, see the reviews of Garland 1994 in *JHS* 116 (1996): 225–6. and *BMCR* 7: 8 (1996): 677–9
6 See Leppmann 1968: 129–54, and plates 13–14b.
7 Kus 1992: 171–2.
8 See Humphreys and King 1980: 40; Meskell 1994b.

Part I

PERFECT BODIES, IMPERFECT BODIES

2

DISABLING BODIES

Nicholas Vlahogiannis

He snatched the golden brooches from her gown,
And, lifting them, struck the centre of his eyes

(Soph. *OT* 1268–70)

Thus the Messenger pronounced Oedipus' self-blinding, punishment for sleeping with his mother and killing his father.[1] Oedipus no doubt suffered the intense pain of his wound, but that was only the prelude to his life beyond the moment: a life of loneliness and unsociability, weakness and dependence, and vulnerability – a forceful juxtaposition with the memory of the proud, authoritative man that he once was.

One does not need to resort to Oedipus' measures to modify or alter the body or physical appearance. Clothing and make-up will change appearance temporarily. Permanent forms of alteration might include body sculpting, be it the swaddling and reshaping of a newly-born child into a desirable shape (Sor. *Gyn.* ii 102–3); the corsets and tight-lacing popular in the Victorian age; working out in the gymnasium; plastic surgery; or tattooing. In a sense, each of these measures fulfils Claude Lévi Strauss' observation that humans transform the body into a product of its own techniques and representations. Each measure changes the body to move it closer to the prevailing aesthetic ideal of a particular social group; each serves as a means of communication, providing symbolic information about the bearer's personal interests, social position, relationship and self-definition.[2]

Modification of the body through disease or deformity, or mutilation of the limbs or senses, also satisfies these aims, albeit negatively. Oedipus' body, already maimed as a child when he was lamed and left to die by his father, was again reworked or retransformed from

13

an imagined, heroic ideal, or socially acceptable physical norm, into a less-than-perfect body. Pertinently, both incidents were punishments for gross transgressions against the divine and natural orders: as a child he was the victim of his father's guilt; the blinding was retribution for his own offence.

In this sense, the premise underlining this chapter is that disability must be extended beyond the physical condition; that physical disability was a metaphor for punishment. The question that stands out is why should disability be used as punishment in mythology, and socially? The answer involves two issues: the value of the body in society, and the socio-religious positioning of disability and the disabled in the community, that would deem disabilities a punishment.[3]

Any discussion of marginalised and minority groups, especially those that evoke emotional responses, automatically raises the basic weaknesses of history writing, namely the fallibility and deficiencies of historical records. Such deficiencies encompass data lost through time, as well as issues that were not generally discussed or did not generate written documentation, for whatever reason. One approach that might help researchers penetrate what Michel de Certeau termed 'zones of silence' (the areas like sorcery, madness, festival, popular literature and the forgotten words of the peasant that traditional historiography ignored) and establish 'historical realities' is *l'histoire des mentalités*, which is based on the construction of beliefs and value systems.[4] These 'historical realities' become the history of representations that stand alongside economic, social and cultural history, and involve the history of ideologies, mental structures, attitudes, intellectual production, imagination.[5] This methodology looks for a relationship between beliefs and assumptions of everyday life, and investigates 'psychological realities underpinning human conceptions of intimate relationships, basic habits of mind, and attitudes towards the elemental passages of life';[6] and shows how the changing relationship between man's rational and emotional faculties reveals the changing shape of human nature. Common attitudes can be found in common codes or 'discourses' of knowledge through which the world is perceived. They are the mental structures (the 'words and things') through which man organises his activities and classifies his perceptions of the world, whether these be aesthetic images, linguistic codes, expressive gestures, religious rituals or social customs.[7]

WHAT IS DISABILITY?

The categorisations of disability in contemporary society, as defined by the World Health Organisation, extend beyond the traditionally obvious physical infirmities, such as blindness, deafness and lameness, to incorporate mental disorders, trauma and injury, communicable and non-communicable somatic diseases, congenital disease, malnutrition, functional psychiatric disturbances, chronic alcoholism and drug abuse.[8] In this way, disability implies a permanent or semi-permanent state that impinges on the ability to function 'normally' within society. As William McNeill wrote, 'a person who can no longer perform expected tasks because of bodily disorder will always seem diseased to his fellows'.[9]

The ancient world did not have conveniently constructed definitions of disability, especially classifications that also connoted social status. Specific terms and a variety of metaphors existed identifying physical conditions, but ancient medical sources did not provide precise taxonomies of diseases and disability to match contemporary medical classifications, only approximations.[10] Archaeopathological evidence and the developing science of pathocoenosis, however, are indicating that a range of conditions was known in antiquity, which included obvious physical disabilities, such as dwarfism, gigantism and focomelia, a myriad of skin diseases, cancerous tumours, tuberculosis, and others.[11]

A number of factors complicates any attempt to distinguish a generic definition of disability in the Graeco-Roman world.[12] The primary concern is the classification of a heterogenous collection of physical conditions, a variety of causes, and ambivalent social attitudes into a common and recognisable group. In *c.* 400 BCE the crippled client of Lysias claimed a pension from the Athenian administration because his impairment prevented him from earning a living (Lys. xxiv 6). Gallus Cerinius, the Augustan senator who suddenly went blind, allegedly found the handicap so traumatic that he resolved to commit suicide by starvation (Suet. *Aug.* 53.3). These conditions fit the broad category, as does leprosy because of the need for social segregation owing to contamination; but why epilepsy or infertility, or skin diseases that are not contagious? Societal constructions also intrude, especially when the functional condition of a handicap is blurred by a physical abnormality that does not constrain effectiveness, but has assumed moral connotations, such as polydactylism or left-handedness.[13]

15

Another factor is the functional demands of society, namely the needs for production, procreation, manpower, and how a disabled individual could satisfy these imperatives. Plutarch's account of customary law as codified by Lycurgus in the eighth century BCE suggested that the exposure of ill-born and maimed children (*agennes kai amorphon*) was motivated by the élite military state's need for able-bodied soldiers (Plu. *Lyc.* 16.1–3). Early pre-Republican laws attributed to Romulus and echoed in the Twelve Tables[14] also emphasised the needs of the state to rear children, especially males. According to Dionysus of Halicarnassus' account of Romulus' statute, a child born 'a cripple or a monster' (*anaperon ê teras*) could be exposed only after the child had been examined by five witnesses (*Ant. Rom.* ii 15.1–2). The weak were weeded out, but the state was not permitting unnecessary infanticide.[15] A similar fate awaited disabled children in the Platonic and Aristotelian utopias; there should be a law, wrote Aristotle, forbidding parents to raise deformed or maimed (*peperomenos*) children.[16]

In all ancient societies the need for security, provision of food and military prowess saw the perfect body idealised in the divine and its representation on earth, in the institution of kingship and hero, and associated with power and the protection of the community. Indeed, the rhetoric of body locates it as a metaphor for holding power and waging war. Hellenic cosmology was based on the survival of the strongest. This theme of the rule of the physically strong also ran through Athenian literature of the fourth and fifth centuries BCE, in the sophistic debates echoed in the speeches of Thucydides, and from the mouth of Thrasymachus and others in Plato's dialogues.

Therefore able-bodiedness is the primary point of reference for disability, based on the notion of an ideal body without blemish or fault, which fulfils the functional needs of the state. The linguistic construction, conceptualisation, classification, metaphorisation – the semiotics of the disabled – becomes a process in opposition to the able-bodied, a contrasting of physical states, and a process of negation: able, disable; Greek *dunatos, adunatos*; Latin *firmus, infirmus*; that is, a focusing on the constraints imposed by the physical state. Without indulging in drawn-out and repetitive definitions, an examination of Greek and Latin semiotics broadly denoting disability collectively signifies an awareness of a *de facto* social group whose numbers arouse unease or revulsion and connote a lesser state. For example Greek *adunatos, asthenês, akikus, anaperos*, and Latin *dehabilitus, infirmus* concentrate on physical or mental weakness, feebleness, the inability to function; the lack of performance; weakness in the mind or moral character; and social conditions such as poverty. They are also of course political and military metaphors. They are the negations of the positive aspects of body, and by extension political power. In the *Crito* 53a3, Socrates admonished Crito for not being involved in the affairs of the city: 'You could not have absented yourself from the city less if you had been lame or blind or crippled' (*anaperos*). In Aristotle's perfect society, only citizens with leisure and undulled sensibilities would exercise the functions of government, religion, defence and property. The remainder, the sub-citizens who provided the labour, were in some ways incomplete men.[17]

Causes of disability must also be a factor in the process of definition, because of the moral value placed on guilt, and the human tendency to attribute blame.[18] Oedipus was stained with guilt: he was born with the guilt of his father, and bore the infirmity of that guilt – his maimed feet. He too committed sins that were marked with a further infirmity, his blindness. In contrast, Cynegeirus, the brother of Aeschylus, who lost his hand and life at Marathon, won eternal fame (Hdt. vi 115). His infirmity resulted from courage and sacrifice, and was therefore to be celebrated, not denigrated with shame.[19] But what was the reaction of a stranger who had neither met nor heard of Cynegeirus, but saw only a man with a handless limb? What did people who encountered a nameless, blind beggar see and think? In other words, the image of disability or physical abnormality does not confront the rational being, but the emotional persona in each of us, and our involuntary responses are preconditioned by long-established cultural images.[20] In popular entertainment, villains have some physical (read: moral) deformity.[21] In the Graeco-Roman world, physically aberrant daemonic spirits such as the Empusa, the Erinyes and Lamia, who stored her eyes each night in a jar (Plu. *De curiositate* = *Moralia* 516a) served a similar purpose, with a similar iconography, and a similar ability to terrify.

A multitude of socially constructed images defining the ideas of disability accompanies the process of classification. What emerges, I would argue, is a broadening of the standard definition of disability to incorporate appearance and socially ascribed abnormalities, such as polydactylism, left-handedness, old age, obesity, impotence, and even those who are socially ill-positioned, such as beggars, the poor, the homeless, the ugly and the diseased.[22] It was not without reason that Spartans stigmatised their 'cowards' with physical shame: an unkempt appearance, marked clothing, and half-shaved beards (Plu. *Ages.* 30.2–3). In short, while disability was the non-perfect body and the inability to function or meet the needs of the community, definitions of disability also adopted ascribed cultural values and ideals, predicated on specific aspects of the body as the norm. Thus the distinction between the able-bodied and the disabled in this broad sense is constructed into what is socially seen as who does and who does not fit into the perceived notion of acceptable community.

ATTITUDES

Breaking the body by destroying the function of limbs or senses would cause pain and suffering. In its reworked form, however, the body also inherited a plethora of emotional responses that are founded on religious, political and social values and attitudes. According to Aristotle, citizenship involved exercising a proper function in government, religion, defence and ownership of property.[23] In this sense, legal restrictions denying a disabled citizen his full role in the functioning of the state would represent undermining the value of citizenship. While a disabled Athenian male did not lose his citizenship rights (as an *atimos* would have), his civic rights were curtailed, in that a disabled male citizen was disqualified from holding an archonship (Lys. xxiv 13), although it is not clear whether all or specific infirmities disqualified candidates from magistracies.

Furthermore, both the Athenian and Roman legal systems, while protecting, also disenfranchised the disabled members of their communities, in that legal and classificatory boundaries, between the normal and the abnormal, competent and incompetent, minors, women, the disabled, create examples and mark the legally incompetent by defining physical weakness.[24] In Athens senility or insanity, which would render the father of the house incapable of maintaining the *oikos*, could be used to displace him as head of the household.[25] Likewise, someone whose judgement was considered impaired by madness, senility, drugs, sickness, or the undue influence of women or force could not serve as *testor*.[26] Roman laws too, while protecting the disabled person or his properties from harm, redefined the disabled individual as a minor by insisting on the appointment of curators or guardians for those deemed insane (*furiosi*), the deaf and mute, and when necessary the blind.[27]

The influence of religion in the forming of attitudes was undoubtedly at the basis of the exclusion. The incidence of physical disability among numerous historical figures outside Athens, however, reiterates the ambiguous attitude the ancient world held towards deformity, and points to the needs of the state and political factions overriding superstition. For example, the congenitally lame Agesilaus was elected king of Sparta in 399 BCE, despite the warnings of an oracle to beware a lame kingship (*cholon basileian*).[28] The Delphic warnings of disaster were fulfilled thirty years later when Epaminondas of Thebes ended Spartan hegemony for ever.

Religion, too, lay at the basis of exclusion in Roman society. Any physical blemish or disability disqualified entry into the priesthood (Plu. *Quaest. Rom.* 73). Indeed, L. Caecilius Metellus who lost his sight saving the Palladium when the temple of Vesta caught fire in 241 BCE, also lost his priestly rights.[29] Religious considerations governed the interpretations of teratologies and *prodigia* that social memory associated with disasters, be it the Athenian plague, the Roman conflict of the orders, or the massive defeat of the Roman forces by Hannibal at Cannae in 216 BCE. Livy isolated deformity and physical abnormality as an inversion of nature (xxxi 12.8). Diviners and soothsayers quickly found causal explanations, and the scapegoats: usually the deformed persons themselves or members of other politically and socially disabled or marginalised groups, whether slaves or aliens.[30]

It would be wrong to suggest that this is the full picture. Not all families in the ancient world discarded their physically and mentally impaired children because they represented evil and danger.[31] Equally, ancient literature and history has its share of physically deformed heroes and leaders. Pericles, described by Plutarch as long-headed and out of proportion, was the brunt of ribaldry from his political enemies because of this 'deformity' (Plu. *Per.* 3–4). Philip II of Macedon had one eye (*Alex.* 3). According to one tradition, Horatius Cocles was already one-eyed before he was lamed defending the bridge against the Etruscans in 508 BCE.[32] Appius Claudius Caecus was blind when in 279 BCE he turned around the war against Pyrrhus by persuading the Senate to reject the king's peace terms.[33] And any number of Roman emperors had some deformity: Julius Caesar was epileptic, as well as being sensitive about his receding hairline (Suet. *Caes.* 45.1, 2); Caligula was also supposedly epileptic, and many other things (Suet. *Calig.* 50.2); Claudius, of course, has become a fictional case study.[34]

The attitudinal ambivalence that runs through literature and mythology further complicates the picture. This was an ambiguous and indeed contradictory discourse that privileged the disabled into positions of status and power: on one hand, heroes and protagonists are marginalised, debased and disempowered by their disability, and on the other they are protected, empowered and privileged in their unnatural state. For example, Teiresias the blind seer was both marginalised by his disability, his punishment for seeing Athena bathing naked, but also privileged with compensatory powers as a prophet, and the space he thus occupied in Greek mythology. Obviously such narratives constitute genres that are using myths paradigmatically. The status and privileging of these, however, contradicts the wider, everyday picture of the disabled in ancient society who lived less than happy lives, thus confusing interpretations.

As a metaphor for punishment, disability represented a greater sin. Disability was linked with aberrations of nature – whether humanly orchestrated such as barbaric mutilation of the body, or with the teratologies that dwelt in the imaginations of the civilised world. Furthermore, the disabled were less than able. They represented misfortune, bad luck, punishment. As marginalised groups they were the foci of blame and persecution. The impetus for such attitudes rested, and rests, within the memories, myths and the semiological system of our societies and ourselves. To quote Roland Barthes: 'the meaning is already complete; it postulates a kind of knowledge, a past, a memory, a comparative order of facts, ideas, decisions.'[35] Such usage of collective memories involves a need to belong to, identify with and function within a community, not to appear different from the norm or assume negative images. The Aesopian fable about a fox that had lost its tail illustrates my point. Realising the attention the lost tail was bringing to itself, and eager to avoid the shame of the disfigurement, the fox tried to persuade other foxes to rid themselves of their tails too.[36] That is, our sense of belonging in a community is determined and shaped by shared blood ties, language, religion, physical appearance, and culture, by sameness, rather than the other of ourselves.[37]

Thus the use of Oedipus as a model is based on a number of premises. The first is the human body as a socio-cultural artefact, a landscape or inscribed surface of events totally imprinted by history. It serves as a metaphor for politics and power, cultural values, sexuality and gender, ownership and privacy, nature and denaturalisation, and self-identification and 'the other'. Disability did not represent the acceptable self, but the opposite. Furthermore the agency of metamorphosis was attributed to the gods. Therefore when communities punished individuals with a disability, their labours were justified with established religio-cultural values.

Before looking at how the ancient world explained the occurrence of disability, I would like to outline briefly the ideal 'norm', the 'perfect body'.

THE BODY BEAUTIFUL

In the following chapter, Richard Hawley demonstrates how male beauty contests in Greek culture were essentially about stressing difference and selecting excellence via perceived ideals of beauty, and how these physical ideals were intimately connected with leadership, whether in a religious or political context. Beauty contests thus also served to marginalise and disempower the disabled by their divergence from perfect somatotypes. These ideals were codified in the so-called 'Canon of Polyclitus', which served as the theoretical and sculptural model for the idealisation of body during the classical period. Written in the second half of the fifth century BCE, the Canon represented the body as a measure of beauty and perfection that was available to all, not only kings and heroes. The perfect body was the result of balance (*symmetria*) and harmony (*harmonia*), perfect proportions being a gift of nature, while ugliness was a lack of this balance.[38] The obvious and direct contrast – that disability, the lack of perfection, disfigurement, was the direct result (implied or overt) of being in disharmony, imbalance, out of step with nature – was taken up by Chrysippus. The third-century BCE Stoic philosopher wrote that asymmetry in the body was illness, in the sinews a lack of toning; and that weakness in the limbs was ugliness.[39] Similar themes had already been broached in the Hippocratic corpus where dysfunction was described as an inability of impaired limbs to work like healthy ones, as well as destroying the bodily balance of left and right.[40]

The ideal of beauty and its application to body was addressed by Michel Foucault. He identified a constant theme in the prescriptive medical writings of the first and second centuries CE, namely attention to the body through measured exercise and rest, diet and sexual relations, which 'served as functional devices that would enable individuals to question their own conduct, to watch over and give shape to it, and to shape themselves as ethical subjects', while deviation could cause any sort of ailment, malaise and disease. Sexual excess, for example, might weaken sight and hearing, the sense organs, and cause loss of memory.[41] Thus, according to Suetonius, Sextus Clodius the Sicilian rhetorician blamed his deteriorating eyesight on frequent late night dissipations with Mark Antony (*Rhet.* 5). In other words, morality was becoming concomitant with the care of the body, complementing the medical advice, recorded by Soranus, on the moulding of young bodies into socially acceptable shapes. An important message of Soranus was the favouring of the right hand to ensure right-handedness, which perhaps emanated from the Hippocratic notion that the male foetus was formed on the right side of the body, while the female came from the left. Right, as maleness, also connoted health, and goodness.[42]

The superiority of the right hand that was ingrained in Greek, and Roman, thinking, crossed into religion and social contexts.[43] Roman pledges were taken with the right hand (Liv. i 58.7), the hand Mucius Scaevola sacrificed when defying Porsenna, this inversion of the oath-taking procedure rendering credible his false testimony that he was the first of 300 Romans waiting to assassinate the Etruscan.[44] The left hand, in contrast, represented effeminacy, weakness, and evil.[45] In Sophocles' *Ajax* (1225) left-handedness (*skaios*) was used as a metaphor for an ill omen. According to Suetonius, Augustus, superstitious at the best of times, thought it a bad omen if his left and right shoes were placed in the wrong order (*Aug.* 92). Laius, Oedipus' father, was left-handed, and this became a metaphor for all of his sexual unbalance: for example, his rape of Chrysippus, the son of his host Pelops (thereby abusing the laws of hospitality), and his abnormal sexual relationship with Iocasta.[46]

In opposition to the elevation of the body beautiful was a wide distaste for the ugly. In the *Iliad*, the combination of Thersites' personality and physical appearance made him the least attractive Achaean at Troy. While the Homeric heroes were fine physical specimens, well built, healthy, durable, and without disabled bodies,[47] the anti-hero Thersites was represented as bandy-legged and lame, with stooped shoulders and chest drawn together, his skull pointed and bald (*Il.* ii 211–19). His physicality is a metaphor for his lowly birth and his audacity in challenging the accepted social order and heroic ideal by speaking out and advocating the abandonment of the Trojan War. Similar contempt, belittlement, and prejudicial stigmatisation of physical characteristics deemed ugly can be seen in the innumerable insults put into verse by the Hellenistic epi-

grammatists collected in the so-called *Anthologia Palatina*, which cover anything from the reshaped faces of boxers (xi 75), to baldness (xi 434), bad breath (xi 239), and noses (xi 203).

Rejection of the disabled and physically abnormal is epitomised in the tradition of Hephaestus, the god of fire and crafts. Apart from the allegorical lame Spirits of Prayer ('lame of their feet and wrinkled': *Il.* ix 502–3), he was the only Olympian with a disability. The reason for a disabled god has been variously discussed. One interpretation is the paralleling of the births of Athena and Hephaestus, both born to one parent alone, and the inherited contest between the Olympians: Zeus conceiving the 'splendid Athena', whilst Hera produced the crippled Hephaestus, and the monster Typhoeus.[48] Another is offered in the fascinating essay by Jean-Pierre Vernant deconstructing Hephaestus' club-footedness.[49] While the essay highlights the deity's skill with metal-working and his cunning (ironically in a trade that causes disability and is stereotypically represented by lame workmen), Homer recorded a tradition in which Hera pushed her son away, rejecting him, because of his deformity;[50] while the gods would laugh at the sight of the hobbling god. Did Greeks identify with Hera's disgust and revulsion as common to their own behaviour, or did they recognise it as expressions of a past time? How are attitudes to be treated and fixed in time? Ordinarily, the historian's training searches for diachronic models, but the search is confounded in the readings of myth by the paucity of material and the longevity and similarity of attitudes across societies, which instill competing synchronic orderings.

The disabled are thus the Other for the able-bodied, challenging the norms of society, and simultaneously defining and being defined by the cult of the heroic body. Just as the perfect bodies of heroes such as Achilles were the result of divine procreation, so too the condition of disability was deemed to have divine causes.

CAUSES OF DISABILITY: FORMS OF MODIFICATION

In reality, disability is caused by many factors. The ancient world generalised the causes into the natural, human and divine. Accidents in the workplace, such as a blacksmith going deaf, or a soldier being wounded, are one cause. Human ephemerality, disease and the ravages of time are more commonplace. In ancient writing, attention was drawn to the decayed and infirm body, and the effects of age and

23

diseases were emphasised through contrasting images of the body. The Homeric heroes were well built, never suffered bad health, and lived long lives. Their antithesis was Hesiod's Iron-Age, fifth generation who suffered disease, old age and death (*Op.* 174ff.). Livy's champions of Rome were blessed with vigour, strength, heroism, striking handsomeness, and proud heritage, such as Papirius Cursor, whom Livy considered a physical and military match to Alexander of Macedon (ix 16.11ff.). On the other hand, the retiring hero's body was decayed, the hearing dulled, memory failing, and the vigour of mind impaired (v 18.4–5). Suetonius contrasted his description of the aged body of Augustus – one-eyed and limping because of his weakened left hip and thigh – with the body represented in official iconography: the clear, bright eyes that personified divine power, the well-proportioned body that distracted attention from his short stature; the official, idealised statuary that emblazoned youthfulness, piety, and bravery.[51]

Self-violation was harder to comprehend, although on occasions it became a source of power or a weapon of the trickster. L. Iunius Brutus is such an example. Perhaps reflecting an attempt by late Republican tradition to reconcile the meaning of *brutus* (dull, stupid) with the cognomen of the traditional founder of the Roman Republic, Brutus was depicted as feigning stupidity to gain a political advantage over Tarquinius Superbus.[52] Hegesistratus' self-disablement by hacking off his foot to escape the Spartan stocks and certain death earned Herodotus' unqualified praise as the bravest act of which he had ever heard (Hdt. ix 37). On the whole, however, disfigurement and mutilation at the hands of others were signs of cruelty, desecration, and denaturalisation of the body.[53] Unlike their creation stories where mutilation and violation abound, Greeks regarded defiling the body and such actions as abhorrent, and associated them with the Asiatic and barbarian Other, rather than with civilised Greekness.[54] In the Greek world, only slaves were mutilated, while the bodily integrity of the citizen had to be preserved.[55] Acts of mutilation recorded by Herodotus were committed by non-Greeks on themselves, on their enemies, slaves, and on Greeks. In contrast, the Romans had no such qualms and provide many examples, notably the actions of dictatorial emperors recorded by Suetonius, such as Augustus (*Aug.* 27) and Nero (*Ner.* 5) gouging out the eyes of Roman nobles, or Caligula disfiguring aristocrats or handsome men (*Calig.* 26, 35).

The development of the so-called 'scientific medicine' embodied in the Hippocratic treatises during the sixth and fifth centuries BCE attributed sickness to natural causes and not superstitiously to divine intervention. Epilepsy is a common example. Known as the 'holy sickness' (*hierê nosos*; Latin *morbus sacrus*), the sufferer was thought to be possessed by a spirit, connoting the presence of evil or madness, and thus attracted stigmatisation.[56] For example, Phaedra's wasting sickness was attributed to possession by Pan, Hecate and other deities (Eur. *Hipp.* 141–7); the cure too was divine. The Hippocratic treatise *Peri hierês nosou*, however, argued that the disease is due to a moistening of the brain, and is curable by natural means.[57]

The Hippocratic treatises examined a myriad of direct causes for specific and sometimes permanent disabilities. A stroke would affect limbs and voice, and deposits of phlegm sight and hearing (*Morb.* i 3). Brain damage could cause hearing, speech, and sight defects and paralysis (*Morb.* ii 4, 6; *Morb.* iii 4, 13). Disease could permanently disable some part of the body, for example, asthma or a cough in pre-puberty could cause a child permanent gibbosity (*Aph.* vi 46). Dislocation and limb fractures were often mendable, unless gangrene had set in due to the severity of the injury, requiring amputation.

While accidents may break limbs, the development of personality and physical character and the propensity for disease were also influenced by climate (hot or cold, wet or dry) and geography (hilly or flat, marshy or barren). Communities in moderate climates supposedly had citizens who were healthy, tall, clear-voiced, better tempered and more intelligent, while extreme conditions, such as those at Phasis, produced tall but fat specimens, with deep voices and a disinclination for anything tiring.[58] These Hippocratic treatises, together with the ethnographic details from Herodotus and Pliny's *Naturalis Historia*, contribute to the fascinating genre of imaginative literature that was intrigued by teratologies and physical oddities and otherness, of peoples sited on the boundaries of the civilised world. Not only were the Cyclopes, for example, one-eyed giants, which relegated them to the realms of teratology, but they also lived and behaved in a manner that was alien and unappealing to civilised life: alone, without consideration even for each other, in a land on the fringes of the world, without laws and government, without marriage, without agriculture, having lost or abandoned the art of smithing (i.e. technology), cannibalistic, and readily defying Zeus' hospitality laws. The Cyclopes were outside civilisation, representing a past era, a time before civilisation.

Aristotle, of course, could recognise imagination for what it was, and looked to causal explanations for such hybridity. He, however, laboured under his own misconceptions, namely the superiority of men and the potency and role in procreation of the male sperm. His notion of *teras* – 'monster, portent' – and his choice of terminology (although he also used the terms *anaperos* and *peperomenos*) stemmed from the theory that nature had not reached a proper stage (*telos*). The *telos* was the male being, and any deviation from that norm, either in terms of maleness, or the body as a whole, was regarded as a deformity or monstrosity (*teras*: *HA* 496b, 507a). Plato had already cast women as the first stage of degeneration from the male (*deutera genesis*; *Tim.* 90e), and Aristotle continued the proposition, ranking living things into an order of perfection (*HA* 588b.21). Thus females were maimed males, because they had not achieved the perfect *eidos* that the male had.[59] A *teras* was anything that is contrary to nature, especially in terms of functionality. In this sense, any congenital disability would be regarded as a degree of monstrosity. Offspring were also ranked in a series of options. Produced in the form of parents, the first step was the child that resembled the father; next the mother, third ancestors, then no one in the family; and at the bottom of the scale was the child that did not have a human appearance (*GA* 715b.12ff.). Every step further away from the replica of the father, therefore, can be termed 'deformed'.[60] Furthermore accidents of nature could occur (*GA* 767b.7); equally deformities could be transmitted from parent to child.[61] Thus any disability could be regarded as having a degree of monstrosity.

I have dwelt on this theme because of the influence language and classifications have on thinking and attitudes. Classifications define and prescribe significance and meaning, they position and con- textualise terms of reference. Language and labels perpetuate pre- judices about differences by propagating the superiority of certain groups, thus subordinating others. Classification also constitutes self-identification, compressing moral sensibilities and making it easier to deny the bonds of human universality. Terms like *adunatos* and *infirmus* contrast physical and mental weakness, and weakness in the mind or character, with the positive aspects of body. In the *Phaedrus* (253 d–f), Plato, expounding on the meaning of true love, the madness inspired by it, and the capturing of that love, divided the soul into three parts: two being like horses, the third like a charioteer. Of the two horses, one is good, the other not. Putting aside any subtextual readings about the insignificance of physical

beauty in love or self-conscious references to Socrates' physical appearance, Plato's descriptions of good (*agathos*) and bad (*kakos*) are what is of interest: the good horse is

> upright and clean-limbed, carrying his neck high, with something of a hooked nose; in colour he is white, with black eyes; a lover of glory, but with temperance and modesty; one that consorts with genuine renown, and needs no whip, being driven by command alone. The other is crooked of frame, a massive jumble of a creature, with thick short neck, snub nose, black skin and grey eyes; hot-blooded, consorting with wantonness and vainglory; shaggy of ear, deaf, and hard to control with whip or goad.

Plato went on to discuss how the bad horse was tamed, but that is not my point: what is striking is the imagery of physicality, of ugliness and beauty, and its associations with morality. The disabled horse is immoral, black, deaf, the eyes grey and bloodshot. In Hippocratic terms, bloodshot eyes were a sign of bad health (*Aph.* vii 3), or a symptom of epilepsy (*Morb. Sacr.* xviii 20), that is, diseased. Grey eyes too are associated with physical weakness. Together with other undesired inherited characteristics, such as baldness and a squint, they are the result of sickly seed, as distinct from good characteristics that emanate from healthy seed (*Aër.* 14).

Such ideas contributed to the positioning of the disabled into a designated cultural space as undesirables on the margins of society, and by emphasising their physical imperfections influenced social responses to disabled persons through stigmatisation and belittlement. The prioritisation and hierarchal positioning of senses as central to information-gathering will illustrate my point. The use of blindness and deafness as metaphors for lack of knowledge and lack of intelligence – because the loss of these senses hampers the ability to collect information – is all too common, and a means of belittlement. Plato's dialogues are strewn with such examples: 'plain enough for a blind man to see' (*Sph.* 241d.9); similarly, Plato's man who has no interest in culture, and whose mind became feeble, and his soul deaf and blind. In his ignorance and ineptitude, he resorts to the habits of a beast; violence and savagery are his means of persuasion, not speech (*Resp.* 411d). This is also the case with the broad use and connotation of *teras* as deformity and its associations with monsters, portents, and threats to community. To quote Geoffrey Lloyd, 'the terminology of mutilation and deformities has its primary sphere of application in ways individual members of a species fall short of the norm provided by the species as a whole'.[62] It was members of these groups who were persecuted or used as sacrificial scapegoats, to save the community and ward off evil.[63] As undesirables, the physically and mentally imperfect functioned materially and symbolically as metaphors or paradigms for religious and social transgressions. Punishment through disability therefore served a double purpose: it was a tool of punishment because it caused pain and physical deprivation; and it consigned to the transgressor the role of symbol or metaphor for punishment, because of the visibility or obviousness of the punishment.

DIVINE CAUSES OF DISABILITY

Running parallel to the scientific developments of the sixth and fifth centuries BCE was what popular imagination believed: namely that the gods brought illness, disease, and disability. This was evident in the earliest literature, and continued as a motif through the tragedians, historical narratives, philosophical treatises and popular literature into the early centuries CE and into Christianity.

Very near the beginning of the *Odyssey* (i 32–4), Zeus, addressing the Olympians about the slaying of Aegisthus, remarked: 'Shame, how mortals blame the gods, For they say that evil (*kakos*) comes from us, In fact it is they themselves who by their own recklessness experience suffering beyond what is fated.' In Hesiod, evil meant sickness and disease. Pandora's box saw to that: 'the earth is full of evil (*kakos*) things and the sea is full of them; these are sicknesses (*nousoi*) that come to men' (*Op.* 101–2). That is, the humans can blame the gods, but it is their own doing that brings punishment, harm. Equally, it is their responsibility to maintain good physical and moral health; and keep out of the way of the gods. Moral questions inevitably prepared the way for socio-religious evaluations of what a moral sign was, why that sign was being flagged, and how the perceived danger might be averted. In the rush to attribute blame and avert the perceived harm, scapegoats became easy prey.

Graeco-Roman tradition had an abundance of daemonic and malicious spirits who wreaked havoc and physical harm on humans. Pandora brought sorrow to mortals, while independent evil spirits destroyed humans – the Erinyes, Mania, Keres (the bringers of blindness and madness), the Harpies and Lamia, and unnamed spirits, such as the one who inexplicably blinded a soldier at

Marathon (Hdt. vi 117). More telling was the work of the gods who punished transgressions with affliction and disability. Every god could punish, and specific punishments were not restricted to specific deities. Disabilities – destruction of limbs through paralysis or injury, loss of the use of senses, personal appearance, sanity, impotence – became intertwined with punishment for violations of divine and moral order. In the search for an explanation for disability, it is a universal human trait that aetiologically evil consequences must have had an evil cause. Even when a natural cause can be shown to explain an incident, the supernatural explanation often replaced it. Hence, Philip of Macedon's eye: although it was lost in battle, the tradition that evolved was that he saw his wife in bed with the god Amon. He saw something he should not have seen (Plu. *Alex.* 3).

Besides the harm brought by Pandora's capricious evils, Hesiod used the anecdote of just and unjust cities to make the point of divine punishment. The just city benefited from fertile and plentiful produce, healthy livestock, and healthy children. Its antithesis was the city punished by Zeus for the crimes of one person: the community dies off; the women no longer bear children, or they are born as monsters that do not resemble their parents. A recurring motif in Greek literature is that of impotence, the bearing of disabled children, and the consequent dying community, as a punishment or curse against enemies. In Callimachus' *Hymn to Artemis*, Artemis' disfavour brought plagues, sorrow, death, and crippled children, in direct contrast to those whom she blessed. The fate of Thebes, Argos and Athens in the tragedies is similar.[64] An Athenian oath sworn before the battle of Plataea in 479 BCE read, 'If I remain loyal to the inscribed oath, may women give birth to children who resemble their parents. If not, may they give birth to monsters (*terata*).'[65] In these examples, it is the community that suffered, and there is a general association between disabilities and disease as punishment. In other incidents, individuals and their family suffer impotence: Glaucus the Spartan thought about deceiving and robbing the men who placed their trust in him, only to be punished by Zeus with impotence for transgressing his laws of hospitality (Hdt. vi 85–6).

The most common punishment by the gods was blindness. Blindness affected the physical condition, but also lifestyle, and social situation, and as such represented one of the worst misfortunes to befall a human being. Blindness signified exclusion, the inability to gather visual information, helplessness, social isolation, and a dependence on others to mediate relations with the physical and social environment. The fear and difficulties associated with a life of blindness drove some to suicide, rather than live in a world of darkness, as in the case of Gallus Cerinius referred to above. But Oedipus is the premier model for the life of a blind person: the beggar, the social outcast, unwanted, feared, ignored and tormented. Spatially severed from urban civilisation, he wandered unknown and unrecognised, alive only because of the care of his daughters. So too Bellerophon! Fabled for his remarkable beauty and valour, the hero who tamed the winged Pegasus and defeated the monstrous Chimaera, was punished by Zeus for arrogantly setting off on the back of Pegasus to join the gods on Olympus (Pind. *Isthm.* vii 60–8). Although the extent of his punishment was embellished by later traditions, he too spent the remainder of his life roaming the 'plain of wandering' (*pedion aleion*), a blind beggar, lonely and accursed, forever avoiding the paths of men. Only slaves and aliens lived outside the cultural setting of the city and all that that entailed: humanity, political and social discourse, even normality.

The otherness of the disabled as outside society, the fear and anxiety that the image generates, the human tendency to blame the weak and the defenceless, and their association with danger, come together as a moralist cocktail in a story in Philostratus' *Vita Apollonii*, written in the early third century CE. In this story, the people of Ephesus, led by the holy man Apollonius, turned on a blind beggar and stoned him to death as a way of expunging the city of the terrible plague afflicting it (iv 10). The important point is not that Apollonius later exposed the beggar as a daemonic charlatan, but that he resorted to the socially marginalised as scapegoats – the lower classes, slaves, social outcasts, the physically odd or curious or ugly or disabled, the socially damned.[66]

The blinding of Oedipus, Teiresias, the poet Phineus, and others, were all punishments linked to transgressions, usually sexual, that overstepped the limits and boundaries set by the gods. Teiresias had seen Athena naked, while Oedipus had committed the primeval taboo of incest.

But it is here that the ambivalence associated with the divine causes of disability becomes pertinent. In many cases of punishment, particularly those of blindness, the victim of the gods is also rewarded, gaining a new voice, function and fame. This is imbued with a universal stereotype linking blindness with powers in music, poetry or prophecy. Demodocus, the bard of Alcinous in the *Odyssey*, had been blinded by the Muses but compensated with the power of song (*Od.* viii 62–4). Teiresias was given the power of prophecy and the ability to move in a cosmological space: he never comes, but just appears. Even Appius Claudius, who according to Livy was punished with blindness owing to the unforgetting anger of the gods (ix 29.11), was according to Ovid blessed with inner light (*Fast.* vi 203–4), as well as possessing a fluency which moved a demoralised Roman people into defying the king of Epirus. Richard Buxton has pointed to the wide cultural understanding of a sixth sense attributed to blind people and the insight traditionally ascribed to poets and musicians, who are deemed as blessed by the gods.[67] The social and cultural status of blindness, and its link with the sacred, emphasises that the manifestations of some disabilities were attributed to realms beyond human knowledge or social control.

The intervention of the divine is also the causal explanation for many 'historical' incidents of body modification or debilitating injuries. Again the implicit subtext is the transgression of boundaries separating the human from the natural and the divine.[68] In Greek literature, Herodotus provides the best examples. The Persians who had offended the sun were struck with *lepra* or white sickness, and expelled from the community (i 138). The paralysis that caused the bodies of the Agyllaians and their flocks and beasts of burden to be crippled and twisted was punishment for stoning to death their Tyrrhenian prisoners, who were women and children. Atonement came with the institution of a funeral ceremony and athletic and equestrian games in honour of the dead (i 167). The Spartan king Cleomenes' self-mutilation and suicide evoked images of violation, barbarism and the denaturalised body, placing him outside culture (vi 75). Herodotus recorded at least five reasons for Cleomenes' change of character and abhorrent behaviour, most of which involved some sacrilege or transgression against deities, including punishment for devastating the sacred land of Demeter and Persephone at Eleusis (vi 84).

Blinding too impinged on the historical context of disabling punishments. Herodotus' fabled eighth-century BCE pharaoh, Pheros, was blinded because in an hubristic and insensate frenzy he threw a spear into the flooded Nile, the life force of Egypt. What is interesting in this anecdote is the secondary discourse of sexual fidelity serving as a cure for his blindness, and infidelity a further motive for punishment. Having remained blind for ten years, he consulted the oracle at Buto, which prophesied that his sight would be recovered when he washed his eyes with the urine of a woman

31

who had remained faithful to her husband. The many women who provided urine unsuccessfully, including his wife, were themselves punished, with death (ii 111).

Blindness is punishment for sacrilege in an anonymous declamatory epigram (*Anthologia Palatina* ix 159). A man passing a skull on the roadside threw a stone at it with his right arm, hitting it. As luck would have it, the stone ricocheted and struck him in the eye, blinding him. But for the poet, the protagonist had not paid proper respect to the dead or acknowledged man's ultimate fate, but sacrilegiously had assaulted the dead with his disrespect. The stone, dumb (*kophon*, a common metaphor for death) but alive with the spirit of vengeance, rebounded, punishing him with the loss of 'his sweet sight' (*glykerou blemmatos*). The emphasis on the right arm, no doubt, served as an ironic contrast between the evil that is represented by left-handedness, and the evil and the profane that had been perpetrated.

There are also examples of the community or state punishing individuals for offences against the community and its welfare. Herodotus' account of Euenius' blinding by the people of Apollonia, because he fell asleep while guarding Apollo's flock of sheep, which was then savaged by wolves, is an example of the state punishing a culprit–victim to deflect feared divine punishment of the community as a whole. The Apollonians, however, had overreacted, and the oracles of Delphi and Dodona exonerated Euenius of blame, and ordered the Apollonians to compensate him with land, while his son, Deiphonus, received the greater power of divination (ix 93–6). Another example is a story retained by Aelian of the severe law codifier Zaleucus of Sicilian Locri, who had decreed that adultery, a violation of the *oikos*, be punishable with blindness (*VH* xiii 24). A similar example of offence against social proprieties is the incident recorded by Pausanius, where the violent Bryas of Argos, appointed commander of the Argive army in *c.* 421 BCE, raped a girl on the way to her wedding. That night, she retaliated by blinding the sleeping assailant (ii 20.2).

All of these examples share one element: a presumably natural incident causing a disability has been reinterpreted and ascribed some divine or extraordinary aetiology. Even the community-induced punishments have connotations or overtones of divine justification, if not intervention of the divine in the affairs of humans, guiding the community to a fitting punishment. In each of these, the punishment involved the attribution of blame and the recognition of a culprit, repentance and retribution. Here disability as a punishment, like the disease cast by Apollo onto the amassed Achaean army waiting to leave for Troy, or that afflicting the people of Thebes, was outside the realm of the human healer.[69]

CONCLUSIONS

According to Bryan Turner, one's body 'is at once the most solid, the most elusive, illusory, concrete, metaphorical, ever present and ever distant thing – a site, an instrument, an environment, a singularity and a multiplicity'.[70] Our body, able-bodied or disabled, is our social self, our social location; it forms our identity within the world beyond. The body of the disabled person, therefore, whose body the community has ascribed with values, has been judged according to the community's ideals of body, community needs, and socioreligious perceptions. Milan Kundera expressed it best in his novel *Immortality*:

> even her handouts to beggars were based on negation: she gave them money not because beggars, too, belonged to mankind but because they did not belong to it, because they were excluded from it, and probably ... felt no solidarity with mankind.[71]

Attributing evil consequences to an evil cause is a universal trait. To the Graeco-Roman world, Oedipus had transgressed natural and social boundaries; and his punishment had to suit the crime. Disability as a punishment served numerous purposes: retribution through physical pain, political disempowerment, and moral and social isolation. As a paradigm, Oedipus' disability served both as a metaphor for his punishment, and as a signifier for the status or social positioning the disabled were ascribed by society. He was placed socially and emotionally outside society.

ACKNOWLEDGEMENTS

My thanks go to Roger Just for his comments on this chapter.

NOTES

1 See Devereux 1973: 36–49.
2 See, for instance, Sanders 1989: 1–22.

3 Very little has been written about disability in the ancient world. Two works have recently appeared: Dasen 1993 and Garland 1995.
4 See Le Goff 1986: 166–80.
5 Le Goff 1992: xiii–xix.
6 Hutton 1981: 237.
7 See Foucault 1973, especially xiv, xx–xxi, 237–9.
8 See Satapati 1988. On appropriate terminology (disability, handicap, impairment), as defined by the World Health Organisation, see Doyal 1983: 12.
9 McNeill 1979: 16.
10 Grmek 1989: 18.
11 See Brothwell and Sandison 1967.
12 On establishing definitions of disability, see Smith and Smith 1991: 20ff., who point out that even thinking about the disabled as a homogeneous group is wrong. By looking for commonness, we neglect or overlook the different physical conditions.
13 On polydactylism and left-handedness respectively, see Barnett 1990: 46ff.; Coren 1992: 1–21.
14 Cic. *Leg.* iii 8.19 = Riccobono *et al.* 1940 i 35; see also Sen. *Dial.* iii 15.2.
15 Watson 1991: 9–10 suggested that the Roman attitude to infanticide had weakened in the three centuries between Romulus and the codification of the Twelve Tables in the mid-fifth century. By now the *paterfamilias* could expose infants without check. The debate on infanticide is growing: for recent bibliography and discussion, see Garland 1995: 1–6 and Harris 1994: 1–22.
16 *Pol.* 1335b.20; also Pl. *Tht.* 160c; *Resp.* 460c.
17 *Pol.* 1328b; Clark 1983: 105–6.
18 Douglas 1966.
19 On the valorisation of wounds in antiquity, see Leigh 1995: 196–9.
20 An analogy is Barthes' example of the 'negro' as signifier: see Barthes 1973a: 116–17.
21 See Bogdan 1988: vii.
22 Compare Aristophanes' image of poverty as degrading, and causing crime and disease: see David 1984: 5–14; equally, beggars as thieves, Pl. *Resp.* 552d; Arist. *Pol.* 1265b.12; and even the derogatory connotations of Greek *ochloi* and Latin *turbae*. On beggars, see Segal 1994: 150–77; for stigmatisation among the disabled, Goffman 1963: 7.
23 Bradley 1991: 29–37.
24 For a cross-cultural parallel, see Minow 1990: 6–8.
25 Ostwald 1986: 51.
26 Harrison 1968: 152.
27 Gardner 1994, especially Chapter 6.
28 On Agesilaus, see Cartledge 1987: 20–6, 112–13.
29 Ov. *Fast.* vi 436–54; Cic. *Scaur.* 48; also D. H. *Ant. Rom.* ii 21.3; Sen. *Contr.* x 4.2. Metellus was punished for violating the taboo forbidding males entering the temple (Dudley 1967: 109). Compare Dio Cassius' account (Liv. 24) of a similar occurrence in 14 BCE, when a fire in the Basilica Pauli spread to the Temple of Vesta. On this occasion the sacred objects were rescued by the Vestal Virgins. Only the eldest priestess did not help because she was blind.

30 E.g. D. H. *Ant. Rom.* vii 69.1; Liv. ii 37.8–9; 42.10–11; iii 5.13–14; xxxi
   12.8; and many more in Julius Obsequens; for a brief discussion, see
   Garland 1995: 65–72.
31 See Meskell 1994b.
32 For the various accounts, see D. H. *Ant. Rom.* v 23.2 (one eye lost in a
   prior battle); Plu. *Publ.* 16.4 (either an eye lost in battle, or had the
   appearance of Cyclops); *Publ.* 16.6–7 (lamed escaping); Pol. vi 55.1–4
   (drowned); also *De fort. Rom.* 3 (317). According to Walbank 1957: 740,
   his lameness, blindness, and even the defence of the Pons Sublicius, were
   later additions to the tradition. In Liv. ii 10.11–12 the account is very
   dramatised, and Horatius heroised. Here, Horatius has no physical
   blemish, survived unscathed, and was honoured with a statue erected in
   his honour. Livy's account was necessary for the narrative, because
   psychologically the rewards of the hero could not be tarnished.
33 Plu. *Pyrrh.* 18.5; 19.1.
34 For example, Suet. *Claud.* 3–4; (see Levick 1990: 13–15).
35 Barthes 1973a: 117.
36 Chambry 1967 no. 41.
37 Anderson 1983: 16.
38 Leftwich 1987 *passim*: see also Moon 1995.
39 Leftwich 1987: 68.
40 *Art.* 51–2; *Fract.* 19.11.
41 Foucault 1985: 13, 15–20; Foucault 1986: 112–13.
42 See Staden 1989: 165.
43 Lloyd 1966: 30.
44 Liv. ii 12–13.1; burning the right hand had the significance of punishment
   for breaking an oath or pledge. The original story may have had C.
   Mucius being punished for perjury, which he endured, hence his
   heroism.
45 Lincoln 1991: 244ff.
46 Vernant 1982: 19–38.
47 Grmek 1989: 24.
48 Arafat 1990: 33.
49 Detienne and Vernant 1978: 270–3; see also Garland 1995: 61–3.
50 *Il.* xviii 394–9: this may be a Homeric invention. Compare the contrary
   Homeric tradition in *Od.* viii 312; xv 18–24, in which Hephaestus was
   lamed when Zeus, exasperated by his defence of Hera, threw him from
   Olympus.
51 Suet. *Aug.* 79–80: for official statuary see e.g. Kleiner 1992: 60 ff. and
   plates 41–2.
52 Liv. i 56–8, 59.2. The Brutus image was constructed in the latter half of
   the first century BC.
53 Mascia-Lees and Sharpe 1992: 1–9.
54 Hall 1989, *passim*. On archaic attitudes see Segal 1977.
55 duBois 1991; Jones 1987.
56 Temkin 1971: 4 ff.
57 See also *Aph.* ii 45 and Lloyd 1979: 16 ff.
58 *Aër.* 5.
59 *GA* 767b.7; 769b.30; 737a.28; Dean-Jones 1994: 182.

60 Pellegrin 1986:109; Dean-Jones 1994: 197–9.
61 *GA* 721b.28f, 724a3f; *HA* 585b.28f.
62 Lloyd 1983: 12.
63 Bremmer 1983: 303; Girard 1983: 18–22.
64 Soph. *OT* 269–271; Aesch. *Eum.* 937–87 and *Supp.* 625–709.
65 Text in Tod 1946: 204.39–45.
66 Bremmer 1983: 300–3.
67 Buxton 1980: 22–37.
68 On law and punishment in Greek penology, see Saunders 1991.
69 Jones 1990: 12.
70 Turner 1984: 8 and 38ff.
71 Kundera 1991: 43–4.

3

THE DYNAMICS OF BEAUTY IN CLASSICAL GREECE

Richard Hawley

Notoriously, there are as many definitions of beauty as there are cultures. This chapter does not aim to define the details of classical Greek concepts of beauty.[1] Rather, it is a corollary to the previous chapter in that it shows how beauty rather than physical aberrance could be used in the classical world as a focus of contention or difference. The first part of the chapter briefly looks at some roles beauty played in classical Greek myth and religion. It then progresses to examine literary treatments of beauty, especially in tragedy, where I demonstrate how Euripides used attitudes towards external appearance, especially that of oneself, as a device to create pity and differentiate character in two plays, *Medea* and *Electra*. Finally I argue that the discourse of beauty and its manipulation becomes very subtle and complex in Athens during the fifth and fourth centuries BCE, and that they play a vital role in Athenian self-definition.

BEAUTY CONTESTS

The second half of this chapter will focus upon outward appearance in classical tragedy. Before that I wish to examine how beauty worked within the general context of classical Greek life. Then beauty was deemed a gift of the gods and was often prized accordingly in religious ritual. Perhaps the most striking example of this is the phenomenon of the beauty competition (*kallisteion*), which figures in many myths and is often adopted and adapted in literature. The most popular role for the myth of the beauty contest is aetiological. While, most famously, Paris' choice of Aphrodite over Athena or Hera caused the Trojan War,[2] beauty contests are more commonly used to explain origins in religious matters. For example,

Athenaeus (xiii 554c) records the foundation myth for the temple of Aphrodite Kallipugos ('of the beautiful buttocks') which also includes a beauty contest. Here two farmer's daughters compete in beauty with one another, making their decision upon the site of the future temple. Again, Athenodorus of Eretria (*FHG* iv 345), drawing on an earlier collection of myths by Antiochus, records that a beauty contest took place in Thessaly between Medea and Thetis. The judge, Idomeneus, chose Thetis over Medea. She then cursed Idomeneus as a liar, thus initiating the Cretans' later proverbial reputation as liars. The result of the contest accords well with the near universal idealisation of Thetis as perfect wife, as against the dangerous Medea.[3] The victory is thus symbolic: virtue over vice, a motif to which I shall return below. A final example might be a fragment of the historian Nicias, preserved in Athenaeus (xiii 609e = *FHG* iv 463), which tells us that the famous tyrant Cypselus held a beauty contest as part of a festival for Demeter at Eleusis. Suspiciously, perhaps, the first winner was his wife, Herodice. The story of the competition performs an aetiological function, for the custom persisted 'to the present day',[4] with the entrants called *chrusophoroi*. Cypselus' choice of his wife may not simply be nepotism, however. It may also underline one feature of the beauty contest to which I shall return below, that of beauty as a criterion for leadership. It may be significant in this connection that the famous chest of Cypselus featured a scene depicting the Judgement of Paris (Pausanias v 19.5).

Athenaeus' sensationalist miscellany preserves references which vouchsafe the popularity of the beauty contest in classical times.[5] He records two fragments of Theophrastus (563 and 564 Fortenbaugh), which relate to a similar religious beauty contest in Elis.[6] Here the winner of the first prize carried the sacred vessels to the goddess (perhaps Hera), the second prize winner led the sacred ox, with the winner of the third prize making the preliminary offerings on the fire. Theophrastus' typically peripatetic concern for antiquarian detail is not entirely free of moral colouring, however. For he adds that beauty was not the only area in which contests were held: there were also contests for sexual morality (*sôphrosunê*) and household management (*oikonomia* F564). We also know of beauty contests held on a similar basis on Tenedos and Lesbos.[7]

But Theophrastus also reminds us of another difference between ancient and modern stereotypical connotations of beauty, for he mentions beauty contests for men, again in Elis (Athen. xiii 565–66a,

609ff.). These contests, he tells us, took place 'with great enthusiasm' (*meta spoudês*), the winners being given arms as prizes, which, according to Dionysius of Leuctra, were later dedicated to Athena. The winner was given ceremonial ribbons to wear and led the procession to Athena's temple. The military nature of the prizes gives us a clue to the slightly different ethos of the male beauty contest. Here beauty seems connected with heroism or martial prowess. Not surprisingly, therefore, we find that male beauty contests formed a part of Spartan culture. Heracleides Lembos (*FHG* iii 168) tells us that in Sparta the most beautiful men and women (*ho kallistos* and *hê kallistê*) are admired above all things, giving rise to the epic description of Sparta as home 'of beautiful women' (*kalligunaika*: e.g. Homer *Od.* xiii 412). At Athens, too, the contest of manliness (*euandrias agôn*), open only to Athenians, was not simply for beauty, but also for 'bodily stature and strength' (*sômatôn megethos kai rhômê*: Xen. *Mem* iii 3.12).[8] This choice of the most beautiful seems primarily a means to select people to perform special religious rites. But we also learn that it can elsewhere be a way to choose a leader. In his *Ethiopian History*, Bion relates that among the Ethiopians, a race about whom many stories circulated, the handsomest men were chosen to be the kings (*FHG* iv 351 F4), 'for it seems that beauty is a criterion of kingship'. Other sources attest the same tradition, including an almost proverbial remark made in Euripides' *Aegeus* (Nauck 1889, fragment 15).[9]

Once lodged in the mythic imagination, the beauty contest motif could also be developed in more literary texts as a way of symbolising a decision between different life styles (Athen. xiii 510c). Prodicus, most famously, presented Heracles with a choice between two women, Virtue and Vice (Xen. *Mem.* ii 1.21ff. = 84 B2 Diels-Kranz). Here, as suited a conservative moralist's view, the beautiful woman was the destructive Vice (cf. Helen's fatal beauty in the Judgement of Paris). Prodicus' fable was enormously popular with later writers, being parodied for example by Lucian in several of his works (e.g. the *Gallus*). Prodicus, however, was not alone in his allegorical use of the beauty contest motif. Sophocles' lost satyr play about the Judgement of Paris, *The Judgement*,[10] seems to have presented the choice between Aphrodite and Athena as one between *Hêdonê* (Pleasure) and *Phronêsis* (Intellect). This allegorical extension of the beauty contest may also contribute to the myth cited earlier where the virtuous Thetis triumphs over the vicious Medea.

ARCHAIC LITERATURE AND COMEDY

So far we have seen beauty being used to single out excellence, or at least difference. Shortly I shall look in detail at tragedy's use of beauty. But before that, and as tragedy derives so much from earlier archaic literature and was contemporary with comedy, it is useful to remind ourselves of how these genres used the motif of beauty. In these texts, beauty was not simply a divine gift: it could also be a source of danger. This potential could also be developed, especially with regard to women, where it appeared a threat to stable male-ordered society.

Priam in the *Iliad* neatly encapsulates the ambivalent attitude towards beauty. He admires Helen's beauty, even though it has led to the loss of countless lives, but does not hold Helen responsible for the Trojan War (*Il.* iii 156). However, later writers were quick to vilify her for her fatal good looks: a classic example is the savage tirade against her in the first choral ode of Aeschylus' *Agamemnon* (60ff.). But Aeschylus' suspicious attitude towards beauty also finds a root in Homeric epic, although not connected with the figure of Helen. In one famous episode in the *Iliad* (xiv 153ff.), feminine beauty is explicitly focused upon *at length and in detail* as a means to deceive the male: this is when Hera takes exquisite care over the details of her appearance in her (later successful) attempt to seduce her husband, Zeus, and so to divert his attention from the battle on earth.

The myth of the first woman, Pandora, as related in Hesiod's *Works and Days* and *Theogony*, firmly cites Pandora's beauty as one of the worst snares for Epimetheus. Here beauty is again an aetiological device. Pandora's beauty epitomises the dangers of mortal women to men. Another early attempt to explain women's nature is Simonides' infamously misogynistic *Satire on Women*. Among his nine types of bad woman, he includes the mare woman, who is excessively concerned with her appearance (57–70):

> She pushes servile work and trouble onto others; she would never set her hand to a mill, nor pick up a sieve nor throw the dung out of the house, nor sit over the oven dodging the soot; she makes her husband acquainted with Necessity. She washes the dirt off herself twice, sometimes three times, every day; she rubs herself with scents, and always has her thick hair combed and garlanded with flowers. A woman like her is a fine sight for others, but for the man she belongs to she proves a plague.[11]

This hostile treatment of women's beauty is inherited and exploited by Attic comedy. In Old Comedy, man's lust for women and their carefully contrived and deceptive beauty may be his downfall, as in Aristophanes' *Lysistrata*. In New Comedy, the dangerous snares of women's beauty are concentrated more within the dramatic figure of the prostitute.[12] She uses her beauty to capture young men, only to drain their finances dry and discard them when they become poor. Moreover, this beauty may not even be skin deep, for the comic writers delight in exposing the elaborate techniques and technology then available for making oneself look prettier by emphasising good points, by underplaying weaknesses, and by sheer lies. The most famous example is a fragment of Alexis.[13] Here the speaker expands upon how prostitutes swindle money from their clients. He catalogues the ways in which a woman can be made more attractive: platform shoes if short, flat soles if tall, a bustle to increase the size of her hips, false breasts, eyebrow highlighter, white lead to lighten the complexion, endless smiling to show off good teeth. This reminds us of the importance of the beauty economy in classical Athens, an economy designed to serve the desires of women. Such goods were probably on sale in the so-called woman's Agora. The lists of unusual and rare words in later grammarians include a large proportion of words for female apparel, accessories and cosmetics.[14]

Comedy's treatment of beauty is therefore relatively limited. It is restricted mainly to sexual crudity or the dangers of socially undesirable women. Respectable young girls are the objects of young men's desires, but seldom is the woman's beauty developed in detail. In Menander's *Dyscolus*, for example, Sostratus falls in love with the unnamed daughter of the old grouch Cnemon, when he catches a glimpse of her creeping outdoors for some water. His subsequent description of her stresses her evident good breeding (384–89) and can be compared to Pan's description of her at the opening of the play (34–9), which stresses her good character and piety. He does not say much about beauty. Archaic literature and classical comedy therefore offer two possible ways of approaching beauty: as a source of male admiration (or pity), or as a threat. In classical Attic comedy, the latter seems to be more prevalent. Is this bias towards the negative treatment of female beauty paralleled in contemporary tragedy?

TRAGEDY

The next section of this chapter will focus upon tragedy, where I shall show that the motif of feminine beauty can be subtly deployed in a variety of ways. Here the dramatist may decide to treat traditional motifs in traditional ways, or to experiment with more innovative and subtle interpretations. One traditional motif traditionally deployed is that of a woman's beauty as dangerous, both to herself and others. The first such use of beauty may be to amplify the pathos of a play. Much of Euripides' emotive description of Iphigeneia's noble self-sacrifice in his *Iphigeneia at Aulis* relies heavily upon the youth and beauty of the victim, as is also the case with Polyxena in his *Hecuba*. In Sophocles' *Women of Trachis*, Deianeira comments sadly upon the dangers which beauty may bring to a young woman.[15] Deianeira's beauty had caused her suitors to fight for her, making her fear that it would bring her only pain (24–25). Later in the play, the silent Iole stands out among the crowd of Heracles' prisoners only because of her beauty and her tears (e.g. 465). This pathetic tone is echoed by a famous fragment of Sophocles' *Tereus* (Radt 1977, fragment 583) where Procne laments that young women are luckiest before they are married off to strangers.

A second traditional use of the beauty motif is as a source of rivalry between women, as with Andromache and Hermione in Euripides' *Andromache*. The noble Andromache, who in many ways epitomises the Athenian ideal wife, reminds Hermione that it is not beauty but virtue which pleases a husband (207–8). This remark may echo a popular view of the time, as it is very similar to several fragments by classical authors often quoted in later times: Gorgias said that a woman should be known not for her beauty but for her reputation (82 B22 Diels-Kranz),[16] Menander that the one sure love-philtre is a good nature (Körte 1953, fragment 571), and Euripides that beauty does not bring a wife a good husband but virtue (Nauck 1889, fragment 909).

This stress on virtue and reputation over beauty may therefore be a sign of a change of emphasis in thought about women taking place during the fifth century BCE. It complements the crystallisation of contrived or self-obsessed beauty as a hallmark of the disreputable prostitute in contemporary comedy and prose literature. As I noted earlier, by the time of Menander's comedy in the fourth century BCE, the young heroines are not described primarily in terms of their looks. Virtuous women should retain a simple, natural beauty. In his idealised picture of conjugal relations, Xenophon's Ischomachus discourages his wife from using cosmetics, fancy clothes and platform boots because they make her like 'women who are deceivers and wear make-up', that is, prostitutes (x 13).[17] She should lead an active life around the home: that will make her more sexually

attractive to her husband (x 12). Here we witness a careful manipulation of the beauty motif. It is based upon the formula 'female
beauty is a threat to male-ordered society'. But instead of simply
prohibiting excessive use of cosmetics or pride in contrived appearance, moralising literature offers women a more pragmatic message:
you will find a better match if you do not count on beauty.
Furthermore, the appeal is spiced with natural human snobbery: such
contrived beauty is the mark of socially disreputable figures, the
prostitutes. Male writers are thus able to shroud their social control
of women under an apparently sympathetic disguise.

The ideality and unreality of these injunctions should be stressed,
however. Evidence from grave-goods, vases and literature, such as
Aristophanes' *Lysistrata* or Lysias i 4, shows that respectable
women *did* use cosmetics. Indeed these seem to have played an
important part in the preparation of the bride for her wedding, one
of the few days in a respectable woman's life when she was on public
display. We may therefore wonder why such an unrealistic ideal was
being thrust upon women. The answer lies in historical context.
These texts are being written and promulgated at a time of upheaval
and change within Athens. They are circulating during and after a
war in which many young, marriageable men have died, probably
leaving a heavy imbalance between the sexes. There is anxiety about
legitimacy, citizenship and inheritance, in which women play an
important, if passive role. Like the contemporary stress on other
aspects of women's respectability, such as chastity (*sôphrosunê*),
outward appearance is targeted as a symptom and symbol of a
woman's virtue. Men looking for wives will want to ensure that they
marry a stable, virtuous, reliable woman. Women who desire husbands will therefore be encouraged by their male relatives to live up
to this ideal as best as they can. One of the worst calumnies that could
be levelled at a woman (and through her at her family) was laxity of
sexual behaviour. Texts that encourage women to adopt restrained
adornment therefore play upon the warning, 'Excessive adornment
makes you look like a prostitute, and you don't want to be taken for
one of them, do you?'[18]

Euripides' *Medea*

I now propose to turn to two tragedies to examine the dramatic use
made of feminine beauty and external appearance. I shall show that
in these two plays we may witness further examples of the con-

temporary discourse about female beauty/female control. I chose Euripides' *Medea* because it provides an illustration of how the traditional literary use of beauty for pathos can be heightened to a level that is close to the grotesque, which is so couched as to offer a moralising message. Particularly interesting is the description of the death of Creon's daughter, which I shall examine in detail.

Medea has heard the news of Jason's new marriage and of Creon's edict expelling her from Corinth. She has secured her later refuge at Athens with Aegeus. She has decided to send the princess poisoned robes and a diadem. We have had several references already to the wealth and luxury contained within the palace. Jason has said that it does not lack its own supply of robes (960) and Medea has referred to the palace as a rich house (*plousious domous* 969), when she sent her children there with her deadly gifts. Euripides has thus created within our mind's eye a traditionally luxurious palace as the setting for the drama to unfold off-stage. The chorus then start to imagine (in lyric) how the princess will react (978–90):

> The bride will take it, she will take the golden diadem's ruin, poor wretch; she will place about her golden hair the adorn-ment of Death with her own hands.
>
> Its charm, and its heavenly splendour will persuade her to wrap around herself the robe and golden-wrought crown; even now she will be getting dressed for a marriage among the dead. To such a bourne shall she fall, to such a mortal stroke, poor wretch; but the disaster she shall never escape.

The picture is one of gold, of light, of deceptive allurement. We retain that image in our mind during the interlude of Medea's deliberations over whether to kill her children. Then the Messenger arrives (1121) to relate the culmination of her revenge (1136–1230). Euripides skilfully recreates the scene off-stage and in the past, thus distancing the audience geographically and temporally. The princess initially scorns the children, 'tossing back her white neck' and veiling herself (1147–48). Her neck is white, and so attractive both aes-thetically and socially, for pale skin was an ideal sign that the woman came from a family who were wealthy enough to excuse her working outdoors. It is perhaps significant that one of the first images that Euripides had given us of Medea, Jason's earlier love, was of her own white (desirable) neck (30: compare 923). Jason intercedes, but what attracts the girl's attention are not his words but the clothes (1156–66).

But when she saw the finery, she did not hold back, but agreed with her man in everything. And before the father and his children had gone far from her room, she seized the richly-decorated robes and wrapped them round her. The gold crown she placed upon her curls, and arranged her hair before a shining mirror, smiling at her lifeless image. Then she arose from her chair and walked through the halls lightly, with her snow-white feet, revelling in her gifts, again and again glancing down to the hem.

So far the image is bright and happy, full of light and laughter. Then the change occurs (1157–75):

But then there was a dreadful sight to see. For she changed her colour, and fell back, trembling in her legs, and scarcely able to collapse into a chair before falling on the ground. And one old servant, thinking perhaps that it was the anger of Pan or another god, cried out, before she saw white froth coming from her lips, and saw the girl's eyes rolling, and her complexion bloodless.

Jason is then notified, as the description continues (1186–1203):

The golden coil which lay on her head began to shoot forth an amazing stream of fire; the soft clothes ... bit into her soft flesh, poor girl. She runs off, jumping up from her chair in flames, shaking her locks and her head this way and that, wanting to throw off the crown. But fixed firmly, the golden chain held fast, and the fire, when she tossed her hair, burned twice as fiercely. She falls to the ground, vanquished by her agony, her face hard to recognise except by her father. There was no calm gaze from her eyes, no beautiful face, but blood dripping from the top of her head, as it was engulfed in flames. Her flesh dripped from her bones like sap from a pine, driven by the poison's invisible feast, a sight dreadful to see. Everyone was afraid to touch the body, for we had learnt our lesson from her fate.

The Messenger then proceeds to relate the death of Creon. But my focus is upon the princess. The scenario is gruesome and gory. Perhaps it is no accident that it may remind us of the agonies of Heracles in Sophocles' *Women of Trachis*, for it is possible that Sophocles' play was produced shortly before the *Medea*.[19] Much of the force of the scene derives from Euripides' careful deployment of the beauty of the princess and of the garments Medea sent her. We may recall that the chorus sang of the princess' fair hair, and of the golden crown, using adjectives such as 'golden' and 'golden-wrought' (*chruseon, chrusteukton*). Their song left a dazzling image. They did refer to the princess' death, but *in no detail*. I suggest that this absence of detail is deliberately designed to enhance the visual effect of the Messenger's vivid description. Medea and Jason had both referred to the palace's wealth. The Messenger's speech closes with a moralising commonplace (1229–30): 'When fortune flows well for you, one man might become more prosperous than another, but not happy.' The wealth which characterised the palace has only brought ruin. Wealth is an illusion of happiness. In the same way, the fine robes, described by the chorus and the Messenger with such initially dazzling vocabulary, are illusions of material beauty. The adornment (*kosmos*) they bring is that of Hades (980–81).

Similarly, the Messenger's speech shows that the princess' initial beauty is illusion. She gazes at her reflection in a mirror, but the reflection is described as 'lifeless' (*apsuchon* 1162) – a proleptic image for the life she is to lose. Euripides develops that scene when the princess poses in front of the mirror and performs her own mini-fashion show in the palace. But this space devoted to the details of her appearance is not merely rhetorical accumulation. It would be unfair to judge Euripides as verbose without a reason. The facets of the grooming scene which he records are designed to parallel facets of the description of the girl's death. She sits and arranges her curls at the mirror (*schematizetai* 1160–61); later Euripides tells us, twice and at emphatic line-beginnings, that she shakes those same curls violently from side to side (*seiousa* 1191, *eseise* 1195). What were delicate curls before (*bostruchois* 1160), become like a horse's mane (*chaitên* 1191). We may recall the mare woman's mane in Simonides. Her face, initially beautiful (*euphues* 1198) becomes hard to recognise (*dusmathês* 1196), and a terrible sight to behold (*deinon theama* 1202). The phrase *deinon theama* was used at the start of this sequence at 1167 to refer to *the whole scene*, but by 1202 it can be interpreted best as referring to the princess herself. It thus neatly telescopes our attention upon the princess and subdivides this segment of the speech. The description of her death focuses very much on her face, head and eyes, with only a brief mention of the rest of her body (1200–1). This again is designed to recall the image of the princess looking at herself in the mirror.

There has been much analysis of mirrors and their use by women in feminist criticism of modern literature.[20] Critics employ psycho-analysis to see in such scenes signs of male oppression. Women, they say, are forced by a society controlled by men to mould themselves physically to accommodate male ideals of feminine beauty. But literature written by men offers women a warning when it presents female characters becoming absorbed with their own reflections. It is fine for a woman to use mirrors to mould herself for her man, but she should not let her reflection replace that man. Women who gaze at themselves in mirrors may begin to believe that they can exist independently from men. That image must be shattered: so male writers show that such exclusive self-absorption, termed narcissism by psychoanalysts, must end in disaster.

While I am not always ready to adopt all modern critical ideas without question, it does seem to me that this scene from the *Medea* would neatly fall into that type of 'destructive narcissism', and that this concept is not anachronistic for analysis of classical Athens because it is echoed elsewhere, as I shall show. The princess does not listen to Jason's words of persuasion, but is instead won over by the sight of the clothes (1156), by a selfish passion, which ignores her man. Medea by contrast would and has already moulded herself to accommodate Jason. The two women are linked by the motif of their beautiful white necks, but the princess' wealth and beauty are shown to be shallow. I believe that we are justified in seeing a message here: that men should value more the devotion of a woman like Medea than the material wealth and all-too-transient beauty of the self-obsessed princess. As the Messenger says as he closes his description of the princess' death (1202–3): 'everyone was afraid to touch the body, for we had learnt our lesson from her fate'. A woman's fatal attraction to mirrors is a motif which Euripides uses on several occasions in the extant plays. Whenever he uses it, it is a symbol of sinister doom. In his *Hecuba*, the Trojan chorus recall how they were fixing their hair in a golden mirror on the night that Troy fell (923–25). In several plays, Euripides partly characterises Helen by her fascination with outward appearances, including her own, which is underlined by her use of mirrors. In her denunciation of Helen in *Trojan Women*, Hecuba says that it was the outstanding beauty of the splendidly-dressed Paris which drove Helen mad with desire (987, 991–92). Hecuba is disgusted that while the other Trojan women are dressed in rags, Helen has decked herself out carefully to win over Menelaus (1022–24). After Helen's departure, the chorus contrast their pitiable lot with the glamorous Helen, who has her collection of mirrors, which bring joy to young girls (*parthenoi* 1107–8). Helen's fondness for mirrors is used again in the *Orestes*. Among her Phrygian attendants are those in charge of perfumes and mirrors (1112). Earlier in that play, Electra had exclaimed to Nature, and thus the audience, that Helen's grief was carefully controlled (128–29): 'Did you notice how she had shorn her hair along the edge, to save her beauty?'[21]

Euripides' *Electra*

In his *Electra*, Euripides also develops the traditional theme of feminine beauty, but once again he does so in a sophisticated manner. He uses it to point a similarity between mother and daughter, but modulated in such a way that mother and daughter are also subtly contrasted. When we first meet Electra she is striking by her appearance. She is wearing tattered robes and has short-cropped hair (108), which was associated in fifth-century Athens with mourning or servile status.[22] This visual characterisation is crucial to Euripides' new version of the famous myth. His Electra constantly refers to her outward appearance: her dirty clothes, her tear-stained face, her short hair.[23] Frequently she will appear to mourn the loss of her father and to desire revenge, but Euripides so crafts her words that we see that it is the loss of the fine clothes and luxury which her position brought her which she mourns, more than her father.

These references to traditional aspects of feminine beauty (hair, face, clothes) heighten Electra's position as exceptional. The women of the chorus invite her to dance in honour of Hera, but she prefers ostentatious mourning (175–80): not fineries or dances, but tears. Here again she refers to her sordid hair and ragged clothes (184–85). When Orestes first sees Electra, Euripides makes him and later Electra refer again to her shocking physical state (e.g. 239, 241). Orestes first thought Electra a servant from her hair-cut (107–8). As Electra relates her situation to her brother, the first things (*prôton* 304) that she singles out are her dirty clothes and squalid living conditions (302–8). Furthermore, she blatantly contradicts what we know from earlier in the play: she says that she has been forced to abstain from dances and fine clothes because of her shameful position (310–11). But the audience know that far from being shunned by the other women, Electra rejected just such offers from the chorus.

The motif of Electra's sordid clothes is developed more subtly as the play progresses. For we later see clothing and physical appearance being used by Euripides both to contrast and to link Electra and Clytemnestra. Both women are made to refer to their appearance on a number of important occasions. They are obsessed with how others see them. We know from her first scene with the chorus, that Electra positively seeks to cultivate an appearance that shocks and elicits pity. In Electra's narrative to her brother, Electra stresses the material deprivation of her sordid lifestyle. This is contrasted sharply with the material luxury in which she envisages Clytemnestra: on a throne among Phrygian spoils,[24] surrounded by Asian slaves, wearing Idaean robes and golden brooches (314–18). Indeed the squalour of Electra's appearance is made the framing device for the whole speech, for she closes with references to it (333–35). When she attacks her mother in the *agôn* of the play, Electra envisages her mother *preening her hair* in front of a mirror, as self-sufficient and self-engrossed, while Agamemnon wages war (1070–71, 1073).[25] Clytemnestra clearly has/had hair to be proud of, while Electra's is cropped short. This imagined image of the past merely serves to confirm Clytemnestra's present appearance. Her entrance is deliberately designed to be stunning. She arrives in a chariot, with attendants, and in fine robes (967). The entrance must surely recall that of Agamemnon in Aeschylus' *Oresteia*. But in Euripides' version, Electra will now parallel her mother's earlier role by luring the Aeschylean 'victor' indoors to her death.

Both women are given a concern for spectacle. Both women want to arouse emotions in those who see them: for Electra pity and shock, for Clytemnestra awe. Clytemnestra arrives as an ideal upper-class wife: concerned to manage her attendants well,[26] striving to wear fine clothes and appear supremely feminine. By contrast, Electra denies her femininity at every juncture: tearing her face, wearing dirty rags, cropping her hair. Electra in fact succeeds in eliciting her mother's pity: her squalid appearance is an explicit reason for Clytemnestra agreeing to help with the sacrifice (1107). Electra even denies her natural *telos* (goal) of marriage, by not consummating her union with the Peasant.[27] Clytemnestra eroticises herself for pleasure-giving spectacle, while Electra anti-eroticises herself. Both women are made to focus this 'eroticisation' upon traditional hallmarks of feminine beauty: skin, hair, clothes. All of these Clytemnestra presents in splendour; all of these Electra masochistically disfigures. The point at which this motif of outward appearance reaches its climax is when Electra finally lures her mother into the cottage. As Electra ushers Clytemnestra in, she warns her mother to 'take care that the smokey roof does not dirty your robes' (1139–40). After the murders, Clytemnestra's body is shown, shrouded in a mantle (1227 31). It is tempting to suggest that she is here covered by the fine robes which so rankled with Electra.

CONCLUSIONS

This chapter has shown different ways in which beauty was treated in archaic and classical Greece. We have seen how the beauty contest was essentially a means of stressing difference and selecting excellence. Such contests were intimately connected with leadership, whether in a religious or political context. But I would suggest that these contests took on a slightly different nuance in classical Athens. Here the 'contest of manliness' (*euandrias agôn*) was not simply one of beauty, but also of more general bodily strength. As far as men were concerned, the emphasis was less on a merely pleasing appearance and more on constructive and useful physical attributes. Mere bodily attractiveness seems to have shifted to become a characteristic of the feminine gender or of boys, whose beautiful characteristics are often suspiciously feminine (e.g. smooth skin).

This shift to the focus on the superficial beauty of women is further refined during the fifth century as social conventions developed to distinguish 'respectable' women from their 'disreputable' sisters by means of appearance. Contrived beauty, such as elaborate coiffures or the use of cosmetics, becomes a hallmark of the prostitute. This is a far cry from the elaborate toilet of the respectable goddess Hera in the *Iliad*. What links the image of Hera and that of the disreputable women is a male anxiety that such women are deceptive and dangerous. Their outward physical deceptions thus symbolise and advertise their innate deceptive nature. This is, of course, an image as old as Hesiod's Pandora. But I suggest that it is developed during the classical period for specific social reasons. This fifth/fourth-century interest in female appearance is evidenced in a convincingly large variety of sources. We find it, for example, in the visual arts, especially in the work of the Meidias painter, whose images of women are clothed in extremely elaborate drapery.[28] In literature it abounds. Advice to respectable women to avoid cosmetics becomes a commonplace in moralising prose, such as Xenophon's *Oeconomicus*. In Old Comedy's *Lysistrata*, the primary characteristic of difference between the Athenian women and the Spartan Lampito is her tan, masculine appearance. Middle and New Comedy dramatically enhance the figure of the prostitute. Mosaics, terra-cottas, and literary sources for the use of comic masks testify to a subtle use of costume, facial appearance and hair-style to differentiate female characters by age and/or status.[29]

Tragedy confirms the argument. We have seen how Euripides exploits an awareness of outward appearance in two plays. In the *Medea*, I argue that the princess is offered as a cautionary example of the dangers of self-obsession, especially as regards external appearances. In *Electra*, physical appearance, beauty versus squalour, is a fundamental aspect of the complementary characterisation of two women, mother and daughter. Both develop their sophisticated concern for external appearances to an excessive degree. I have also pointed to other tragedies where Euripides and Sophocles develop the more traditional use of beauty for tragic pathos, and to the figure of Helen, who comes to epitomise excessive susceptibility to physical beauty. Indeed, one of the many innovative aspects of Euripides' *Helen* is that the protagonist knows how to manipulate her famed beauty to achieve her escape: her self-mutilation in feigned mourning is a powerful weapon in persuading Theoclymenus to allow her to board the ship on which she will make her eventual escape.

The argument that beauty becomes more strongly 'feminised' in the fifth and fourth centuries is also more conclusive when one compares the references to male and female beauty in tragedy. The world of epic was quite able to accommodate favourable remarks about male beauty. Priam, for example, passes such a comment about the kingly beauty of Agamemnon (*Il.* iii 169). Such remarks about men, however, are significantly rare in tragedy.[30] Paris may be described as 'outstanding in beauty' (*kallos euprepestatos*) by Hecuba in Euripides' *Trojan Women* (987), but that is primarily to denounce Helen as interested only in appearances. One might expect to find such references in Euripides' *Hippolytus*, a play about a woman's desire for an athletic youth. But one would look in vain. There are references to Hippolytus' body, but they are few and vague and mainly refer to the destruction of his body by the chariot crash (1239, 1342–44, 1359).

The unusually selective treatment of beauty in the classical period is also highlighted when one looks at later Greek literature. Hellenistic and imperial literature is not averse to praising male beauty in detail. Indeed, in moralising prose about the choice of a marriage partner, beauty is a quality to be desired in both man and woman.[31] The beauty contest also reverts to its pre-classical, non-Athenian type. It becomes a literary adornment, devoid of deeper social significance. It can be an excuse for flirtation with eroticism. A splendid example is an outdoor party described by Alciphron (iv 14.4–7), where two women gradually undress before others to compare one another's hips, breasts and buttocks. The same tone is caught by epigrams by Rufinus in the *Anthologia Palatina* (v 35–36 = Page 1978 XI, XII).[32] Or again, it can be used humorously to characterise an eccentric philosopher. Diogenes Laertius (ii 67) records that Dionysius once asked the philosopher Archippus to choose one from three prostitutes. Archippus promptly takes all three, commenting on how unlucky Paris became after he chose only one in similar circumstances. Again, it can be used as a motif to adorn moralising fables. Babrius (*Fable* 56) imagines a beauty contest among the animals before Zeus and the gods, where a snub-nosed monkey causes laughter by offering herself as a beautiful mother, finally admitting that Zeus is more beautiful.[33]

There is even a further example where it appears that life imitates art. We have already seen that Cypselus may have deliberately imitated Paris in instituting his own beauty contest. Nearly 1,500 years later, the Byzantine chronicler Zonaras records that around 830 CE, the emperor Theophilus was the judge of a beauty contest for marriageable young women from all over his domain in order to choose his bride. He too played the role of a Paris, aiming to give a golden apple to the most beautiful. Walking along the line-up, he was attracted by a girl named Cassia. However, he made the mistake of commenting to her that only ill came from women. The quick-witted Cassia retorted that women are also the source of much good. Angered, Theophilus promptly gave the apple to (later Saint) Theodora. Cassia missed out on becoming empress but went on to become a respected holy woman, honoured by God. The pious Zonaras leaves us in no doubt which was the more desirable fate.[34]

This chapter has argued that in classical Athens the discourse of beauty was concentrated, complex and common to written, spoken and visual media. It was manipulated to perform a definite social function to differentiate men from women, men from boys, reputable from disreputable women. It was enhanced to take on allegorical and symbolic resonance: Heracles' or Paris' choice between women becomes a choice of lifestyle. Such a shift in the dynamics of beauty must therefore be seen as another important aspect of the social self-definition and development taking place within Athens during the crisis period of the fifth and fourth centuries.

ACKNOWLEDGEMENTS

This is an elaborated version of a paper given at the Warwick University *Anthropometamorphosis* conference. I am grateful to all present for their comments and enthusiasm.

NOTES

1 For a detailed analysis of female beauty in Greek poetry, see Jax 1933.
2 For an analysis of the myth: Stinton 1990: 17–76. See also *Anthologia Palatina* xvi 169, 170, 172, 174, 181.
3 The two women are also linked in a myth recorded in Plu. *De Herodoti malignitate* 39c = *Moralia* 871b. Medea is connected with a temple of Aphrodite, one explanation being that Aphrodite cured Jason of a love for Thetis.
4 This probably refers to the time of Nicias rather than Athenaeus, who is likely to be absorbing Nicias' words here.
5 Compare the kissing competition alleged to take place at Megara: Theocr. xii 29, with the Scholiast and Gow *ad loc*. There may have been another at Didyma: Varro ap. Schol. Stat. *Theb*. vii 198.
6 Numbered as L123 and L124 in Fortenbaugh 1984; for commentary see Fortenbaugh 1984: 320–22. See also Fortenbaugh 1992.
7 Athenaeus xiii 610ab collects references. Tenedos: Nymphodorus cited in Athen. xiii 609e. Beauty contests among Lesbian women: Alcaeus fragment 130b.17–18 in Voigt 1971, on which see Page 1955: 168 n.4; *Anthologia Palatina* ix 189 (in honour of Hera); Hesychius ii 4342; Scholiast A on *Il*. ix 129; *RE* xii 2122.38–45.
8 For the 'contest of manliness', see *RE* vi 839.31–54. Note that Athen. xiii 565ff. only mentions a contest of beauty. I return to this contest below.
9 The Euripides fragment was much quoted: see Nauck 1889 for the parallels. See also Hdt. iii 20; Arist. *Pol*. iv 3.7; Nicolaus of Damascus *On customs* 90 (= *FGrH* IIA.385, fragment 103m): where no heir is apparent they select the most beautiful and most warlike as leader.
10 Radt 1977, fragment 361 = Athen. xiii 687c.
11 Translation by Lefkowitz in Lefkowitz and Fant 1982: 15. All other translations in this article are my own.
12 On prostitutes in comedy, see Henry 1985, with the review in *CR* n.s. 37 1987: 99–100.
13 Kassel and Austin 1991, fragment 103.
14 For the woman's Agora, see Thphr. *Char*. ii 9, 22.10, Pollux x 18. See further Brock 1994: 345 n. 53.
15 See also Eur. *Hel*. 27.
16 Plutarch uses this as a suitable opening to his *Mulierum virtutes* = *Moralia* 242e.
17 See further discussion and references in the editions by Pomeroy 1994 and Holden 1885.
18 For the vernacular use of such texts, see Montserrat 1996a: 71–72.

19 Page 1938: xxvi.
20 For a discussion (with bibliography) of women and mirrors in Latin literature, see Wyke 1994.
21 Compare the descriptive context in Athenaeus for Sophocles' *Judgement* (Radt 1977, fragment 361, discussed above): Athen. xiii 687 c describes Aphrodite as representing Pleasure and as looking at herself in a mirror (*katoptrizomenên*).
22 It is because of her cropped hair that Orestes first assumes that Electra is a slave: *El.* 107.
23 E.g. 146–50, 184–85, 501. Note that at the very close of the play her face is described as damp again with tears, this time those of parting: 1339.
24 Clytemnestra herself refers to the same luxurious spoils in 1000–1.
25 Compare Electra's remarks about Helen in Eur. *Orestes* 128–29.
26 E.g. addressing them with instructions at 998, 1135–36.
27 Note how after the murders, she wonders who will marry her: 1198–200.
28 See Burn 1987.
29 See references in e.g. Wiles 1991.
30 In another paper (Hawley forthcoming) I discuss in much greater detail the treatment of the male body as spectacle in Greek literature, especially tragedy.
31 E.g. Musonius Rufus 13b. See also Isidore of Seville, *De ecclesiasticis officiis* ii 20: *de coniugatis* (= *PL* 83.812) and his *Etymologiarum* ix 7.29 (= *PL* 82.367) 'item in eligenda uxore, quatuor res impellunt homine ad amorem: pulchritudo, genus, divitiae, mores.'; also Treggiari 1991: 86–87, 100–1. However, Treggiari nowhere discusses beauty contests.
32 See the commentary by Page 1978: 82–85.
33 Compare *Fable* 614 in the Appendix to Perry 1965, where an owl steals the rose meant as a prize for a beauty contest among the birds. As punishment the owl is condemned to fly only by night. In Babrius *Fable* 65 a crane and a peacock compete in beauty, but here the moralising tone is more dominant.
34 Zonaras, *Epitomae historiarum* xv 25.10. On these Byzantine imperial bride-shows, see Treadgold 1979. The historicity of these accounts has been questioned by Rydén 1985, who suggests that the bride show is a literary topos.

Part II

BODIES AND SIGNS IN LATIN LITERATURE

4

EXUVIAS EFFIGIEMQUE
Dido, Aeneas and the body as sign
Angus Bowie

It is an odd feature of the narrative of this episode that Dido places on her pyre an effigy of Aeneas which will have no further role to play and is never mentioned again (iv 504–8):[1]

> at regina pyra penetrali in sede sub auras
> erecta ingenti taedis atque ilice secta,
> intenditque locum sertis et fronde coronat
> funerea; super exuvias ensemque relictum
> effigiemque toro locat haud ignara futuri.

The queen built a pyre under the open sky in the centre of the palace, piled high with pine logs and cut holm-oak; she hung garlands round the place and decorated it with funereal branches. On top, not unaware of what the future held, she put the couch with the things he had left behind, his sword and an *effigy*.

According to the historians Timaeus of Tauromenium and later Pompeius Trogus,[2] Dido, faced with marriage to the Libyan king, again builds a deceptive pyre, pretending to perform a rite to free her of her love (in this case, for her former husband); she then commits suicide on it. In neither, however, is there any effigy. We have therefore a feature which Virgil himself seems to have introduced into the story, and its apparent lack of functionality demands closer attention. One could, with Austin, see the effigy as made of wax and intended for sympathetic magic,[3] but the attempt to reduce the text's problems by constructing an apparently satisfactory 'reality' behind them runs the risk of closing off potential areas of meaning:[4] it is often precisely at such problematic points that literary texts reveal something of their functioning. I want here to look at this effigy, using some of the theoretical work that is currently being done on the body in literature, and to suggest that an account may be given of the effigy through a study of how the body generally operates in this episode.

It may appear prima facie paradoxical that the stimulus for interest in literary bodies is psychoanalysis, but from Freud onwards, psychologists and psychoanalysts have pursued the theory that our experience of our bodies creates and conditions our attitudes to the world. Freud argued that our earliest experiences are autoerotic, that is driven by desire, and this has been variously developed.[5] Essentially, the body is seen as the origin of that sense of difference that is the basis of language. To quote Brooks:[6]

> Bodily parts, sensations, and perceptions (including the notorious recognition of the anatomical distinction between the sexes) are the first building blocks in the construction of a symbolic order, including speech, play, and the whole system of human language, within which the child finds a libidinally invested place.

Currently, the most influential theory is that of Jacques Lacan.[7] At the risk of simplification and distortion of his protean writings, one can say that he posits an original state called the 'Imaginary', in which the child, believing itself part of its mother, acknowledges no difference between itself and the rest of the world. This ends with the 'Oedipal crisis', when the father breaks this unity, becomes a third term and so introduces the idea of difference to the child, who thus enters the 'Symbolic Order', essentially the world as culturally constituted. The father also, by the 'Law of the Father' which Lacan represents by the phallus, forbids the child continued access to the mother's body, and thus imposes a sense of loss on the child through its desire for the lost body of its mother which must be suppressed. This 'first repression' opens up the unconscious and is contemporaneous with the acquisition of language: the child can now distinguish 'I am', 'you are' and 'he is'. Language creates the unconscious: there is no pre-linguistic state. Most famously, Lacan claimed that 'the unconscious is structured like a language',[8] that is, the unconscious acts like language in its constant move from object to object in search of that plenitude it enjoyed with the mother's body, which corresponds to language's constant movement from signifier to signifier: meaning can never be fully grasped, and similarly our desires can never be fulfilled. The body that is sought *par excellence* is, therefore, that of the mother.

These theories have a consequence for reading, through a parallelism that will be central to our inquiry:

> a protagonist often desires a body (most often another's, but sometimes his or her own) and that body comes to represent for the protagonist an apparent ultimate good, since it appears to hold within itself – as itself – the key to satisfaction, power, and meaning. On the plane of reading, desire for knowledge of that body and its secrets becomes the desire to master the text's symbolic system, its key to knowledge, pleasure, and the very creation of significance.[9]

The character's pursuit of the desired body, which is absent in different ways, is analogous to the pursuit by the reader of the signs constituting the constantly deferred meaning of the text. Brooks goes on: 'narrative desire . . . becomes oriented toward knowledge and possession of the body. Narrative seeks to make such a body semiotic, to mark or imprint it as a linguistic and narrative sign.'[10] The reader thus pursues the semiotic, the lover, the physical aspect of the desired body. Such texts must end in paradox: possession of the body may bring a closure to the narrative, but the nature of the linguistic sign ensures that the meaning of the narrative cannot be grasped in its entirety.

THE BODY IN VIRGIL

I begin with some highly selective remarks about bodies in the *Aeneid* generally,[11] to show that the body and what happens to it is a notable aspect of the work.[12] It is foregrounded in different ways at crucial points in the narrative, where the plot takes a significant turn, or where prophecy or important information is given. In this context, the whole narrative is first set in motion through the agency of a desired body.[13] To persuade him to create the storm, Juno offers Aeolus a bride, and the text emphasises her physical attractiveness (i 71–3):[14]

> sunt mihi bis septem praestanti corpore Nymphae,
> quarum quae forma pulcherrima, Deiopea,
> conubio iungam stabili propriamque dicabo.

I have seven Nymphs of outstanding beauty. Of these I will unite Deiopea to you in a lasting marriage and call her yours; she is the most beautiful.

His desire for Deiopea is such that to possess her Aeolus will bend Jupiter's rules under which he controls the winds, and so sets the story on its way.

Violent physical effects on bodies mark cardinal moments.[15] Sometimes these effects are mysteriously harmless: an omen of fire enveloping a child's body persuades Anchises to leave Troy (ii 682–6) and prevents Latinus from marrying Lavinia to Turnus (vii 71–8). By contrast, psychological effects undergone by characters are often described in strongly physical terms. Compare the impact of the hellish Allecto on Amata and Turnus, the physical violence of which leads to bacchic frenzy among the women and passion for war among the men. With Amata (vii 351–3),[16]

> fit tortile collo
> aurum ingens coluber, fit longae taenia vittae
> innectitque comas et membris lubricus errat.

The huge snake became a golden torque around her neck, became the ribbon of her long headband, wound itself through her hair and slithered over her body.

As for Turnus (vii 456–60),

> facem iuveni coniecit et atro
> lumine fumantis fixit sub pectore taedas.
> olli somnum ingens rumpit pavor, ossaque et artus
> perfundit toto proruptus corpore sudor.
> arma amens fremit . . .

She hurled the torch into the youth's face, and fixed the torches that smoked darkly in his breast. Great terror broke his sleep and sweat broke out all over his body. Madly he calls for arms.

A violent physical effect of a less destructive kind is found in the encounter between Venus and Vulcan. When the goddess wants to persuade her husband to make arms for Aeneas (viii 387–92):

> niveis hinc atque hinc diva lacertis
> cunctantem amplexu molli fovet. ille repente
> accepit solitam flammam, notusque medullas
> intravit calor et labefacta per ossa cucurrit,
> non secus atque olim tonitru cum rupta corusco
> ignea rima micans percurrit lumine nimbos.

In her snow-white arms the goddess fondled her hesitating husband, moving him this way and that in a soft embrace. Suddenly he felt the accustomed flame, and the familiar warmth entered his body and ran through his yielding limbs, just as at times a flash of fire burst open by the thunder runs through the clouds with a blazing light.

The result of this thunderous effect is the making of the shield which reveals so much of Rome's future, and bodily effects and prophecy are again linked in Apollo's effect on the Sibyl when she gives her prophecies (vi 47–50, 77–80):

> subito non vultus, non color unus,
> non comptae mansere comae; sed pectus anhelum,
> et rabie fera corda tument, maiorque videri
> nec mortale sonans . . .
> at Phoebi nondum patiens immanis in antro
> bacchatur vates, magnum si pectore possit
> excussisse deum; tanto magis ille fatigat
> os rabidum, fera corda domans, fingitque premendo.

Suddenly, her face and complexion changed; her hair was in disarray; her chest heaved as she breathed and her heart swelled with wild madness; she seemed to grow in stature and to speak in a tone that was not mortal . . . No longer able to bear mighty Phoebus, the priestess raved in the cave to see if she could shake the great god from her breast; all the more he harassed her rabid mouth, dominating her wild heart and moulding her by his pressure.

Here her body is very much the source of the narrative, as the god forces the prophecies physically from her: Aeneas is thus given an outline prophecy of his time in Italy (vi 83–97).

A final category of bodily manifestations prepares the way for how the body works specifically in the Dido episode. Prophecy or revelation is frequently given by ghostly bodies,[17] often of those specifically marked as desired in one way or another by the characters (compare Sychaeus, discussed below).[18] These figures are often referred to as *imagines*, a word used to translate Greek *eidola*, which, for the Atomists and Epicurus are the physical images cast off by bodies which not only enable us to see those bodies but also form the ideas with which we think.[19] Thus, Creusa, sought throughout Troy, flees as an *imago*. Aeneas attempts to embrace her after she reveals the fate he must follow (ii 771–95); Hector, his appalling physical state described at length (ii 270–9), is then addressed (ii 281–3) as *spes ... quae tantae tenuere morae? ... expectate* ('our hope ... what delayed you so long? ... we waited for you') before he gives Aeneas instructions and 'the eternal fire of Troy' (ii 296–7); Deiphobus, hideously disfigured, was also sought in vain (vi 494–508).[20] These *imagines* of desired people and their ultimate inaccessibility are one way in which the *Aeneid* marks the way Aeneas' desire cannot be allowed to dictate the course of events when that desire does not coincide with divine plans.[21] Furthermore, they thus illustrate an aspect of the body's functioning in the *Aeneid* which will be important in the Dido episode. The *imagines, effigies* etc. are 'signs' in the now traditional linguistic sense of anything which stands for, and so indicates the absence of, something else:[22] the desired bodies are tantalisingly present and yet absent. There are also problems of interpretation of the signs. Epicurus again provides an ancient parallel: though for him all sensations of these *eidola* are true, it is our judgement which introduces false opinion and interpretation:[23] a gap opens again between sign and meaning. So it will be for Dido.

DIDO AND AENEAS

The importance of the body and its connection to narrative is thus a notable feature of the epic. In concentrating on the function of the body in this episode, and especially on that of Aeneas, we shall also be able to show not only how the effigy takes its place in a sequence of other similar 'substitutes' or 'signs' for Aeneas, but also to plot both Dido's and the reader's relationship to this somatic/textual sign. There are various kinds of sign for Aeneas' body: they may be linguistic (as in a story about a person), physical (such as artistic representations of the person, or people who resemble them), or what one might call 'psychological' (such as dreams). Dido will be found to be implicated with all of these types, as her determination to maintain her loyalty to Sychaeus involves repeated attempts to use various substitutes for the body she desires. By a cruel twist, the one time when she seems to possess that body is precisely the time that the text's signs become most opaque, and Dido's problems in 'reading' the signs becomes comparable to the reader's.

Before turning to the episode with Aeneas, we may note that Dido has been this way before. It is her tragedy that twice in her life she seeks possession of a desired body, but both times is left with nothing but signs of its absence. The dilemma she faces with Aeneas is in effect a repetition in a slightly different form of her problems over the death of her first husband. The episode concerning Sychaeus' body provides a paradigm for a simple 'somatological' reading of a text.

Pygmalion murdered Sychaeus (i 351–6, 358–9)

> factumque diu celavit et aegram
> multa malus simulans vana spe lusit amantem.
> ipsa sed in somnis inhumati venit imago
> coniugis ora modis attollens pallida miris;
> crudelis aras traiectaque pectora ferro
> nudavit, caecumque domus scelus omne retexit . . .
>   veteres tellure recludit
> thesauros.

For a long time he hid the deed and with every deception deluded the sick and loving wife with empty hopes. However, the ghost of her unburied husband came to her in a dream, lifting strangely its pallid face; he laid bare the cruelty at the altar and his breast pierced by the sword, and unveiled all the house's secret crime . . . He revealed ancient treasures hidden in the earth.

This episode of the appearance of Sychaeus, like the effigy, seems to have been invented by Virgil.[24] Many details of the episode are missing, but, importantly for our purposes, the text concentrates on the absence and reappearance of Sychaeus' body, and the deception practised by Pygmalion. Her husband's body is missing and in its place Dido is faced with the deceptive signs of the 'empty hope' offered her by Pygmalion. This problem is in part resolved by the reappearance of the desired body: the idea of revelation occurs three times in *nudavit*, *retexit* and *recludit*. Sychaeus thus reveals both his body and the solution to the problem facing Dido: 'nudavit' is used, in a notable zeugma, both of his body and of the site of his death. The body inscribed with 'signs', made 'semiotic', gives Dido the answer to her problem. However, her husband does not come in actual bodily form, but only as an *imago*: the signs solve the immediate problem, but merely confirm the absence of her husband. The continued frustration of Dido's desire for Sychaeus means her story is not at an end, but she must go into exile and further experiences. Desire and narrative are coextensive, and only when she

possesses Sychaeus among the shades will her story finish.[25] There
will be a similar frustration in her relationship with Aeneas, when
again apparent possession turns out to be illusory.

This first presentation of Dido's story by Venus itself combines
deception and the body in a way that curiously prefigures their
functioning in the main part of the story. Venus appears to Aeneas,
but disguised as a Spartan or Thracian huntress, pretending to be
searching for a sister who does not in fact exist. There is a physical
description of her which is unusually full for the *Aeneid*, but this
description is employed not to convey a 'true' picture of the goddess
but a false one:[26] the body as sign is no window on 'reality'. The
problem of her identity is alluded to by Aeneas immediately
(i 327–8): *o quam te memorem, virgo? namque haud tibi vultus /
mortalis, nec vox hominem sonat; o dea certe* ... ('How am I to
address you, young lady? Your face and voice are not those of
mortals. A goddess, surely ...'). At the end, he will complain
(i 407–8): *quid natum totiens ... falsis / ludis imaginibus?* ('Why
do you so often deceive your son with false images?'). The episode
ends with the re-establishment of identity and certainty, as Venus
reveals who she really is (i 402–5) and with an omen assures Aeneas
of the truth of what she has told him (i 389–99). The tale of Dido is
thus doubly presented under the sign of bodily deception: an *imago*
tells the story of an *imago* and the possible deceptiveness of the
physical body and its meanings are underscored.

Before Dido meets Aeneas she has already been involved with
'signs' about him. Not only has she heard the story of the Trojans
and Aeneas from Teucer (i 619–26), but later we learn that she has
been warned in the past about Aeneas in oracular utterances (iv
464–5); her failure earlier to call to mind these ambiguous signs
prefigures her failure to comprehend what is happening when Aeneas
is there. More significantly, she has also installed a bodily image of
him on the doors of the temple of Juno (i 488). These images, though
'an empty picture' (*pictura ... inani*, i 464), are the first things which
give Aeneas cause for hope (i 450–2). This is in strong contrast to
Dido, whose attempts to console herself with images will fail: the
signs are empty, for Dido in more ways than one. Commentators
have worried how Aeneas could recognise himself when no specific
action is mentioned, and how Dido could know what he looked like
never having seen him. Once again, however, the point of the episode
may not be simply the realistic representation of actual events: we
seem yet again to have an anomaly which by its very strangeness

suggests, like the effigy, that representations of Aeneas are an important signifying system in the text.

It is at the end of Aeneas' scrutiny of the pictures that Dido appears in person. The text locates her in a significant fashion. The last figure described on the temple is Penthesilea, an Amazon, who like Dido plays male roles: 'and dares, though a woman, to confront men' (*audetque viris concurrere virgo*: i 493). Dido is then compared in bodily appearance to another figure who points to her repression of her sexuality, the chaste goddess Diana (i 498–502). Paradoxically, at the same time, she takes her seat on the throne outside the temple of Juno, the goddess of marriage. The body of Dido is therefore situated uncomfortably amidst figures representing the chastity of the unmarried girl, the man-hating Amazons and the goddess of marriage.

Before Venus leaves Aeneas and Achates, she wraps them in a cloud, thus once more instituting a deception wrought through the body. When Aeneas and Dido first coincide, he is still wrapped in the cloud. There are of course good practical reasons for this (i 411–14), but it also well emblematises the problems Dido will have with Aeneas' body, which will be variously both present physically before her, but also 'absent', in the sense of unattainable. Dido's 'pursuit' of Aeneas is foreshadowed by her reaction to Ilioneus' mention of him, when, in her desire to see this great leader who stands hidden before her, she intends to send out a search party (i 575–8). Her wish is immediately fulfilled as the cloud is dissipated.[27] It is significant however that her first gaze on Aeneas is on an artificially enhanced version, not on Aeneas as he 'really' is: the body deceives again. He appears like a god (i 589–93):

> namque ipsa decoram
> caesariem nato genetrix lumenque iuventae
> purpureum et laetos oculis adflarat honores:
> quale manus addunt ebori decus, aut ubi flavo
> argentum Pariusve lapis circumdatur auro.

> Since the goddess herself had inspired grace in his hair, given
> him the noble glow of youth and a happy sparkle in his eyes;
> as when a craftsman decorates ivory, or mounts Parian marble
> or silver with flaxen gold.

The simile of the craftsman underlines the fact that Dido has no access to the 'true' nature of the man. Similes are, of course, a rhetorical device that simultaneously does and does not say what a person is 'like', and as in the case of the disguised Venus, this rare physical description does not in fact give access to physical truth.

To ensure all goes well, Venus again resorts to trickery, and again the body is the crucial medium. Cupid is instructed to take on the 'form and face' of Ascanius (*faciem mutatus et ora Cupido*: i 658). Whilst everyone admires Cupid (i 713–18),

> expleri mentem nequit ardescitque tuendo
> Phoenissa, et pariter puero donisque movetur.
> ille ubi complexu Aeneae colloque pependit
> et magnum falsi implevit genitoris amorem,
> reginam petit. haec oculis, haec pectore toto
> haeret et interdum gremio fovet . . .

Dido cannot satisfy her desire and burns as she looks, affected equally by the child and the gifts. When Cupid had hung in an embrace around Aeneas' neck and satisfied his false father's great desire, he sought the queen. Her eyes and heart were obsessed by him, and at times she dandled him on her lap.

But why is Dido described as so passionate about the child, if the claim is that it is Aeneas' body that is in question? The answer lies in the description of Ascanius in iv 84 as 'the image of his father' (*genitoris imago*).[28] There, as here, in an image of considerable erotic power, Dido seeks to console herself with a bodily substitute for Aeneas. Thus Cupid disguises himself as the absent Ascanius who looks like Aeneas, in order to make Dido fall in love: this elaborate double similarity immediately delineates the gap that exists between Dido and Aeneas' body. She is moving closer to that body, via stories, oracles, a physical representation, cloud-shrouded presence and actual presence, but she is yet merely fondling one who looks like one who looks like Aeneas.

Dido is yet resisting her passion, and in a classic example of how desire can create narrative, she employs the story of Aeneas' experiences as it were as a substitute for him. Here we and Dido come closest to each other in our relation to the text, in that, though the story is actually addressed to her and the Carthaginians, the length and complexity of the narration naturally cause the reader to forget that context. That the story is being used to defer the problems is suggested at the start of Book IV, when she is showing Aeneas round the new city (iv 76–9):

> incipit effari mediaque in voce resistit;
> nunc eadem labente die convivia quaerit,
> Iliacosque iterum demens audire labores
> exposcit pendetque iterum narrantis ab ore.

She begins to speak, but stops as she does so. Now, as day declines, she commands a repetition of the feast, and in her madness demands to hear the travails of the Trojans once more, and hangs on his words as once more he tells them.

Unable to speak herself, she has recourse to further repetitions of his story. In 'pendetque iterum narrantis ab ore', the Lucretian intertext describing a passionate scene between Mars and Venus, 'his breath hangs on your lips as he lies back beside you' (*eque tuo pendet resupini spiritus ore*: i 38), comes cruelly close to suggesting a kiss that is not taking place.

But this deferral cannot go on for ever, any more than the narrative can stand the simple repetition of the same stories. When Aeneas' narrative is over, the problem re-emerges. Dido's passion is depicted in strikingly violent physical terms (iv 1–2, 4–5):

> at regina gravi iamdudum saucia cura
> vulnus alit venis et caeco carpitur igni . . .
>   haerent infixi pectore vultus
> verbaque . . .

But the queen, now long grievously wounded, feeds the wound in her veins and is consumed by a hidden fire. . . . His features and his words have transfixed her breast.

Dreams, presumably of the absent Sychaeus, and the physical presence of Aeneas combine to torment her (iv 9–11). Then (iv 83–5):

> illum absens absentem auditque videtque,
> aut gremio Ascanium genitoris imagine capta
> detinet, infandum si fallere possit amorem.

Though apart from each other, she sees his face and hears his words; or, taken by Ascanius' likeness to him, she keeps him with her and holds him in her lap, to see if she can beguile the love she dare not speak of.

Her passion is such that she can summon up a picture of his body when it is absent: Aeneas' simultaneous presence and absence is graphically portrayed. The interpretation of the next sentence is disputed: does she, as Page suggests, actually fondle Ascanius 'as a substitute for Aeneas', or is it, as Austin argues, that 'Dido sorrows alone in the empty palace, Aeneas is there, the child is there, the whole vivid scene is present again'? Is the substitution single or double? The lines may pose difficulties in realist terms, but less so for a bodily reading: the body of Ascanius is again substituted, whether in fact or imagination, for that of his father. Dido's love is 'unspeakable', not (yet) to be put into language, so that it has to be dealt with by other means. The problem with this resort to substitutes for Aeneas' body is given in the next lines: all activity stops (iv 86–9):

> non coeptae adsurgunt turres, non arma iuventus
> exercet portusve aut propugnacula bello
> tuta parant: pendent opera interrupta minaeque
> murorum ingentes aequataque machina caelo.

The towers she had begun did not rise, and the young men did not practise with their weapons, nor construct the harbours or defences for war. The work suspended stood idle, along with the threateningly high walls and the crane that reached the sky.

And not only activity on the building of Carthage: Aeneas' mission and the divine plan are also impeded.

Now the goddesses step in with their plan to bring Aeneas and Dido together in the cave. The episode is notoriously problematic, but it is also of great interest for our 'bodily' study, since at last the bodies are brought together in an erotic context. However, by not making absolutely clear what happened, and more importantly by having Aeneas and Dido interpret it differently, Virgil plunges both the reader and Dido into uncertainty: Dido's control of the story is finally lost, and the reader's certainty is also shaken. As with Sychaeus, we have an erotic meeting which does not resolve the problems, but intensifies them.

There are hints aplenty as to the meaning of the scene, but they do not allow an authoritative account. Juno proposes to Venus a 'marriage pact', in which Dido 'serves a Trojan husband, and the Carthaginians come to you as a dowry' (iv 99, 103–4). If Venus is willing, 'I will join them in a lasting marriage and pronounce her his; this will be their wedding day' (*conubio iungam stabili propriamque dicabo. / hic hymenaeus erit:* iv 126–7). Events turn out as Juno says (iv 166–72):

> prima et Tellus et pronuba Juno
> dant signum; fulsere ignes et conscius aether
> conubiis, summoque ulularunt vertice Nymphae.
> ille dies primus leti primusque malorum
> causa fuit; neque enim specie famave movetur
> nec iam furtivum Dido meditatur amorem:
> coniugium vocat, hoc praetexit nomine culpam.

First Earth and Juno, goddess of marriage, gave the signal: lightning flashed and the air aware of the marriage; the Nymphs cried out on the mountain top. That day first was the cause of her death and of her troubles. Dido was moved no more by appearances or what people said; she no longer dwelt on a secret passion: she called it a marriage, and with this word hid her shame.

It is hard not to take this as an actual wedding:[29] we have witnesses, *pronuba*, the sign 'as if for the bridal procession', lightning as the marriage torch, the technical terms *conubium, dicare, hymenaeus*, and the wedding song. The wedding is thus in some ways 'ritually correct', even if there are oddities: no mortal witnesses are present and 'ulularunt' can be a cry of horror as well as a ritual one.[30] The text encourages both us and Dido to see a marriage involved, but what exactly happened is clothed in secrecy. To twist Virgil's language, Juno and the Earth may 'give the sign' (iv 166–7), but the meaning of the sign is unclear.

This problem of interpretation is underlined by the text itself, through its juxtaposition of the cave episode with the reaction of Fama, 'Rumour', who is described in full bodily detail (iv 180–3), followed at iv 188–90 by the information that she is:

> tam ficti pravique tenax quam nuntia veri.
> haec tum multiplici populos sermone replebat
> gaudens, et pariter facta atque infecta canebat.

A messenger as keen on the false and malicious as the true, she then gleefully spread ambiguous reports among the peoples, and told alike of things done and not done.

Thus her reports of their wallowing in debauch and luxury (iv 192–4) are not to be trusted[31] (Virgil calls them 'foul', *foeda*: iv 195), and they are as useful as our own speculations and attempts to fill the gaps. Dido's attempt to possess Aeneas' body and our attempts to grasp fully the narrative thus seem to suffer from the same problems of having nothing certain to work with, merely signs that must be interpreted as best they may be. The ambiguity therefore over the meaning of the cave episode might be said not to be a problem to be solved in 'realist' terms by ever closer reading of the text or weighing of probabilities, but as a device that puts the reader in the same position as Dido in her perplexity. Judging the characters on the basis of this crucial episode becomes problematic because there is no authoritative account of what happened, either from the primary narrator or from any of the actors.

Dido is in no doubt, and shortly after we (and Mercury) see Aeneas engaged in building work (iv 261–4):

> atque illi stellatus iaspide fulva
> ensis erat Tyrioque ardebat murice laena
> demissa ex umeris, dives quae munera Dido
> fecerat, et tenui telas discreverat auro.

He had a sword studded with yellow jasper, and a cloak hung from his shoulders glowing with Tyrian purple, gifts which wealthy Dido had made, embroidering the cloth with gold thread.

The wife's task was making clothes for her husband, and that is what Dido has done for Aeneas. Again the situation is expressed in bodily terms, though it will transpire that Dido has only affected the external accessories of Aeneas' body.[32] Dido's apparent progress in her desire restarts the building work that had earlier come to a halt. At the same time, the gods are once again intervening to see the narrative resumes its allotted course, as Jupiter, in an imposition, as it were, of the Law of the Father, forbids Dido's desire to reach fulfilment.

We and Dido might reasonably decode the above description of Aeneas as signifying that he is now the Carthaginian husband of Dido, but how Aeneas originally understood the implications of the cave episode we are never explicitly or unambiguously told, because all his behaviour and remarks postdate the intervention of Mercury. There are however enough hints concerning his feelings before this to suggest that Dido is not entirely wrong. We are told that he found Carthage very pleasant (*dulcis . . . terras*: iv 281) and that Dido 'did not expect so great a passion to be broken off' (iv 291–2), both of which suggest strong emotional involvement on his part. Furthermore, Jupiter sees them both as 'lovers forgetful of their good reputation' (*oblitos famae melioris amantis*: iv 221), and complains that Aeneas is not fulfilling his destiny (iv 224–31); Mercury will call Aeneas *uxorius* and *oblite* (iv 266–7). Later, Dido tells Anna to inform Aeneas that 'I do not ask any more for that old marriage that he has betrayed' (*non iam coniugium antiquum, quod prodidit, oro*: iv 431), and refers to 'the marriage bed where I was undone' (*lectum . . . iugalem, / quo perii:* iv 496–7). Uncertainty is created however by his denials when Dido, calling him 'guest' (*hospes*) and commenting 'since this name is all that is left from what was once "husband"' (*hoc solum nomen quoniam de coniuge restat*: iv 324), begs him to change his mind 'by our nuptials, by the marriage we contracted' (*per conubia nostra, per inceptos hymenaeos*: iv 316). He replies 'I never handed you the bridegroom's torch, nor made any such contract' (*nec coniugis umquam / praetendi taedas aut haec in foedera veni*: iv 338–9): the first clause may be technically acceptable, since lightning played the role of the torches, but the second we cannot judge. We are left therefore with ambiguities: Dido's position is clear, Aeneas' denials equally so, but the narrator intrudes enough hints to suggest that to begin with Aeneas interpreted the signs in the cave and reacted to them in the same way as Dido, or at least acted as if he did. One should not easily presume, as many (male) commentators have, that Aeneas is correct and Dido deluded.

If the reader has begun to share Dido's uncertainties,[33] when she appears to have lost Aeneas and her good name and broken her vow, she begins gradually once again to take control of the story and its meanings and to bring this narrative and her life to a close, her passion finally thwarted. Once again, deception is tried against her, as Aeneas gives orders to his men to prepare departure (iv 290–1), but now this does not work (iv 296, 305–6). This time even Fama is reliable in her report that the Trojans are preparing to leave (iv 298–9). A little later, Dido ends a speech to Anna with a line that has been described by Conington as 'the most difficult in Virgil': *extremam hanc oro veniam (miserere sororis) / quam mihi cum dederit cumulatam morte remittam* (iv 435–6).[34] The positioning of this 'outstanding example of Virgilian mystery' (Austin) is significant: from this point on, she becomes less the victim of deception and misunderstanding and more the operator of deception which makes others misunderstand the signs.

Even here however she turns again to those substitutes for Aeneas which she tried before, but the subjunctives suggest the impossibility of her desires (iv 328–9):

> saltem si qua mihi de te suscepta fuisset
> ante fugam suboles, si quis mihi parvulus aula
> luderet Aeneas, qui te tamen ore referret,
> non equidem omnino capta ac deserta viderer.

If only I had had some child by you before you left, if only
some little Aeneas played in my halls whose face would remind
me of you, then I would not feel so completely betrayed and
devastated.

The signs given by Aeneas' body are now unambiguous: 'Did he
grieve when I wept? Did he turn his gaze away? Was he won over
to tears or did he pity the one who loves him? No.' (*num fletu
ingemuit nostro? num lumina flexit? / num lacrimas victus dedit aut
miseratus amantem est?*: iv 369–70). Similarly, the plan to make
Aeneas stay until the spring fails, which is yet another attempt to
make up for the impossibility of possessing him: externally Aeneas
weeps, but his tears are merely *inanes* (iv 449). Knowing now that
these external signs are no guide to internal feelings, Dido 'longs for
death' (iv 451).

As things begin to move towards their close, we have a repetition
of motifs from the start of the episode. Dido told of her *insomnia* (iv
9), and now again she is caught between visions of the two men. In
the temple of Juno, she hears Sychaeus calling her (iv 460–1), and
later (iv 465–7)

> agit ipse furentem
> in somnis ferus Aeneas, semperque relinqui
> sola sibi ... videtur ...

In her dream wild Aeneas himself drives her to madness, and
she seems always to be left alone.

The dream combines truth (she is left alone) and falsehood (the image
of Aeneas pursues her), and encapsulates the problem of her relationship with him: at one minute he is her lover, the next not, after
a sudden shift of intention. This passage concludes with a simile
comparing Dido to various figures who suffered terrible visions in
tragedy (iv 469–71):

> Eumenidum veluti demens videt agmina Pentheus
> et solem geminum et duplices se ostendere Thebas,
> aut Agamemnonius scaenis agitatus Orestes ...

Like Pentheus when in his madness he saw appear the ranks of
the Eumenides, the double suns and double Thebes, or Orestes
driven over the stage . . .

The problem of perception is doubly involved here. First, in
Pentheus' double vision: Dido too is, as it were, 'seeing double'
when she looks at Aeneas;[35] secondly, reference to tragedy brings
with it the notion of the deceptiveness of drama, noted from at least
Gorgias on.[36] This sole reference to theatrical representation in the
Aeneid is thus not casually placed but marks Dido's entrapment in
an ambiguous world.

She goes again to Anna, and now uses her own body to disguise
her intentions: 'she hides her intentions by her expression and
showed hope on her face' (*consilium vultu tegit ac spem fronte
serenat*: iv 477–8). She orders a pyre on the pretence that it is part of
a magical rite to bring him to her or to get rid of her love for Aeneas
(iv 479).[37] On the pyre are to go all the things that are associated with
Aeneas, his 'arma', all the *exuviae*, and the *lectus iugalis*: everything
that recalls him (*monimenta*) is to be destroyed (iv 495–8). Anna is
fooled into doing her will, failing to interpret properly Dido's 'pallor'
(iv 500–3). When the pyre is ready, Dido places the effigy upon the
arms and *exuviae* (iv 507–8). The effigy is her final substitute, which
takes her back to the equally lifeless image on the temple, which was
all she had before she met Aeneas, and Cupid came in disguised as
Ascanius, the *parvulus Aeneas*. The substitutes for the body of
Aeneas are thus at the centre of things: both the *exuviae* and the
effigies are clear 'signs' for the absent Aeneas. *Exuviae* can be an
animal- or snake-skin,[38] or items which suggest one has the form or
status of another,[39] as well as spoils taken in battle that stand as signs
of the defeat of an enemy. In this context of apparent ritual magic,
as Austin says, they will be not just some token given by Aeneas but
also something 'symbolic of himself', something which stands for
him in the rite and will (normally) suffer the things which Dido
wishes to happen to the man himself. Atop the whole is the
culminating item in our list of substitutes, the actual image of Aeneas'
body: Dido and the effigy on the wedding bed make a pitiful parody
of the marriage she sought, a suitable image for the way her
relationship to Aeneas has been so much at one remove, and she both
has and has not possessed him. This effigy is also an ambiguous sign:
it is apparently meant to signify to Anna that Dido really is
conducting a ritual to win back her lover, but for Dido it means

something else, even if we are not told exactly what that meaning might be.

Indeed, if the ritual as a whole deceives Anna, it is also problematic for us, in part because we too are uncertain what Dido has in mind. As Eitrem pointed out,[40] the ritual is rather curious. He makes three main points: (1) the pyre is odd in such a ritual and is never lit during it, nor is any use made of the effigy; (2) the magic ingredients have to be fetched just at the moment when one expects the rite to be completed (iv 513–14); (3) for the rite to succeed, the performer must wish for its success, but Dido is ashamed of her use of magic, describing herself as *invitam* ('unwilling', iv 492–3), and one would have expected her to have prayed to chthonic deities in iv 519–20.[41] If the reader earlier shared Dido's uncertainties about Aeneas, now Dido is in control[42] and we are paired more closely with Anna in our attempts to make sense of the signs in the text. The meaning of the whole ritual, let alone of the effigy, is opaque: it does not correspond in its details to its avowed purpose.

Dido's control of events, of the narrative, is most strikingly manifested in her use of prophecy combined with curse. Her first (iv 382–7) was somewhat unspecific,[43] the second is much more significant. Earlier, her desire for Aeneas generated a narrative of the past, and her hopes were that the fulfilment of that desire would generate a future of marriage and safety. Deprived of that hope, she now seeks to determine the future in another way. The effects are impressive.[44] Her curse on Aeneas and the Trojans (iv 607–29) seems to ensure the future course of tragic history for Carthage and Rome: her desire and fate coincide (cf. i 19–22). Her suicide even manages to change fate, since she dies 'neither as determined by fate nor as she deserved' (*nec fato merita nec morte*: iv 696), with the result that she is, ironically, trapped in her own body until freed by Iris. More importantly for our purposes, she also specifies the fate she wishes to befall Aeneas' body: 'may he fall before his time is due and lie unburied on the wide sand' (*sed cadat ante diem mediaque inhumatus arena*: iv 620). Intriguingly, Servius preserves a tradition that, sacrificing after a successful battle, Aeneas fell into the Numicus river and his body was never found.[45] Is she left, therefore, with the final say over this body which has so shaped her own life? Since Virgil gives two accounts of Aeneas' end which contradict each other (and, apparently, Dido's curse),[46] we shall never know.[47]

Dido's death brings an end, not to her desire, which continues in Hades,[48] but to its frustration. Dido loves on,[49] but at the third attempt, she possesses the desired man, and her desires are matched by his: 'her original husband Sychaeus reciprocates her cares and matches her love with his' (*coniunx ... pristinus illi / respondet curis aequatque Sychaeus amorem*: vi 473–4). Sychaeus is again a ghost, but so is she. They have now achieved a kind of plenitude, in Lacanian terms almost a regression to the pre-specular stage. Earlier, Dido had problems with her perception of Aeneas and his body, but here it is Aeneas who has the difficulty (vi 452–4):

> agnovitque per umbras
> obscuram, qualem primo qui surgere mense
> aut videt aut vidisse putat per nubila lunam.

> He caught sight of her dimly through the shadows, like a man who, as the month begins, sees or thinks he has seen the moon rise through the clouds.

The clouds that once obscured Aeneas now surround Dido. She need no longer look at Aeneas' body which caused her such pain, and keeps her eyes turned away: (*illa solo fixos oculos aversa tenebat*: vi 469; cf. 465).[50] With the possession of Sychaeus and the fulfilment of their mutual desire, her story effectively comes full circle, the presence of Aeneas' mortal, physical body of little interest.[51]

We can summarise as follows. Dido's involvement with Aeneas can be divided into five stages. (1) Before Aeneas arrives, the 'signs' lurk, their significance not yet clear. (2) Before the cave scene, Dido is silent about her love and uses a number of substitutes for Aeneas' actual body; despite the fact that she is the victim of deceptions whose nature is clear to the reader, she nonetheless retains some control over her life and so the narrative. (3) After the cave scene, we begin to share her perplexity about her relationship to Aeneas and his body. She obviously knows what happened physically in the cave, but this is not the important point; what matters is the significance of it. (4) In the period leading up to her death, Dido loses control of Aeneas but takes control of the narrative and of deception, so that it is the reader who is now uncertain about the meanings in the text. (5) United with Sychaeus, Dido has no further interest in Aeneas and her story closes; this closing episode brings no clarification to the earlier uncertainty. In this shifting relationship between Dido and Aeneas, there is a similar shifting relationship between reader and text. We do not move from desire to comprehend the text to the possession of its meaning. Rather, our grasp of the text changes from comprehension to uncertainty.

The advantage of using Aeneas' body as the *file-conducteur* of our analysis is that it makes plain how nightmarish Dido's relation to the body has been. It also helps plot the broad outlines of reader-response, from sympathy, both for the deceptions which we see and she does not and for the attempts she makes to find surrogates for her passion, to shared perplexity over the cave-episode, and finally to a separation from her shared with Anna, as Dido goes her own way and herself exploits ambiguity to bring about her end. This 'bodily' reading has shown too that the ambiguities in a text are not always to be resolved in realist terms, but may have a crucial function in our own uncomfortable reading of the text. It has also suggested a solution to the question of the *effigies*.[52]

NOTES

1 See iv 646ff. where she mentions sword, clothing, couch and *exuviae*, but not the effigy, which is also ignored when she refers to Aeneas himself (iv 660).

2 Timaeus, *FGrH* III b.566, fragment 82; Justin xviii 4–6. For effigies as erotic substitutes in mythology, see Laodamia (Hyginus, *Fab.* 104; she too used the effigy 'as if she were carrying out some religious rite' (*sub simulatione sacrorum*), and leapt on the pyre lit by her father to burn the image) and Pygmalion (Ov. *Met.* x 253ff.).

3 Austin 1955: 151. For the magical use of effigies, see Pease 1935: 416–17.

4 On the opposing camps in Virgilian criticism which line up on either side of this divide, see Fowler 1990: 42–63.

5 A convenient summary is in Brooks 1993: 1–27.

6 Brooks 1993: 7.

7 On Lacan, see Benvenuto and Kennedy 1986; Raglan-Sullivan 1986; Bowie 1987; Bowie 1979: 116–53; for a very succinct account of this aspect of Lacan's work, see Moi 1985: 99–101. A seminal text on the body in literature is of course Barthes 1973b *passim*, esp. 122–3; see further Moriarty 1991: 186–94.

8 See Bowie 1979: 126:

> he points out that the human subject, as he acquires speech, is inserting himself into a pre-existing symbolic order and thereby submitting his libido (*désir*) to the systemic pressures of that order: in adopting language he allows his free instinctual energies to be operated upon and organised. It is the peculiar privilege of man the language-user to remain oblivious, while making things with words, of the extent to which words have made, and continue to make, him.

9 Brooks 1993: 8.

10 Brooks 1993: 8.

11 For a different and fuller account of the body in Virgil, see Heuzé 1985.

12 Both in Dido's case (e.g. i 673) and those of others, the language used often is that of the capture and destruction of cities, so that the violence against individuals becomes by synecdoche symbolic of the effect of fated history on nations.

13 Note that Juno is initially described as 'nursing an eternal wound in her breast' (*aeternum servans sub pectore vulnus*: i 36).

14 Ominously, line 73 will be repeated in the Dido episode (iv 126).

15 See also Heuzé 1985: 67–206.

16 vii 355 *ossibus implicat ignem* repeats i 660 (of Dido). See too what happens to Laocoon and his sons (ii 212–24) before the horse is brought into Troy.

17 See also Heuzé 1985: 407–15.

18 In Lucretius, it is a predisposition or desire of the mind to see certain *imagines* that permits their perception: *et quia tenuia sunt, nisi quae contendit, acute / cernere non potis est animus ... / ipse parat sese porro speratque futurum / ut videat quod consequitur rem quamque* (iv 802–3, 805–6).

19 '*Imagines, quae eidola nominant, quorum incursione non solum videamus, sed etiam cogitemus*' (Cic. *Fin.* i 6.21); see Alexander, *De sensu* 56.12; Long and Sedley 1987: i 72–86 and ii 75–91. Lucretius (iv 722–822) expounds the theory at length, but as often Virgil replaces the randomness of Epicurean atoms with *imagines* that have a role in a more ordered universe: see Hardie 1986: 157–240. On the word generally in Virgil, see Gagliardi 1985 *s.v. imago*. On the social symbolism of *imagines* at Rome, see Leigh 1995: 207–9.

20 The Parade of Heroes at the end of Book VI is a further example on a larger scale.

21 The Penates also appear in a dream; Aeneas has saved these and they will stay with him, but it is significant that they are divine. On the way Aeneas may not enjoy the presence of those he loves, see Feeney 1990.

22 This distinction between sign and referent, 'signifiant' and 'signifié', is not evoked anachronistically here: it is found in the Stoic distinction between *semainon* and *semainomenon*: see Sext. Emp. *Adv. Math.* viii 11–13; Graeser 1978: 77–100.

23 See Sext. Emp. *Adv. Math.* viii 63 on Orestes: 'when he seemed to see the Furies, his sensation, being moved by the images, was true, in that the images objectively existed; but his mind, in thinking that the Furies were solid bodies, held a false opinion'; see below on *Aen.* iv 469–71.

24 See Austin 1971: 129.

25 Though Dido has vowed faithfulness to Sychaeus, the text makes plain that her *resides animos desuetaque corda* (i 722) are not entirely quiescent.

26 The goddess of sexuality is dressed in a manner better suited to the virgin goddess, Diana. Disguise as Harpalyce also involves reversals: she was a woman who took on male roles (see DServius on 317). This confrontation of Aeneas and 'Diana' foreshadows his meeting with Dido compared to Diana in i 498–502.

27 This dissipation of the cloud might be compared with the use of the novelistic device of the shattered window-pane to create significant gazes; see Brooks 1993: 89–90.

28 There is a stronger physical sense to this use of *imago* than in, say, Cicero's use of *effigies* in a comparable context at *Fin.* ii 18.58: *Ser Pedacueus reliquit effigiem et humanitatis et probitatis suae filium.*

29 See for the details Austin 1955: 57–9, 69–70.

30 In the *Aeneid* it is used elsewhere only in painful circumstances: Dido's death (iv 667); the women accompanying Amata on her bacchic frenzy (vii 395); Euryalus' mother on hearing of his death (ix 477); mass funeral of warriors (xi 190).

31 Equally unreliable is Iarbas' xenophobic description of Aeneas at iv 215–18.

32 Contrast the way that Aeneas' gifts of clothes and accoutrements belonging to an adulteress (Helen) and a suicide (Ilione, i 648–54) have a prophetic quality.

33 Later, Dido describes Anna as the one to whom Aeneas confided his 'secret feelings' (*arcanos . . . sensus*: iv 421–2). *Arcanos*, with its intimations of 'some inner "mystery"', into which she was not initiated' (Austin 1955: 129), sums up the problem Dido has faced in interpreting the outward signs given by Aeneas. Neither she nor we have been privy to Aeneas' meetings with Anna.

34 Austin 1955: 132 translates: 'and when he has granted this kindness to me, I shall repay it a thousandfold at my death'; see the commentators for discussions ancient and modern.

35 See above n. 23.

36 Grg. 82 B 23 DK; *Diss. Log.* iii 10. The prevalence of tragic intertexts in the episode should also be considered in this context.

37 The echoes of the Nurse's ambiguous remarks in the *Hippolytus* about her own love-cures emphasise the deceptive nature of this remark (see Eur. *Hipp.* 509ff.). The uncertainty over the precise role of the witch of iv 480ff. is a further example of Dido's deceptiveness.

38 See e.g. *Aen.* ii 473, ix 307, xi 577.

39 Suet. *Aug.* 94.

40 Eitrem 1933.

41 Note also *simulatos* used of the water from Avernus (iv 512): Austin 1955: 153 quotes Servius' comment *in sacris . . . quae exhiberi non poterant simulabantur, et erant pro veris* ('in ritual, those things they could not bring forth they imitated, so that they stood for the actual objects').

42 Contrast *haud ignara futuri* (iv 508) with *fati nescia* Dido (i 299).

43 It employed the kind of paradoxical language which characterised her relationship with Aeneas: 'absent, I shall pursue you' (*sequar . . . absens*: iv 384) and 'a shade, I shall be with you' (*umbra . . . adero*: iv 386). This prophecy was followed by collapse and tender care from her servants; the main one carries much more power, and is followed by commands coolly given to a servant.

44 Note that she prays that an avenger should arise *nostris ex ossibus* (iv 625).

45 Servius on iv 620: *alii dicunt quod victor Aeneas, cum sacrificaret super Numicum fluvium, lapsus est et eius nec cadaver inventum est.*

46 See i 265–6 and vii 764–5.

47 Her final deception is of Aeneas who, as he leaves and sees the flames, has difficulty interpreting this sign: 'the cause of so great a fire was unclear' (*quae tantum incenderit ignem / causa latet*: v 4–5).

48 See vi 444, 'their cares do not leave them even in death' (*curae non ipsa in morte relinquunt*).

49 She bears, like Sychaeus, the signs of her suffering: *recens a vulnere Dido* (vi 450).

50 vi 469 = i 482 of Athena's reaction to the robe offered by the Trojan women, a clear indication that the imperfects of 468 are conatives, not inceptives.

51 Turnus, in many ways Dido's counterpart in the second part of the *Aeneid*, is also involved in an incident where a substitute for Aeneas' body is used in an attempt to ensure safety. In x 633ff., Juno makes an *imago* (see x 643, etc.) of Aeneas for Turnus to chase, whose description recalls features of Dido's experiences (see x 633–42), but, just as Dido's safety from the consequences of her passion is restricted by the wishes of the goddesses, so Jupiter has told Juno Turnus can only have a brief respite (x 622). The image cannot save him in the end, any more than Dido's substitutes can save her: Turnus will also die by a sword belonging to Aeneas.

52 This type of reading may explain the 'dissatisfaction' some feel at the *Aeneid*'s ending. Aeneas and Lavinia never meet, as intertexts like the *Odyssey* suggest they will. Furthermore, Aeneas has never seen Lavinia and expresses no emotion about her (he refers to her non-committally once at xii 194). He completes his task (even finding his 'ancient mother' [iii 96]) and closes the narrative, but the desiring subject is Turnus, not he. Desire is thus frustrated for the reader and Turnus, and apparently absent for Aeneas (only on the divine level is desire for union fulfilled [xii 791–842]). At the end, instead of Aeneas and Lavinia, we get Aeneas and Turnus (made all the more uncomfortable by verbal and other echoes of Dido's suicide). The decoration on Pallas' fatal belt symbolises this 'dissatisfaction' at the end of the work: 'a band of young men foully murdered on their wedding night and blood-stained bedrooms' (*una sub nocte iugali / caesa manus iuvenum foede thalamique cruenti*: x 497–8), i.e. the murder of the sons of Aegyptus by the Danaids. We and Turnus are thus like the sons of Aegyptus, disappointed of the married bliss they legitimately expected at the end of the story. Is this why some readers sympathise with Turnus' soul as it goes to Hades *indignata*?

5

BODIES IN FLUX
Ovid's *Metamorphoses*
Penelope Murray

Ovid's *Metamorphoses* presents us with the ultimate in anthropo-metamorphosis. In this poem the human body is not simply modified, but unrecognisably transformed into animal, plant or tree, sometimes disappearing altogether like Echo, who becomes merely an incorporeal voice (see frontispiece). This is a world in which all conventional boundaries are dissolved: at any point you might find your hair sprouting horns, your feet rooted to the spot or curving into claws, your arms bristling with coarse black hair, bark surrounding your thighs; you might find you were growing leaves instead of hair, or had hideous gaping jaws instead of a once beautiful face. What happens to a human being when his or her body undergoes such drastic modification? How important is the body to our understanding of what it is to be human? These are some of the questions which Ovid's poem invites us to consider, questions which are, of course, central to the theme of this book.

Generalisations about the *Metamorphoses* are difficult; even the question of the significance of the theme of metamorphosis itself is controversial. Some scholars regard it as merely tangential to the poem, pointing out that it is no accident that paintings and works of art inspired by it tend not to take the moment of metamorphosis as their theme.[1] Ovid's delight in describing the process of change, in capturing that stage of transition between one shape and another when his subject is neither human being, beast or tree is not reflected in the enormously rich artistic tradition deriving from his fleshly and corporeal poem.[2] But then how does an artist represent fluidity and flux in the static and inflexible medium of painting, sculpture or woodcut?[3] The result can easily be a static image of bodily otherness, an exotic prop in an environment, from which the experiential aspects of humanity have been evacuated (see Plates 5.1a and b).

Ovid's tales of transformation are immensely varied: sometimes the metamorphosis is instant and miraculous, as when the nymph Syrinx, pursued by Pan, prays desperately to be changed in order to elude his grasp. Pan, thinking that he has at last caught hold of her, finds that instead of the nymph's body he is holding a handful of marsh-reeds (*Met.* i 703ff.). At other times the process is gradual and depicted in minute detail, as in the examples I am going to discuss. Very often the transformation is incomplete: when Apollo puts his hand on the laurel tree he feels Daphne's heart still beating and kisses the wood as if it were limbs, but even as a tree she shuns his kisses (*Met.* i 553ff.). Usually the metamorphosis is permanent, which paradoxically introduces an element of fixity into an otherwise constantly changing world. This is particularly the case in stories of transformation into birds, plants and stones, which as Forbes-Irving has shown,[4] tend to be both aetiological and terminal.

Often it is not clear how we are supposed to respond to these stories – indeed Ovid delights in exploiting the existential ambiguity involved in the very idea of metamorphosis. Myrrha (see frontispiece), unable to endure the burden of her incestuous guilt and not knowing what to pray for, at last begs to be transformed (*Met.* x 481ff.):

> o siqua patetis
> numina confessis, merui nec triste recuso
> supplicium! sed ne violem vivosque superstes
> mortuaque extinctos, ambobus pellite regnis
> mutataeque mihi vitamque necemque negate!

> Oh gods, if there be any who will listen to my prayer, I have deserved grievous punishment, nor do I shrink from it: but in case I should contaminate the living by my presence if I live, or the dead if I die, banish me from the realms of both, and deny me life and death, by changing me into some other form.[5]

Similarly, Anius (*Met.* xiii 670ff.), describing how Bacchus miraculously changed his daughters into birds, relates how the god brought them help,

> if you can call it help to bring about their destruction. How they lost their human shape I could not discover, nor can I tell you now, but I do know the final issue of this calamity. My daughters took wings, and were changed into snow-white doves (*niveas abire columbas*).

81

Plate 5.1a and b The transformations of Lycaon and Daphne (left) and
Actaeon (right).
(Details of engravings from Sandys' translation of Ovid's *Metamorphoses*, London
1632: photographs reproduced by courtesy of Michael Whitby.)

That use of *abire*, a favourite expression for change both in relation to whole bodies as here, and in cases where parts of bodies are changed, highlights the paradox of simultaneous presence and absence that is involved in metamorphosis: despite their continuing corporeal existence, Anius' daughters as individuals have disappeared, transformed into nameless members of another species.[6] For Anius this disappearance is a calamity, but often the response to metamorphosis is more equivocal as, for example, when the companions of Daphne's father do not know whether to congratulate or console him after she has been turned into a tree (*Met.* i 578). Transformed into a laurel, she both is and is not Daphne. The theme of metamorphosis thus tends to avoid tragedy, but the human suffering remains. (See Plate 5.1a.)

It is interesting that in all these tales of metamorphosis, none is described as being physically painful; what Ovid concentrates on is the mental anguish involved in bodily transformations.[7] Part of the fascination of the poem lies in the way in which it explores feelings of entrapment, feelings of a person being imprisoned within a body that is not what he or she essentially is. The nightmarish quality, so often commented on, in tales of metamorphosis from Ovid to Kafka, depends largely on this sense of bodily imprisonment, particularly when the body is that of an animal. It is this aspect of the metamorphosis theme which will be the focus of my chapter.

As a starting point I shall take the story of Io in *Met.* i. Jupiter, having raped Io, then turns her into a cow in a futile attempt to prevent Juno from finding out about his misdemeanours. The jealous wife, well aware of the attractions of her rival, even though she is only a cow (*bos quoque formosa est*: *Met.* i 612) sets the hundred-eyed Argus to guard her. During the day she is allowed to graze, but at night she is locked up, 'an ignominious halter round her neck'; the Loeb translation quoted here gets across correctly the sense of *indigno ... collo* (*Met.* i 631) – it is not simply that she does not deserve it, but also that to be shackled like a cow is degrading for a human being. She feeds on grass that is bitter (*amara*: *Met.* i 632), continuing the human perspective, drinks muddy water and, instead of on a bed the poor thing has to lie down on the ground. When she wanted to stretch out her arms in supplication she had no arms to stretch; when she opened her mouth she could only moo. She was afraid at the sound of her own voice, and when she saw her gaping jaws and strange horns reflected in the waters where she used to play, she fled, terrified, from herself (*Met.* i 636–41).

This would all be funny if it were not for the fact that it is presented to us from Io's point of view; we are not allowed to keep ourselves outside the mind of the victim. The overwhelming sense we have is that of the human consciousness helplessly trapped inside an alien body, powerless to act, and unable to communicate. If only the words would come she would beg for help, speak her name and tell of her misfortune (*Met.* i 647–8). Instead of words she traced letters in the dust 'as a sad indication of her changed form' (*corporis indicium mutati triste*). The two simple letters IO communicate not only her name, but also her misfortune and perhaps too her cry for help. Her father's repeated *me miserum*, emphatically placed at the beginnings of lines 651 and 653, remind the cognisant reader that *io* is a standard exclamation of woe in Greek tragedy, which can also be used for invoking aid. 'Io' thus encapsulates what she would have said could she but speak. Of course there is humour in the situation, but the mental suffering caused by her transformation remains at the centre of this story. 'My sorrow was less keen when you were lost than it is now that you have been found' (*tu non inventa reperta / luctus eras levior*), as her father says (*Met.* i 654–5). Even Jupiter cannot bear to witness her sufferings any more, and causes Argus her guardian to be killed, which only increases her pain because Juno now sends a Fury, an Erinys, to pursue her Argive rival around the world. Finally Io reaches the Nile, where in desperation she sinks down on her knees (*Met.* i 729 ff.) and, with head bent back, raises her face, the only thing that she can raise, to the stars above, and begs with sorrowful mooings to be released from her travails. The contrast between her bestial form and her human feelings is especially brought out by line 731, *quos potuit solos, tollens ad sidera vultus* ('raising her face, all she could raise, to the stars'), which echoes the description of the creation of human beings earlier in *Met.* i. Here the creator 'made man stand erect, bidding him look up to heaven, and lift his head to the stars' (*os homini sublime dedit caelumque videre / iussit et erectos ad sidera tollere vultus*). Io's inability to raise more than her head to the stars epitomises her loss of human status; but because she retains her human consciousness she is not a cow either. Poised between two states, she is neither one nor the other, she feels herself still to be Io, but she is not recognisably so to anyone else, even to herself: 'frightened and dismayed she fled from herself' (*pertimuit seque exsternata refugit*: *Met.* i 641).

Hermann Fränkel has written interestingly about the psychological significance of the theme of metamorphosis and his perceptive, if quaint, analysis of this episode is worth quoting:

> Why is it that in spite of the fantastic plot, we are moved by Ovid's tale and feel concern for the cow-woman? It is, I think, because we have lived through similar experiences ourselves, although a miracle has never come our way. We understood all too well what it means to try to escape from our own self. And we also remember the shock we received when, in our adolescence, we were standing before the mirror and for the first time with an adult perception realised how plain and homely we looked to others; or when we were speaking and it happened that our voice sounded wrong and hideous, utterly incapable of conveying what we felt; or when growing old, we discovered that we were no longer the person we meant to be. There is much in Ovid's metamorphosis fables which can easily be divested of the miraculous element and translated into everyday occurrence.[8]

What Fränkel brings out here very well is that the question of human identity is bound up with the way in which other people see us; but our external appearance does not necessarily tally with what we feel ourselves to be. The mirror is revealing not because it shows us our true selves,[9] but because it shows us as we appear to other people; and human identity depends amongst other things on having a social identity. Io, trapped inside a hideously transformed body, is both herself and not herself, as the mirror cruelly shows.

At first sight this feeling of entrapment which many of the stories explore looks as though it depends on the familiar Orphic/ Pythagorean, Platonic and subsequently Christian idea of the body as a kind of prison-house of the soul.[10] The definitive opposition between body and soul, so firmly established in the western tradition, is nowhere more graphically presented than in Marvell's *Dialogue between the Soul and Body* (see Figure 5.1).

Ovid often seems to be working with the same set of ideas as those of Marvell's poem, particularly in view of Pythagoras' speech in *Metamorphoses* xv, which has often been seen as the philosophical key to the poem as a whole. Pythagoras' account of the nature of the universe ties up with the creation at the beginning, and appears to provide a theoretical background to the theme of transformation. Finally, after all these tales of apparently meaningless and endless

A Dialogue between the Soul and Body.

Soul.

O Who shall, from this Dungeon, raise
   A Soul inslav'd so many wayes ?
With bolts of Bones, that fetter'd stands
In Feet ; and manacled in Hands.
Here blinded with an Eye ; and there
Deaf with the drumming of an Ear.
A Soul hung up, as 'twere, in Chains
Of Nerves, and Arteries, and Veins.
Tortur'd, besides each other part,
In a vain Head, and double Heart.

Body.

O who shall me deliver whole,
From bonds of this Tyrannic Soul ?
Which, stretcht upright, impales me so,
That mine own Precipice I go;
And warms and moves this needless Frame:
(A Fever could but do the same.)
And, wanting where its spight to try,
Has made me live to let me dye.
A Body that could never rest,
Since this ill Spirit it possest.

Soul.

What Magick could me thus confine
Within anothers Grief to pine ?
Where whatsoever it complain,
I feel, that cannot feel, the pain.
And all my Care its self employes,
That to preserve, which me destroys :
Constrain'd not only to indure
Diseases, but, whats worse, the Cure :
And ready oft the Port to gain,
Am Shipwrackt into Health again.

Body.

But Physick yet could never reach
The Maladies Thou me dost teach ;
Whom first the Cramp of Hope does Tear :
And then the Palsie Shakes of Fear.
The Pestilence of Love does heat :
Or Hatred's hidden Ulcer eat.
Joy's chearful Madness does perplex :
Or Sorrow's other Madness vex.
Which Knowledge forces me to know ;
And Memory will not foregoe.
What but a Soul could have the wit
To build me up for Sin so fit?
So Architects do square and hew,
Green Trees that in the Forest grew.

Figure 5.1 Facsimile of *Dialogue between the Soul and Body*, from Andrew
Marvell's *Miscellaneous Poems*, London 1691.

change, the words of Pythagoras suggest a way of connecting and
explaining the disparate material which Ovid has woven together. In
the ever-changing universe, one thing remains constant, the *anima*
or soul (xv 165–72):

All things change, but nothing dies (*omnia mutantur, nihil
interit*); the spirit wanders hither and thither, taking possession
of what limbs it pleases, passing from beasts into human bodies,
or again our human spirit passes into beasts, but never at any
time does it perish. Like pliant wax which, stamped with new
designs, does not remain as it was, or keep the same shape, so
I tell you that the soul is always the same, but incorporates itself
in different forms.

This emphasis on the immortality of the soul as opposed to the
fleeting and transient configurations of the body does confer a kind

of unity on the poem and doubtless has some serious import – when Ovid proudly proclaims in the final lines of *Met.* xv that, though his body will die, the better part of himself will be immortal, surviving the wrath of Jupiter and the gnawing tooth of time, it is difficult not to be moved by his words, particularly by the emphatic 'I shall live' (*vivam*) with which the poem ends. Yet the voice of Pythagoras is only one among many and, as commentators are now fond of pointing out,[11] the apparent gravity of his speech is undercut by the context in which it is set, and the use to which it is put. Pythagoras offers a superb and lengthy argument for vegetarianism (you might be eating your grandmother when you eat beef, as it were); but its levity somewhat undermines the potentially more serious theme of metempsychosis, and that theme itself does not really provide any moral or spiritual justification of the poem as a whole, because no moral explanation is given for the soul's constant migration from one body to another; the speech merely affirms the principle of endless change, change without purpose or meaning.

Furthermore, if one tries to apply Pythagorean principles to the stories Ovid tells, it does not work. According to Ovid's Pythagoras the soul is the vehicle of continuity, but in the rest of the poem Ovid shows very little interest in the soul as such, or in the body/soul dichotomy. That hopeless disparity between body and soul, so powerfully expressed in Marvell's poem, finds no analogue in Ovid's narrative. Nowhere in the *Metamorphoses* is there a sense in which the *human* body is seen as a prison-house, it is only when changed into something non-human that the body becomes a trap. In general it is the body that is the focus of attention and, in so far as Ovid acknowledges a distinction between body and soul at all, it is the body that is privileged. Indeed the human body is presented as the defining characteristic of what it is to be human,[12] and change or loss of that body is presented as diminution.

On this point it is instructive to look at Ovid's treatment of bestial metamorphosis alongside Plato's. In the myth of Er at the end of *Republic* x 620, Er watches the souls of the dead choosing their next incarnations and observes that for the most part, they follow the habits of their former life: Orpheus chooses a swan, Thamyris a nightingale, Ajax a lion, Agamemnon an eagle, Thersites an ape, and so forth. In other words there is a direct correlation between the animal shape they choose and the kind of soul they are: indeed, their bodily incarnation expresses what they are. It is true that this does

happen in Ovid too, and that Ovid often revels in pointing out why a particular metamorphosis is appropriate. The transformation of the murderous and cannibalistic Lycaon into a wolf, the first genuine metamorphosis of the poem, is an example (*Met.* i 233–9).

His clothes changed into bristling hairs, his arms to legs (*in villos abeunt vestes, in crura lacerti*) and he became a wolf. His own savage nature showed in his rabid jaws, and he now directed against the flocks his innate lust for killing. He had a mania, even yet, for shedding blood. But though he was a wolf, he retained some traces of his original shape. The greyness of his hair was the same, his face showed the same violence, his eyes gleamed as before, and he presented the same picture of ferocity.

Solodow regards Lycaon's transformation as programmatic precisely because his chief characteristic is made manifest in his appearance; his essence, externalised and given physical form, is made clearer.[13] For Solodow an essential feature of Ovid's concept of metamorphosis is continuity between the original person and his or her metamorphosed state. What I want to stress is that the continuity often takes the form of a continuity in human consciousness, which, paradoxically, means that the changed persons are all too aware of the *discontinuity* between their metamorphosed state and their former selves. I think, in fact, that this is a distinctive feature of Ovid's poem; the retention of human consciousness within a bestial or other kind of form enables Ovid to explore questions about human identity in a peculiarly disturbing way.

The way Ovid gets inside the skin of the changed person is well brought out by comparing his account of Circe's transformation of Odysseus' men into pigs with Homer's (*Od.* x 237ff.), on which it is closely based. Odysseus relates how he watched his men drinking from the dishes Circe set before them:

when they had drained their bowls in which she had served them, she struck them with her wand, drove them off and penned them in their pigsties. For now to all appearance they were swine: they had pigs' heads and bristles, and they grunted like pigs; but their minds were as human as they had been before the change. Indeed, they shed tears in their sties. But Circe flung them some acorns and cornel-berries, and left them to eat this pigs' fodder and wallow in the mud.

Here the change is instant and described from the outside by an observer, and although we are told that the men retain their human minds inside their pig bodies, we only witness this from the outside – we have to take it on trust. Compare Ovid's version, which is told by Macaraeus, who had been the victim of Circe's magic himself (xiv 276–84, excerpted):

> We took from the goddess' hand the cups she gave us, and drained them greedily ... as soon as we had done so, the dread goddess touched our hair lightly with her wand and at that – ashamed though I am, I shall tell you – my body began to bristle with stiff hairs, and I was no longer able to speak, but uttered harsh grunts instead of words. My body bent forward and down, until my face looked straight at the ground (*in terram toto procumbere vultu*) and I felt my mouth hardening into a turned-up snout, my neck swelling with muscles. My hands, which lately held the goblet, now left prints (*vestigia*) like feet upon the ground.

This is comical, but somehow also uncomfortable because we are really made to feel the powerlessness of the human being whose body, bit by bit, is turned into that of an animal. Similarly with the pigs' transformation back into men; in Homer it happens more or less instantaneously: Circe smears the pigs with a potion, whereupon 'the bristles which her first deadly poison had made them sprout dropped off their limbs, and they not only became men again but looked younger and much handsomer and taller than before' (*Od.* x 393–7). The only physical difference remarked on here is the bristles, and the transformation is instant. Ovid's version is again far more detailed, and dwells on the process of change: Circe chants her spells over the pigs and 'the more she recited, the more we raised ourselves erect (*erigimur*), lifting ourselves up from the ground. Our bristles fell out, the split disappeared from our cloven hooves, shoulders, upper arms and forearms were restored to their proper shape' (*Met.* xiv 302–5). The gradual restoration of human shape is described in such a way that we almost feel it physically ourselves because we are experiencing it from the point of view of the pig–man himself.

A particularly horrific example of this phenomenon is provided by the story of Actaeon – not a typical metamorphosis (but then what is?) in that his transformation is the cause of his death rather than a means of escape from it. Wandering by chance in a sacred wood, the hapless Actaeon comes upon Diana bathing in a spring (see

Plate 5.1b). She, in a fury, sprinkles him with water, and turns him into a stag (*Met.* iii 194ff.); she gives horns to his head, lengthens his neck, sharpens the tips of his ears, substitutes feet for hands, and covers him in a spotted skin. Actaeon is amazed at how quickly he can run, and it is only when he sees his own reflection (the mirror again)[14] that he realises what has happened to him. He thinks as a human being: what is he to do, go home or stay, hidden in the woods? Shame blocks one course, fear the other. But he can only act like the stag which he has apparently now become, and flee in terror at the sight of the hounds who now pursue him. His inability to speak (*'me miserum!' dicturus erat*; *vox nulla secuta est*) is highlighted by the epic catalogue of dogs' names, thirty-six in all, which Ovid proceeds to list (*Met.* iii 206–25). By contrast their master longs to cry out 'I am Actaeon' (*Actaeon ego sum*) but no words come, only the sound of the baying dogs fills the air. As the whole pack sinks their teeth into his body he groans unrecognisably, neither man nor stag. He turns his silent face as though in supplication, and as his companions shout out his name, the *clamant* of line 245, the repetition of the accusative *Actaeona* in the same place in the lines 243 and 244 contrast chillingly with his own inability to speak his name; all he can do is turn his head in silent supplication until he is torn to pieces by his own hounds, their master still despite his false corporeal form (*dilacerant falsi dominum sub imagine cervi*: *Met.* iii 250). What is terrifying here is Actaeon's intermediate status between man and beast. Severed from humanity by his bestial shape and particularly by his inability to speak, his retention of human consciousness makes him more than just a stag – he is neither one thing nor the other. He is a stranger to the world around him, unrecognisable to his companions who look for him as though he is absent, but also a stranger to himself (*lacrimaeque per ora non sua flexerunt*: *Met.* iii 202–3). To me this is much more than the witty exploitation of a paradox.[15] Ovid's emphasis on the feelings of the human trapped within an animal body is deeply disturbing: if only he could see from without rather than feel from within. To lose control over one's appearance, one's gestures, one's voice, of all one's human attributes save consciousness, is indeed to be caught in a nightmare world in which none of the distinctions which we use to make sense of our everyday experiences applies.

J.-P. Vernant has suggested that individual human identity has two aspects, a name and a body;[16] and it is precisely these aspects which are at the centre of Actaeon's story. In contrast with other species, all human beings have names which differentiate one individual from another, but Ovid's narrative reverses that norm with characteristic relish, by giving individual names to the dogs and depriving the master of that vital marker of human identity. As his companions vainly search for Actaeon, all they see before them is a nameless stag. Together with his body, Actaeon loses his ability to speak which, as Aristotle pointed out, is another vital marker of human as opposed to animal existence:

> Nature ... has endowed man alone among the animals with the power of speech. Speech is something different from voice, which is possessed by other animals also and used by them to express pain or pleasure ... speech, on the other hand, serves to indicate what is useful and what is harmful, and so also what is just and what is unjust. For the real difference between men and other animals is that humans alone have perception of good and evil, just and unjust.[17]

Aristotle's confidence in the moral superiority of human beings over animals is by no means unequivocally echoed by Ovid. Indeed, many would argue that there is no morality, no order, no meaning in the *Metamorphoses*, only an endless process of purposeless change. In particular the standard hierarchy of god, human being, beast is said to be destroyed in this chaotic world of fluid interchange, where the crossing of all boundaries, the mingling of all categories is possible. Human beings, poised between god and beast, have the potential for both divinity and bestiality,[18] and it is traditional to assume that bestial metamorphosis represents a move downwards, a degradation of the human state. But some, like Solodow quoted below, would argue that this scheme is confounded by Ovid's poem:

> Animals are ordinarily ranked lower than men in the scale of animate beings, as gods are ranked higher, the criterion being rationality. This scheme hardly belongs in Ovid's poem, however, and has been a source of confusion in understanding metamorphosis. Changes from man to beast or divinity do not represent movement up or down in the quality of being. Many critics have assumed without hesitation that metamorphosis into an animal ... is a form of degradation. But Ovid refrains from rankings of every sort and gives no warrant for the belief that the animal kingdom (not to mention the vegetable) is

inherently inferior. He attaches no moral connotation to the turning of men into animals. An animal is not a degraded but a clarified form of man. It is simply a character that has no inner life or concealed character, whose appearance and customs declare everything about it.[19]

Yet to deprive a character of its inner life is to deprive it of something valuable. Perhaps Io's transformation into a heifer is not degrading; but it is certainly a diminution of her humanity. Her retention of human consciousness, her desire to communicate and the way in which Ovid underlines her inability so to do suggest strongly that her severance from the world of human beings is something both pitiful and frightening. Thus her father laments his daughter's transformed state (*Met.* i 655ff.):

> Alas, are you the daughter I have sought the world over? My sorrow was less keen when you were lost than it is now that you have been found. You do not speak, do not answer my words, but only heave sighs from deep down in your heart, and make lowing sounds in reply – all you can do. And I knew nothing of this, I was preparing a home and marriage for you, hoping for a son-in-law, first of all, and then for grandchildren. Now you must have a bull from a herd for a husband, and your children will be cattle.

This comical yet touching speech reminds us of the pleasures of human life, and particularly the social life of human beings, which are not available to a cow. Equally the longed-for return to human shape which later follows (*Met.* i 744–5) is presented as an un-doubted blessing.

Though the boundaries between god, human and beast are certainly fluid in this poem, I think it does make us aware of the qualitative differences between human and other forms of life. Segal is right to point out that Ovid is still 'well ensconced within classical humanism';[20] to lose one's human characteristics is to lose something of irreplaceable value; and one's human characteristics include the human form. That form is by no means always represented as an unqualified good, but it is impossible to be human without it. And I would argue that bestial metamorphosis in particular tends to be seen as a form of degradation.[21] Macaraeus in the passage quoted above is ashamed (*et pudet et referam*) to relate how Circe turned him into a pig, and the contrast between beasts who are forced to look down to the ground and humans who can stand on two legs and look up at the stars is presented to us right at the beginning of the poem (*pronaque cum spectent animalia cetera terram / os homini sublime dedit caelumque videre / iussit et erectos ad sidera tollere vultus*: *Met.* i 84–6). Needless to say, this essentially Stoic view of the human being as 'sanctius animal' is not one that is consistently maintained. Indeed typically in this fluctuating and unstable poem, it is almost immediately undermined by the emphasis on human wickedness in the account of the four ages of man which follows, and in the story of Lycaon's metamorphosis into a wolf. Similarly the benefits conferred by the human form are presented in a decidedly equivocal light when Daphne, desperate to avoid the clutches of the relentlessly pursuing Apollo, prays for escape from her own body: 'O father, help! if your waters hold divinity; change and destroy this shape by which I pleased too well' (*qua nimium placui, mutando perde figuram*: *Met.* i 547). Here, in the first of many stories of young nubile virgins being pursued by rampant males, usually gods, the body is explicitly presented as the cause of its own destruction.[22] Yet when the metamorphosis occurs in the next line, it brings with it fixity, restriction and loss.[23]

The cumulative effect of all these bizarre, sometimes terrifying, sometimes amusing transformations is to remind us of what it is to be human. For Ovid this is not primarily a question of having a human soul, which elevates us above the brute forces of nature, nor of our being morally superior to other creatures in the world around us. By focusing in minute detail on the *physical* changes which his mythological protagonists undergo in the transition from one form of life to another – changes to hands, feet, eyes, ears, nose, mouth and so on – Ovid places the human body firmly at the centre of our understanding of what it is that differentiates human beings from bird, beast or tree. To deprive individuals of their human shape is to deprive them of their humanity.

ACKNOWLEDGEMENTS

I am most grateful to Alison Sharrock for sending me a copy of her paper on the *Metamorphoses* in advance of publication, and to Jasper Griffin for pointing out the relevance of the Marvell poem to my theme.

NOTES

1 Bernini's famous *Apollo and Daphne* is thus not typical of the tradition as a whole: see Kenney 1967: 52 and Galinsky 1975: 3–4.

2 See Llewellyn 1988: 151–66 and the comments of Barkan 1986: 88: 'the heritage of the *Metamorphoses* is a vision of the universe under the metaphor of things. Metamorphosis becomes the quintessential corporeal metaphor, the belief that the nature of a thing can be read in its shape. That may explain why Ovid's poem was such a magnet for the visual arts.'

3 On this question see Barkan 1986: 168–9; Sharrock 1996.

4 Forbes-Irving 1990: 96.

5 Unless otherwise stated, translations of the *Metamorphoses* are taken from the Penguin version by Mary Innes (1955).

6 Skulsky 1981: 34–5 notes that it is typical of Ovid's narrative for individuals of one species not to be turned into individuals of another, but simply into another species.

7 Riddehough 1959: 206 also makes this point. Physical pain is suggested when Phaethon's sisters are in the process of being turned into trees and their mother tries to tear their bodies out of the tree trunks: she

> broke off the tender branches in her hands; but drops like blood trickled from the gash, as if from a wound. 'Oh mother, please, don't hurt me!' was the cry of whichever girl she touched. 'Do not hurt me, please! It is my body you are injuring, though it has been transformed into a tree.'
>
> (*Met.* ii 358–62)

But this emphasis is unusual.

8 Fränkel 1969: 80.

9 Although it may, of course, do this. See Barkan 1986: 45–58 for an analysis of the mirror motif in the *Metamorphoses* from this point of view.

10 See Plato, *Phaedo* 82e–3e, and for the implications of this idea see e.g. Vernant 1989; Loraux 1989: 13–45; Brown 1988: 26–9.

11 See e.g. Feeney 1991: 205; Solodow 1988: 162–8; and on the relationship between Pythagoras' speech and the rest of the poem Segal 1969a.

12 It is no accident, therefore, that the moment when Pygmalion's statue comes to life is marked by the words, 'it was a body' (*corpus erat*: *Met.* x 289). As Barkan 1986: 89 notes, 'human nature in the metamorphic universe is inextricable from the human body'.

13 Solodow 1988: 175–6.

14 See above, p. 86. This moment in Ovid's story is picked up by Seneca, whose brief account of Actaeon's fate at *Oedipus* 750–63 is shot through with Ovidian echoes: see Töchterle 1994 *ad loc.*

15 Galinsky 1975: 133 speaks of Ovid 'dwelling on the pose, which is more grotesque than pitiful, of Actaeon the stag trying to act like Actaeon the man'. Martindale 1993: 60–3 offers an alternative reading of the Actaeon episode, based on an analysis of Titian's paintings *Diana and Actaeon* and *The Death of Actaeon*.

16 Vernant 1989: 40.
17 *Politics* 1253a. The connection between metamorphosis and loss of
    speech is a notable feature of the *Metamorphoses*: see e.g. ii 363, 477–88,
    65/–/5, 829 32, iv 412–13, 576–89; v 465–7; viii 712–19; ix 367–93; xi
    731–5; xiii 565–9; xiv 91–100. See also Riddehough 1959; 206 and Forbes-
    Irving 1990: 37.
18 See e.g. Detienne 1981: 215–228; Thomas 1984: 36–41.
19 Solodow 1988: 190–1.
20 Segal 1969b: 90. But we do not need to go as far as Riddehough 1959:
    209, who maintains that 'throughout these changes from human form to
    some other shape, the reader is constantly reminded how precious it is,
    in Ovid's eyes, to be human and a member of kindly and civilised society,
    and how wonderful a thing is that *humanitas* which we so readily take
    for granted'. Daphne might not have agreed.
21 See Forbes-Irving 1990: 62 ff., 79, 112 and especially 136 on the difference
    between animals and plants: 'a plant can suggest all the metaphors of
    love and luxurious growth and fruitfulness, and yet since plants do not
    reproduce by sexual intercourse it can avoid the suggestion of pollution
    and sickness that invariably accompany the transformation of a lover of
    a god into an animal.'
22 Compare e.g. *Met.* ii 474–5, 572; iii 270; v 580–4; viii 434–5.
23 Solodow 1988: 189 remarks pertinently that the limitation placed upon
    Daphne's movement 'is virtually a symbol of the person's inability to
    grow, develop, alter'. Compare Barkan 1986: 66.

Part III

MODIFYING THE EARLY CHRISTIAN BODY

6

BODIES AND BLOOD
Late Antique debate on martyrdom, virginity and resurrection

Gillian Clark

Martyrdom was intended, by those who sentenced martyrs to die, as a permanent and degrading transformation of the body: it 'inscribed on the body', to use Foucault's now famous expression, the contempt and hatred of the non-Christian population. But the Christian church succeeded in reinterpreting martyrdom not only as the triumph of faithful spirit over vulnerable body, but as the triumph of the body over torment and death. As the post-Constantinian church established its identity, martyrdom supplied a history and a dominant image of what it is to be Christian. The bodies of martyrs, and of the ascetics who undertook the 'long martyrdom' of renunciation, exemplified major shifts of thought about the body, both in its relation to the soul, and as flesh and blood and bones. This paper explores some of those shifts, and some of the paradoxes they entail.

Martyrdom was a public, humiliating, cruel death. The bodies of martyrs were torn, broken, dismembered and burned. Torture, designed to force admission and recantation, made use of the rack, and of red-hot metal plates laid on the skin, and of the metal 'claws' which lacerated flesh and exposed bones and internal organs (see Figure 6.1). There may have been a peculiar horror in this opening of the body: medical schools were not usually allowed to practise dissection.[1] Sometimes death was inflicted in ways which look like an enactment of the worst human fantasies. There are notorious examples: the respectable new mother Perpetua, stripped and thrust into the arena to be tossed by a mad cow; the slave Blandina, scourged, hung on a post for wild beasts to tear, forced into a red-hot iron chair, what was left of her flung into a basket and given to a bull to toss.[2] As the illustrations show (Figure 6.1), Christian tradition has sometimes sanitised martyrdom, but that is unlikely to

99

TABULA VII.

A Martyres quandoque roris, mucronibus undique affixis, ligati, super cuspides ferreos circumagebantur.
B Aliu ndo, quibus affixi non erant præacuta i mucrones, super cuspides item ferreos.
C Aut saltem, ut misere vitam finirent, super ardentes pruinas.
D Henum rotarum convexis alligati, e loco sublimi præcipitabantur.
E Aut rotarum radiis intexti, sic ad plurimos dies, ut interirent, relinquebantur.

TABULA XX.

A Sanctæ Christi Virgines ignominiæ causa vel ad meretricem prostibula vi ducebantur,
B Vel sic ad turpitudinem radebantur.

TABULA XXIII.

A Christianorum aliqui vel muribus rodendi, ea, quam hæc figura demonstrat, forma, tradebantur, B Vel unus super alium perinde ac agmina locustarum in angustioribus custodiis includebantur, C Vel etiam immissis equitibus oburebantur.

TABULA XXVI.

Instrumenta Martyrii Romæ in cœmeteriis reperta.

Figure 6.1 The torments of early Christian martyrs, as recreated by an anonymous artist to illustrate the *Patrologia Latina* volume of Prudentius.

(Tabulae VII, XX, XXIII and XXVI in J.-P. Migne, *Patrologia Latina* 60, Paris 1862).

happen in the late twentieth century: there are still martyrs, including Christians, and anxieties about the public spectacle of violence.[3]

In the early centuries CE, martyrdom was institutionalised violence. Roman law allowed the condemnation of low-class or especially appalling criminals to 'exaggerated penalties', typically *crematio*, burning alive, or *ad bestias*, exposure to wild animals. These penalties were inflicted in public, as part of the spectacle offered at games in honour of the gods. They took place in purpose-built amphitheatres, which were also used for fights to the death between wild animals, or wild animals and humans, or humans and humans. Fantasias were performed upon the basic themes: convicted persons were sometimes made helpless and sometimes allowed to fight, and at times their deaths became part of a drama, enacting a scene from mythology or from their own career of crime.[4] Classical scholars have rightly asked questions about the extraordinary willingness of the Romans to make extremes of pain a public spectacle. The people who watched and yelled are all too familiar, but how can we explain a society which legitimised such violence inflicted on those it saw as criminals, caused its officials to finance gladiator fights as a popular entertainment, and built amphitheatres to display, with no danger to the spectators, the slaughter of humans and animals?[5]

The most positive readings of the Roman mentality associate gladiators not with cruelty but with the military virtues. Gladiators, it is said, demonstrated the fighting skills required of soldiers and the triumph of the human spirit over death, wounding and the fear of death; even watching gladiators required courage and discipline.[6] (Similar arguments are now deployed whenever another boxer suffers brain damage.) Dramatic physical punishments, according to the more pessimistic among modern scholars, were an opportunity for the underclass to torment a victim more wretched than themselves. According to the more optimistic, assaults on the body acted out the rejection of the criminal from the human community, by his or her reduction to the level of a beast – a body without rationality – or of a corpse. Such punishments might even give him or her the opportunity to escape degradation by dying bravely.[7] There is also a practical consideration: physical punishment was usually inflicted on people of low social status, who had little or nothing else to lose. It was, therefore, peculiarly degrading for the 'more respectable', the *honestiores*, who from the second century on were formally exempted – unless their crime was exceptional, or (in some cases) they were Christians.[8]

Christians insisted on remembering and retelling how their fellow-Christians died like this, commemorating the martyr's 'birthday', *natalicium*, with the story of his or her arrest and trial, imprisonment and death. These martyr-acts are another display of violence.[9] They relate the *passio*, the suffering, of the martyr, with precise detail of what happened to the martyr's body. They also make claims about the martyr's long survival and unshaken defiance which are very difficult to believe. So questions arise about the kind of writing this is. One explanation offered is that martyr-acts were addressed to an audience of the simple faithful (or, less kindly, the vulgarly credulous), and that educated persons knew one was not meant to believe it. A refinement of this explanation is that all fourth-century audiences, however well educated, had an appetite for the marvellous and a readiness to believe it.[10] But it is not certain that Christian texts were written for the simple: simplicity can be a rhetorical strategy. Nor is it certain that the martyr-acts were expected to be read as fiction. They are presented as an expression of truth, even if that truth is (in Aristotle's terms) poetic rather than historical, an account of what could happen rather than what did happen.[11] The obvious stylisation of stories and repetition of motifs in the immense range of Acts of the Saints makes it hard to decide what did happen; and 'compassion fatigue', which rapidly sets in after the reading of several martyr-acts, makes it easy to forget what has in fact been done by humans to humans, and what some humans have endured for a cause.[12]

The narrative display of a tortured and exposed body, especially when that body is female, prompts further questions about the motives of writers and readers. The body of a chaste woman was normally concealed, and a female body on display marked that woman as sexually available. So, even though the sufferings of martyrs were not usually adapted to their gender, the public torture of a woman made a different impact from the torture of a man. It was also, apparently, a rarer event: there are fewer records of women criminals and of martyred women.[13] Some accounts of martyrs cannot claim to be popular literature, addressed to those who know no better. This applies especially to the carefully crafted poems of Prudentius *On the Martyrs' Crowns*, the *Peristephanon* (henceforward *Pe.*). At first sight they are consciously simple, but they imply a reader who is sensitive to the classics of Latin literature.[14] They include two narratives of nubile girls, just emerging from childhood, who insist on proclaiming their Christian faith and not

only accept, but welcome, the consequence: torture and death. Eulalia, literally, asks for it: 'come, torturer, burn, slash, cut up the limbs which are put together from clay. . . .'[15] Agnes' desire for martyrdom is even more explicit (*Pe.* xiv 69–80):[16]

> When Agnes sees the harsh man stand
> with naked sword, more happily she says:
> 'I exult that such a man comes –
> crazy, savage, violent armed man,
> rather than a languid tender youth
> soft and scented with perfume
> who would destroy me by the death of my chastity.
> This lover, this one I want, I confess it.
> I shall meet his onrush half-way
> and not postpone his hot desires.
> I shall take the sword's length into my breasts
> and draw the force of the sword to my inmost heart.
> Thus wedded to Christ I shall leap up
> above the darkness of the sky . . .'.

Both the martyrdom and its retelling may seem suspiciously close to the reassertion of male control over the eroticised body of a girl who refuses her sexual destiny.

Late twentieth-century commentators have seen an analogy with other displays of narrative violence, especially in film, which are often interpreted as a reaction to feminist assertion.[17] But there are important differences in the social context and in the overt purpose of the narrative. Slasher movies present violence which is, by the standards of their time, not only unlawful but aberrant. Martyr-acts, even when they were composed long after the end of persecution, come from a social context in which the public torture of suspected criminals, and the brutal public death of convicted criminals, continued unmodified by Christian belief in a loving God. Thus an early fifth-century Pelagian treatise protests against the Christian magistrate who lolls on his cushions ordering torture, and discusses over dinner the contradictions of his job.[18] Even Ambrose, according to his biographer, ordered the torture of suspects as part of his attempt to convince the people of Milan that he, as their provincial governor, was not a suitable choice for bishop.[19] The first Christian emperor had imposed some limits. Constantine forbade branding on the face and the use of crucifixion as a penalty, and also banned gladiator fights – ineffectively, for they continued, even at Rome, until the

reign of Justinian. But the lawcode of Theodosius II, a militantly orthodox Christian, is notorious for its use of burning, beasts and specific mutilations.[20] So the kind of public violence inflicted on martyrs was still familiar, and still legitimate, even if Christians were no longer at risk (except, sometimes, from other Christians) because of their faith. Such things happened, and Christians might feel an obligation to remember exactly what had happened to their own, just as people now feel an obligation not to let the Holocaust be forgotten. Trial records perish, but according to Prudentius (*Pe.* x 1121–30)

> an angel, standing in God's presence,
> recorded all the martyr said and all he bore;
> the pen recorded not only the words he spoke
> but the wounds in his sides, his cheeks, his chest, his throat.
> Every measure of blood was noted,
> and how the furrow ploughed each gash,
> deep, gaping, close, long, short,
> the force of the pain, the extent of the cut;
> he lost no drop of the blood shed.

It remains possible that some of those who composed, or listened to, martyr-acts were engaged in fantasies of punitive repression, in which recalcitrant bodies were slashed and burned and amputated in a hideous extension of surgery and cautery.[21] But such people might imagine themselves as enduring, rather than as inflicting, pain. The overt purpose of reading martyr-acts was both to commemorate the suffering which the martyr had, with God's help, endured, and to inspire the hearers with resolution to follow the commands of God: as Augustine neatly phrases it, 'that we may delight to imitate what we delight to celebrate'.[22] When martyrdom itself was no longer an immediate threat, the stories of martyrs were used to exhort Christians to put God first, before worldly interest or the pull of family ties. In particular, they were used to inspire the choice of virginity or of celibacy over marriage and family commitment. Family pressure to conform, and the long, bleak struggle against sexual desire, were presented as analogous to the experience of martyrs. Augustine, in a recently rediscovered sermon on the 'birthday' of a martyr, manages to shed the glamour of martyrdom even over the married man who resists temptation to have lawful marital intercourse more than is necessary for the procreation of children.[23]

It may be unjust, or simply anachronistic, to assume that the authors and audiences of martyr-acts were deriving sadistic or masochistic pleasure from the spectacle of pain. Martyr-acts described the suffering of the body in order to re-enact the triumph of the body. The martyr may be shown declaring that what is done to his or her body does not affect the soul, but the suffering of the body is of central importance: it is not a temporary and finally irrelevant anguish, left behind as the triumphant soul ascends to God, but a glorious demonstration of God's power manifested in what seems most vulnerable, human flesh and blood. Present-day commemorations of the Holocaust seek for triumphs of the human spirit, or manifestations of goodness, to challenge and alleviate the horrors. Late Antique martyr-acts find beauty and significance even in the torture and destruction of the body. Thus Prudentius describes witnesses of the martyrdom of Vincent kissing the marks left by metal claws on his flanks, and licking the blood he shed. This would be bestial if done by the magistrate who ordered the martyr's death:

> the good ruler, the great judge
> feeds on innocent blood
> and gasping for pious bodies
> he rends their sober entrails.[24]

In another of these poems, a mother watches the torture of her little son, urging him to laugh at the pain.[25] Eulalia tells the governor who condemns her, and the executioner who carries out his orders, that the claw-marks inscribe on her body the name of Christ. Her deathplace is transformed into beauty and serenity, full of brilliant colour: green river-water flows past her city, she has a marble tomb with a gilded roof and a mosaic floor like a flowery meadow, where boys and girls offer violets and blood-red crocuses. The worst of horrors can be made beautiful and lovable, and if the description evokes an erotic pleasure in torture, the narrative may correct the reader's desire and redirect it, with the martyr's, to God.[26]

But there is one horror which is not made the object of loving description and reinterpretation: rape. It must in practice have been a danger for women martyrs and confessors who were imprisoned. It was also, presumably, a danger for men and especially for boys, but that danger was not openly acknowledged, whereas Justinian ruled that women should not normally be kept in custody, but if it was absolutely necessary, they should be held in a convent.[27] In a martyr-act rape may be threatened, as it is when the martyr Irene is condemned to stand naked in a brothel, but it does not happen.[28] But why not describe a female martyr triumphing over this invasion of her body? Augustine showed what could be said when he discussed the nuns who were raped in the Gothic sack of Rome in 410 CE. Rape, he argued, was irrelevant to their chastity, because their will did not consent: damage to their physical *integritas* did not entail loss of *sanctitas*, and indeed the continuing commitment of the will might sanctify the physically violated body.[29] It has been argued that narratives of women martyrs are not punitive but empowering, and that some were written by and for women: for instance, the adventures of Thecla in the second-century *Acts of Paul and Thecla*, or the long-drawn-out account of Febronia, her community of women and her appalling death.[30] If this is right, women might particularly be expected to reassure women that rape is not the destruction of their essential self and their personal integrity.

But there is a special cluster of associations here. Christians inherited a discourse of sexuality as invasive and violent. Intercourse, especially first intercourse, was thought to make women's blood flow.[31] First intercourse was described in overwhelmingly negative language of corruption and contamination, and the vocabulary applies also to corruption in death: the Greek verb *diaphtheiro* means both 'destroy' and 'seduce'. This fitted very neatly with the story of the Fall in the book of Genesis, in which sexual awareness was the first sign that humans had acquired knowledge of evil, and with it mortality – double corruption. The third-century writer Methodius, in a treatise on virginity, uses the image of the virgin's body as meat which will putrefy unless it is salted with Christ's words and regularly wiped clean of desires.[32] So the closed body of the committed virgin symbolised her triumph over generation and corruption, and thus over mortality.[33] The body of a female martyr might bleed to death under torture, and that torture might be described in consciously erotic language, but the body was not described as bleeding because of a sexual assault which forced her into corruption.

Female bodies also bleed in menstruation: this bleeding is a sign of the potential for generation, and its absence signifies either infertility or pregnancy. In Greek and Roman culture girls were usually (though not always) married as they approached puberty; so a young girl, almost ready for marriage, might be imagined as not yet having reached menarche, and one of the explanations for bleeding on first intercourse was the release of accumulated menstrual blood as the cervix relaxed. It is unclear how perceptions of menstrual bleeding related to perceptions of other blood-flows. There is evidence that menstruation was associated with desire, and that some Christians thought it religiously polluting. Other Christians strongly disagreed, regarding menstruation as a natural physical event. Augustine declares it to be a natural happening, which does not damage the integrity of the female body, and which required purification under Jewish law only because its 'formlessness', like that of seminal emission, was an image of sin.[34] Christian ascetics recommended drastic fasting, often combined with physical stress, as a remedy for desire. Such fasting might cause amenorrhoea, and Late Antique medical theory had expectations that it would do so. Popular wisdom saw a connection between sexual desire and lavish intake of food and drink, and medical theory explained that the surplus which was not required to maintain the body was available for reproduction. In women not pregnant or lactating the surplus was shed as menstrual blood, in men it was refined into semen: fasting was intended to eliminate the surplus.[35] Some ascetics may have been motivated by punitive hatred of the body, or by the kind of anxiety about the body which now manifests as anorexia, but this cannot now be demonstrated. The overt purpose of ascetic practice was to transform the body, to overcome the sexual division and desire which declared its separation from God.[36]

The body of an ascetic became charged with spiritual power, which could be conveyed even by the clothing he or she had worn. Thus Melania's belt rescued a woman who had been unable to deliver her child, and Melania herself was buried in clothing which carried the blessing of other saints.[37] The body of a martyr likewise retained significance: it was not a husk to be discarded, but stored power awaiting the resurrection. It could not be destroyed by those who had condemned the martyr. It could not even be moved with reverence to a shrine, if the martyr did not approve.[38] Fragments of hair and bone and skin, scraps of clothing, even dust which had gathered on the martyr's tomb or cloths which had been lowered through a grating to touch it, had power to protect and heal because the martyr had suffered and died.[39] Christians tried especially to retrieve bloodstained clothing, or to collect blood on cloths.[40] The martyr's blood had special power. Just as 'suffering', *passio*, became a metonymy for martyrdom, so 'shedding blood' became a metonymy for the death of a martyr, no matter how he or she died. Blood was a symbol of life in both Graeco-Roman and Jewish religious tradition, and according to medical theory it was blood, collected in the uterus or refined into semen, which went to make a new living creature. When Tertullian declares that the blood of martyrs is seed, *semen*, from which Christians multiply, this transformation underlies his words.[41] So abundant blood meant abundant life. When Polycarp was stabbed by a soldier, because the fire had not killed him, so much blood poured from the wound that the flames were put out.[42] Stories that the long-buried bodies of martyrs were found uncorrupted and full of blood symbolise the continued potency of the martyred body. Thus Ambrose reports to his sister the discovery at Milan of Gervasius and Protasius, martyrs under Nero: their bones were huge, 'such as the olden times (*prisca aetas*) produced', and there was much blood. In Ambrose's preaching to the people, there was even more: 'the tomb is wet with blood, the marks of triumphant gore are visible'. In his sermon next day, the blood testifies yet more powerfully than those healed by the presence of the relics: 'you have read God's words, "your brother's blood cries out to me", and this blood cries out by the proof of its colour; the blood cries out by the triumph of the *passio*'.[43]

Ambrose's discovery of these heroic bones, and his reinterment of the bones under the altar of his new church, is both similar to and different from the hero-cults of almost a millennium earlier. The bones of Orestes and of Theseus were also huge, and also stored up protection for the place where they were buried and where sacrifice was offered.[44] The blood of the sacrifice perhaps symbolised the continuing power of the heroes, but their own blood would have been a sign of pollution, and further pollution would have been caused if other mortals had been buried in their sacred precinct. Hero-cult had no implications for ordinary mortals, whose mortality was still alien to the deathless gods, the *athanatoi* of the Greeks, and was thus a source of horror.[45] In Ambrose's time, there was still unease about having the dead in close association with the living, and this emotional resistance was expressed in laws against bringing the dead inside the city. His new church, the Basilica Ambrosiana, was outside the walls of Milan; but he had violated a tomb and moved the bodies of the dead. This had been forbidden in an imperial ruling given at Constantinople a few months earlier, and perhaps prompted by earlier transfers of relics.[46] But the Christians of his congregation competed for the privilege of burying their dead *ad sanctos*, near the martyrs, because the continuing power of the special dead was a token of the resurrection. Christian dead were asleep in a cemetery, derived from the Greek *koimeterion* or sleeping-place, with the implication of course that they would wake. Mortal flesh and bones could not be alien or insignificant to God, who had taken on human flesh in the Incarnation; the central Christian symbol is the sharing of Christ's fragmented body and shed blood in the Eucharist, in remembrance of his suffering and death, and in acknowledgement of his continuing presence.

These basic Christian claims allowed much diversity of interpretation and of practice.[47] Greeks and Romans, accustomed to collecting bone and ash after cremation, and to commemorating their special dead, might find it natural to do so for a martyr: thus the Christians of Smyrna collected the bones of Polycarp, made a shrine, and met there on the anniversary of his death not only to remember him, but to re-enact the death in narrative.[48] But some people, including some fourth-century Christians, experienced revulsion and contempt at the reverence shown for bodily remains, the collection of bits of bone and skin.[49] 'They take a pinch of dust, put it in a valuable container, wrap it round with a cloth, and kiss it and venerate it': why, Vigilantius asked, make use of a candle when you can have the sun?[50] Martyr-cult expanded as the later fourth-century church established itself. Ambrose in Milan, and Damasus in Rome, restructured the capital cities with martyr-shrines, just as Prudentius reclaimed classical poetic discourse for the martyrs' crowns. The fourth-century church in Italy was constructing a history and a tradition from the deaths of martyrs.[51] But that implied a new kind of patronage and privilege in access to their physical remains. Ambrose was prepared to distribute fragments of relics; the Roman church distributed only contact relics. Prudentius makes Fructuosus and his companions ask that their ashes should be kept together, not distributed among eager Christians.[52] Interring martyrs under the altar should mean that everyone in church benefits from their presence, just as everyone shares in the Eucharist which is consecrated on the altar. But the privilege of burial near the martyrs, *depositio ad sanctos*, worried Paulinus of Nola, who consulted Augustine on proper care for the dead and prompted his treatise *On the Concern to be Shown for the Dead* (*de cura pro mortuis gerenda*).[53] Augustine's mother found that Ambrose discouraged the practice of taking food and wine to the memorials of the saints, partly because some people drank too much, partly because it looked like the Roman *parentalia*, the pagan offering to the *manes* of the dead; and possibly because he wanted to keep attention to the dead under proper supervision.[54]

The practical questions implied the major theological question of what happens to the body after death. Christian teaching on the resurrection of the body was attacked by non-Christians and not always believed by Christians.[55] It is a puzzling claim to make about God's continuing love. Most Greeks and Romans thought that the soul leaves the body at death, and could not understand why Christians wanted to believe that the soul will take the flesh with it. Many twentieth-century Christians think the central claim is that nothing can separate us from the love of Christ; there is an important philosophical question of how far our human identity is dependent on the endlessly changing body, but the nature of the resurrection is not our problem. But for fourth-century Christians, the incarnation of God in Christ declared that the flesh (*caro*) cannot be un-important. Humans are a compound of rational soul and body, and the body is not just a temporary residence to be discarded. There was intensive fourth-century debate on what exactly is meant by incarna-tion, that is, how it is possible to describe the union of divine nature with human nature, given that humans are rational soul and body. There was further debate on what the body would be like in the resurrection.[56]

Paul had interpreted the resurrection of Christ as the first-fruits of those that sleep: if Christ took on humanity, and Christ was raised from the dead, then all human beings will be raised from the dead. But Paul also made a contrast between the physical body and the spiritual body which is raised, using the analogy of the grain of wheat which falls into the ground and dies. This image allows the argument that there is nevertheless a continuity between the grain and next year's wheat crop, but also the argument that the stalk of wheat which bears seed is as different from the grain as the resurrection-body will be from the natural body.[57] Someone who had not seen wheat growing would be unable to extrapolate it from the seed. Origen's answer was to distinguish the changing 'material substrate' from the 'distinctive form', arguing that the resurrection body will have the distinctive form, but with a different substrate appropriate for heaven. The Greek theologians sometimes call this distinctive form the *logos spermatikos*, the 'seed-like principle' (as in the seed which dies).[58] Gregory of Nyssa suggested that the soul can recognise its physical elements, and at the resurrection will draw to it what it needs – even if those elements have, for instance, been digested by a lion. (Cannibalism posed a fascinating difficulty, much debated by scholastics: whose soul could claim the elements?[59])

111

Gregory thought that the resurrected body will be restored to the condition of humanity before the Fall. Augustine began with a Platonist belief that we are essentially souls fallen into bodies, and a speculation that bodies are themselves a consequence of the Fall; he moved to a belief in the 'conjugal union' of body and soul, which will be maintained in the resurrection. The natural body will be raised, but it will be freed from any deformity, and flesh will be subject to spirit, not resistant.[60]

The Christian doctrine of the incarnation of God entailed a revaluation of the human body in relation to the soul and to God. The proclamation of Christ crucified presented as a central religious symbol the public spectacle of a tortured human body. In the central Christian ritual of the Eucharist, the church, symbolised as the fragmented body of Christ, is united by sharing his body and blood. As the fourth-century church moved from danger to establishment, its discourse of the body was shaped by its theology and ritual, by inherited discourses and practices concerning sex and death, and by the historical experience of Christians in a specific cultural context. The bodies of martyrs and the bodies of ascetics demonstrated the power of God in flesh and blood; and bodily resurrection will be the ultimate transition.

ACKNOWLEDGEMENTS

I am also indebted to Anna Wilson for discussion and exchange of papers. I owe the interpretation of Tertullian *Apol.* 50.13 to a paper by Aline Rousselle given at the Institute of Classical Studies, London, on 10 March 1994.

NOTES

1 The practice of dissection is discussed in Edelstein [1967] 1987: 247–301; compare Bynum 1992: 271–2 for medieval parallels.

2 Perpetua: text and translation in Musurillo 1972: 106–31, and an important discussion in Shaw 1993: 3–45. Blandina: Eus. *h.e.* v 1–51 (Musurillo 1972: 62–85). Further examples in Jones 1993: 23–34.

3 See Wood 1993 for a range of discussion.

4 The infliction of penalties is discussed by Garnsey 1970; Coleman 1990. See Most 1992 for the possible effect of these enactments on literature of the Neronian age. Compare Prud. *Peristephanon* xi 65–88 for a wide variety of deaths, culminating in a suitable fate for a prisoner called Hippolytus, who is torn to death by wild horses.

5 Further discussion in Auguet 1972; Hopkins 1983; Wiedemann 1992; Brown 1992: 180–211.

6 See further Wiedemann 1992; Welch 1994.

7 For these arguments, see Auguet 1972; Wiedemann 1992; Coleman 1990; Barton 1993: 11–46.

8 See further Garnsey 1970. In Prud. *Pe.* x 108–20, a governor substitutes flogging with a lead-tipped scourge for the rack, 'lest he should condemn a man of distinction to a plebeian punishment'.

9 For visual representations, see Roberts 1993: 138, and Grabar 1945–6.

10 Palmer 1988: 32–56.

11 Cameron 1991: 112, 118–19.

12 Stylisation: see Delehaye 1966. See also Davie 1992: 329–42 for the treatment of pain and torment in later Christian literature. Authenticity is discussed by Brock and Harvey 1987: 17.

13 Brock and Harvey 1987; see further on the displayed body Castelli 1992; Shaw 1993: 13.

14 See further Palmer 1988; Roberts 1993.

15 *Pe.* iii 91–2; compare Ach.Tat. 6.21, on which see Goldhill 1995: 117–18.

16 See now Burrus 1995: 25–46.

17 I am indebted to Elizabeth Castelli for her papers on this subject.

18 *De div.* 6, *PL* suppl. 1.1325–6.

19 Paulinus, *vita Ambrosii* 7–8; McLynn 1994: 44–5 argues that Ambrose had routinely used torture.

20 Grodszynski 1984: 361–403; Wiedemann 1992: 153–60.

21 The medical comparison is explicitly made in *Pe.* x 496–505; later in the poem, 896–905, a doctor excises the martyr's tongue, and reports (981–1000) on his continued power to speak.

22 For instance, in Mainz Sermon 42.1, in Dolbeau 1992.

23 Mainz 42 in Dolbeau 1992.

24 *Pe.* v 337–40, see also 151–2; iii 86–90: *dux bonus, arbiter egregius / sanguine pascitur innocuo, corporibusque piis inhians / viscera sobria dilacerat.*

25 *Pe.* x; see further Hahn 1991.

26 *Pe.* iii 186–205; see also *Pe.* x 127–30 for brilliant colour in a picture of the martyrdom of Hippolytus, and *Pe.* xii 31–54 for the churches of Peter and Paul. Further discussions of the martyr as spectacle can be found in Castelli 1992; Roberts 1993; Shaw 1993; and compare Miller 1993 on 'rewriting' the body of the female virgin.

27 *Nov. J.* 134.9 (556 CE); compare *C. Th.* 9.3.1 (320 CE) for prison conditions.

28 Martyrdom of Agape, Irene and Chione 5–6: Musurillo 1972: 291–2. See Prud. *Pe.* xiv 25–56 for the same threat to Agnes. On penetration by the sword, see further Goldhill 1995: 117–18; Burrus 1995: 33–43; Wilfong in this volume.

29 *Civ. Dei* i 16–19, 28; see further Trout 1994: 53–70, and Clark 1996.

30 Davies 1980; Brock and Harvey 1987.

31 See further Fowler 1987; Winkler 1990: 101–26; Goldhill 1995: 33–9. For relevant medical theory, see Dean-Jones 1994: 50–5.

32 Meth. *Symp*. 1.1.

33 See van Eijk 1972 and Clark 1996 on the image of Mary as uninvaded female body.

34 *Civ. Dei* 14.26; *De bono conj.* 20.33. See further on purity rules Cohen 1991; Dean-Jones 1994: 226–53 on menstrual taboos.

35 On the impact of fasting, see Rousselle 1988: 160–78.

36 See further Brown 1988, and a range of discussion in Wimbush and Valantasis 1995.

37 *Vita S.Melaniae* 60, 69; on ascetic clothing, see further Clark 1995.

38 e.g. Prud. *Pe.* v 385–524, the body of Vincentius; the body of Febronia resisted movement (Brock and Harvey 1987: 175); other instances of intact bodies with healing powers in Van Dam 1993: 89–90, 112, 165–6.

39 See Brown 1981: 82–5 on the 'psychodrama' of disintegration and reintegration.

40 For instance, Prud. *Pe.* xi 131–44, on Christians collecting the remains of Hippolytus.

41 *Apol.* 50.13.

42 *Martyrdom of Polycarp* 16 (Musurillo 1972: 15).

43 *invenimus mirae magnitudinis viros duos, ut prisca aetas ferebat. ossa omnia integra, sanguinis plurimum*: Ambrose, Ep. 77(22).12, *CSEL* 82.134. See McLynn 1994: 209–19 for the context in Ambrose's political and ecclesiastical struggles; and Dassmann 1975: 49–68. Note also Victricius of Rouen, *De laude sanctorum* 9 (*CCL* 64: 84), who affirms that the healing power of relics proves that they are complete in flesh, blood and spirit; these relics had been sent him by Ambrose.

44 Hdt. i 67–8; Plu. *Thes.* 36.

45 See Brown 1981: 5–6.

46 *C. Th.* 9.17.7 (February 386 CE); see further Harries 1992: 56–67.

47 On the shift from cremation to inhumation, see Bynum 1995: 51–3, and add to her references Morris 1992: 31–69.

48 *Martyrdom of Polycarp* 18 (Musurillo 1972: 17).

49 This is evoked, and apparently shared, by Lane Fox 1986: 446–50.

50 Quoted, perhaps misquoted, by Jerome, *Contra Vigilantium* (*PL* 23.357–8); further discussion in Bynum 1995: 92–4.

51 Markus 1988: 90–5, 98–9.

52 *Pe.* vi 130–8; see further Roberts 1993: 14–16, and Brown 1981 *passim* for relics and patronage.

53 For an appreciation of *de cura pro mortuis gerenda* (*PL* 40: 591–610) see Bynum 1995: 103.

54 Ambrose's regulations at Milan: Conf. 6.2.2. On martyr-cult in relation to Roman tradition, see Harries 1992; on Ambrose's (mis)interpretation of food for the dead, McLynn 1994: 236; and on North African commemorative practices, Saxer 1980.

55 Augustine, *Serm.* 361 (*PL* 39: 1599–611); see Bynum 1992: 239, 'to twentieth-century non-Christians and Christians alike, no tenet of Christianity has seemed more improbable – indeed, incredible – than the doctrine of the resurrection of the body'.

56 Bynum 1995: 43–51 links concern for resurrection, especially in second-

and third-century discussion, with the wish to compensate martyrs whose bodies were fragmented and were denied burial.

57 1 Corinthians: 15. Bynum 1995 especially 3–8, 21–58, discusses 'seed' and other images.

58 See further Bynum 1995: 63–8.

59 Bynum 1992: 244, and Bynum 1995: 81–6 on Gregory.

60 For Augustine's developing beliefs on resurrection, see Rist 1994: 110–12; Bynum 1995: 95–104 argues for an underlying anxiety about change.

7

READING THE DISJOINTED BODY IN COPTIC

From physical modification to textual fragmentation

Terry Wilfong

Conceptions of the body in Late Antique Egypt have been the focus of some scholarly attention in the past, but such work has, in general, concentrated on Greek-language Patristic sources and only used Egyptian evidence as illuminative of the larger Mediterranean world. Individual studies have concentrated on the body in Late Antique Greek papyrological evidence and Gnostic texts,[1] but there has been little work done on the conceptions and constructions of the body specific to the Coptic-speaking milieu of Late Antiquity in Egypt. The Coptic sources[2] approach the body in a variety of ways and the present study does not attempt to cover all of this potentially large subject, but will, instead, focus on selected sources that illustrate the distinctive modifications of the body found in Coptic. Physical modifications of the body are attested in certain contexts, but far more frequent are the textual modifications practised by Coptic authors, especially the disjoining and fragmenting of the human body along gender lines. In general, Coptic texts treat women's bodies in terms of their parts, rather than as a cohesive whole. This disjoining of the gendered body in Coptic is found in a variety of genres, reaching its culmination in the Coptic martyrdoms, where the usual fragmentations are reversed. These Coptic fragmentations and modifications hint at the highly complex constructions of the human body that had developed in the milieu of Late Antique Egypt.

This study is centred on Coptic language sources in order to look at the specifically Egyptian components of Late Antique culture in Egypt. Since Coptic did not exist in any significant way outside

116

Egypt, its use in both original compositions and translations indicates an audience that knew and used the native Egyptian language at a time when it was not the official language of government. The sources examined in this study span an approximately 600-year period from *c*. 400 to 1000 CE, a period during which the non-native rulers of Egypt used Greek, Latin and Arabic, and a time when these languages (or at least Greek and Arabic) were in common use throughout Egypt. The extent of bilingualism in Egypt in this period cannot be measured quantitatively, but is assumed by many scholars to have been great. Nevertheless, the long survival of the Egyptian language in its latest form attests to the importance of this Egyptian element in a culture that is the product of a large number of indigenous and outside influences. The Coptic sources under consideration here represent what was theoretically accessible to the literate Coptic-speaking Egyptian from the Late Antique and early Islamic periods.[3]

Before going on to the 'literary' modifications of the body found in Coptic texts, it is useful to examine the actual physical modifications of the body attested in such documentation. These can be grouped into two categories, impermanent and permanent, and there is some evidence to suggest that Coptic writers categorised them in a similar way. Cosmetic modifications of the body, such as the application of make-up, the cutting and arrangement of hair, the clothing and adornment of the body, are well-attested in Coptic evidence.[4] For the most part, however, these temporary modifications are treated with disapproval and distrust. This is not surprising when one considers that references to such practices are found almost exclusively in the writings of male religious leaders directed towards women in a secular context. These writers upbraid women for the attention they pay to their appearance, almost exclusively in terms of body parts – hair, eyes, faces. At least one form of attention to one's hair was, however, considered laudable. This was the shaving of the heads of monks, particularly those in the initial stages of their monastic careers. Shaving heads was particularly common among early monks who were converts from paganism. The best example of this is from Paphnutius' *History of the Monks of Upper Egypt*, in which he recounts Macedonius' destruction of pagan idols and the subsequent conversion of a pagan priest's sons: once they are well advanced in their studies, he shaves their heads himself.[5] Even this practice was not universally approved; the monastic rules of Pachomius warn against monks cutting each other's hair,[6] although Pachomius' concern is clearly less with the attention to the monks' hair than with the potential for physical contact between the monks.[7] Archaeological and representational evidence for the clothing and adornment of the body is good for the predominantly Coptic-speaking milieus in Egypt. Indeed, the remains of clothing are extremely extensive and well-preserved, thanks both to the post-mortem practices of the Egyptian Christians and the arid climate of Egypt.[8]

The more permanent modifications of bodies attested in Coptic non-literary texts are not many in number. The piercing of bodies, specifically the ears of women, is well known from representations and from physical remains of earrings worn through holes in the ears; the practice is implicitly recorded in mentions of earrings in the textual sources.[9] Other modifications include circumcision among males, which was traditional, although the documentation is reticent on this subject. This apparent discretion can be ascribed as much to the fact that these kinds of activities do not generate written documentation as to the possibility that notions of prudery or taboo were associated with it. Those documents which do make mention of the practice are mostly concerned with the circumcision of Jesus; the implication is that when circumcision was practised among Egyptian Christians it was done in imitation of Christ and not in deference to the earlier Egyptian tradition of circumcision. Female circumcision or female genital mutilation is not explicitly attested in Coptic documentation, and its occasional occurrences among modern-day Copts probably have no precedent in Late Antique (or earlier) Egypt. Among the more extreme surgical modifications of the body possible, castration is known from Coptic sources, but, in humans at any rate, it is invariably seen as a 'Roman' (i.e. Byzantine) practice – not an Egyptian custom – with the sole purpose of creating eunuchs.

As Peter Brown and Aline Rousselle have shown, ascetic practice among Egyptian monastics, both male and female, occasioned bodily changes that were perceived to be permanent and deliberate; examples of this kind of body modification will be discussed below in relation to textual fragmentation of the body. Pre-existing permanent modifications such as scars are used for identification purposes in Coptic legal documents, just as in earlier Greek papyri. These modifications are treated as regular physical characteristics – height, weight, skin or hair colour. The connection with Graeco-Roman legal practice of such identifications by appearance is underlined by the use of Greek for such descriptions, even in Coptic texts. Thus in an application for a travel pass the three applicants identify themselves in Greek as 'Joseph, son of Patjuen, stout, yellowish

(-complexioned) . . ., Theodore, son of Athanasius, dark . . . and Mark, son of Taurinos, big-boned (?). . . .'[10] The way that the documentary texts use standard sets of metonymic body descriptors almost as a *pars pro toto* to describe real individuals prepares us for the Coptic literary descriptions. These too employ the same kinds of phrasing, whereby whole bodies are evoked through attention to their individual parts.

The permanent body modification most commonly associated with Christianity in Egypt is tattooing. Tattoos occur among Egyptian Christians primarily as a notation of pilgrimage – a permanent and often visible corporeal reminder of a visit to a particular shrine. Tattoos also serve as the visible identifying mark of a Christian in post-Muslim conquest Egypt. Although known from anecdotal evidence, there is little textual attestation for the purpose or even the existence of tattooing in Coptic; the few references that are known are condemnations of the practice by religious writers from a time well before tattooing became an accepted part of Egyptian Christianity. 'You shall not shave your beards, nor shall you prick your bodies with marks . . . [concerning unclean men] Their own bodies do they injure, pricking them with names and other designs, for those foolish ones did not know their dishonour.'[11] There is very little modern scholarly work available on the subject; some collections of Coptic tattoo designs and anecdotal surveys of the practice exist, but the study by Montserrat appears to be the only recent work on the subject.[12]

Then there are the most extreme forms of bodily modification: those practised on martyrs, that ultimately or immediately resulted in death. These fatal modifications are as much textual as actual, and will be discussed below. Finally there are the modifications practised on the body after death. The elaborate preparations of the dead body carried out by earlier Egyptians had largely ceased by the time the Coptic language had come into common use; the body was still covered, often dressed, but no longer eviscerated or embalmed.[13] Coptic writers were aware, though, of some of the embalming techniques of the past, in large part because many of the monastic writers spent at least some time living in ancient tombs in the desert, surrounded by the remains of dead ancient Egyptians. The most graphic account is found in the life of Pisentius, Bishop of Coptos in the seventh century, written in the Bohairic dialect of Coptic. When Pisentius takes up residence in a tomb, he and his disciple find many mummified bodies in it, which give off a 'sweet smell' (from the spices used in embalming) and have their fingers and toes individually bandaged.[14] Accounts of post-mortem modifications are otherwise rare; the extreme pre-mortem injuries and dismember ments of the Coptic martyrdoms often led to further post-mortem changes in the body, all of which will be discussed later on. Having quickly surveyed the actual physical modifications to the body described in Coptic sources, the way is clear to examine the textual modifications of the body and their resulting disjointedness.

Disjointedness of the body is at its most basic in Coptic medical and 'medico-magical' texts. Coptic medicine is an amalgam of Graeco-Roman and later Arabic traditions with the earlier medicine of Pharaonic Egypt. Indeed, this ancient Egyptian element is highly influential and appears to have helped to shape ideas about the functions of the human body in Coptic sources.[15] The normative body in Coptic medicine (as in many ancient cultures) is male. The patient is generically referred to as 'man', 'he', 'him'; the body in such texts is treated as a whole, and conceived of, in varying degrees, as a system. The specific treatment of women in Coptic medicine is done separately. Illness specific to women is discussed solely in terms of the specific body parts affected, most often the womb and the breasts. Very often the prescribed treatment for these parts is topical and local: ointments for the breasts, fumigations and pessaries for the womb.[16]

Taken alone, the nature of medical texts in general might account for such disjointedness in the treatment of women's bodies, but women's bodies are subject to similar and even more explicit fragmentation outside the Coptic medical corpus. Indeed, the ma-gical spells that often accompany the medical prescriptions reflect further fragmentation, even when not intended for use in treatments specific to women. The same is true of non-medical magical texts; women are involved, described and even enchanted by the parts of their bodies. The complex of texts representing what is often referred to, somewhat misleadingly, as 'Coptic magic' shows a wide range of the use and understanding of bodies.[17] And characteristic of the use of the body in these texts is the oppositional pairing of the disjointed female body versus the whole male body. Not surprisingly, as in medical texts, we get the female body fragmented when specific body parts are the focus of magical attention, such as blessings or curses. But magical action taken against or in favour of a woman in general is also often expressed in terms of parts. Thus one general curse against a woman has a detailed description of how the spell should affect individual parts of her body:

I, the poor wretched sinner, I call unto the Lord God almighty that you will do me justice with Tnoute, [who has] divided my son from me so that he despises me. Do not listen to her, God, [...] when she cries out to you. Make her be without hope in this world: strike her womb [and mak]e her barren, make her devour the fruit of her womb. Cause a demon to come upon her, [who will cas]t her into a burdensome sickness and great distress. Bring a fever upon her and a [... and a] cold and a numbness of heart and an itching. You bring upon her the twelve [...] a worm come forth from her with blood, all the days of her life. [...] take them. She does not live while approaching death. Cause her mouth to go astray.[18]

Comparable curses directed at men do not include such information.[19] The use of women's bodies in pieces is also seen in what are usually called 'love' spells, but are more accurately sexual spells or spells of compulsion.[20] In these, women are usually compelled to love and/or have sexual intercourse with the conjurer, and this is often expressed in terms of the woman's body parts. Women are also frequently likened to animals in such texts: 'like a bitch on the prowl, a cat going from house to house, like a mare submitting to the lusty stallions'.[21] Such spells, in a group of texts designed to cause impotence in men, also provide a notable exception to the usually complete and unitary condition of male bodies. There the male body is reduced to what is, at least for the purpose of the spells, its most important part: the penis.[22] The purpose of the spells is to attack specifically the function and power of the man's penis, to make it like 'a rag on a dung-heap' or 'a corpse lying in a tomb' or even more graphically 'like an ant in winter, tiny and frozen'.[23] In doing so, the conjurer concentrates on this one part of the male body to the exclusion of the rest. Whether this is an attempt to 'feminise' the body of the man being cursed through fragmentation is unclear. Otherwise, in Coptic texts of magic the male body does not normally appear in *disjecta membra*, while the female body rarely appears otherwise.

This is not to say that women's bodies have no significance in the Coptic magical texts, nor that they have no power. The bodies of religious women possess inherent magical power, especially that of the Virgin Mary, but again only in terms of their parts, unlike the whole bodies of male divinities. Thus in Coptic magical spells, one conjures and swears by body parts of the Virgin Mary – specifically her breasts and womb. In spite of the more frequent invocations of Jesus Christ, there are no conjurations by the corresponding body parts (or any other body parts) of Christ in these texts.[24]

More explicit manifestations of the disjointed female body are found in Coptic literary texts of various genres. Indeed, the most venerated body in Coptic hagiography, that of the Virgin Mary, is very baldly disjointed in a number of texts for the edification of readers. A good example comes in a parchment fragment in the British Library (BM 178=BL Or 3581 (A) 7), a fragment of a homily attributed to Cyril of Jerusalem in which the body of Mary is identified part by part with various things and concepts. Selected identifications from this text include:

> The ten fingers of Mary are the ten strings of the harp of
>   David. . . .
> The two arms of Mary are the strength of the steadfast. . . .
> The heart of Mary is the treasure of wisdom. . . .
> The two breasts of Mary are the place of nourishing those who
>   are great against wickedness. . . .
> The entrails of Mary are the holy of holies. . . .
> The womb of the Virgin is the tabernacle of the almighty. . . .
> The navel of Mary is the mixing-bowl of wisdom,
> The navel of the Virgin is the pool of baptism,
> The womb of Mary is the dawn of the light.[25]

There are certainly parallels for this elsewhere in Christian literature, but grammatically this text is very reminiscent of much earlier (pagan) Egyptian religious texts, in which the body parts of a deceased person are individually identified with the corresponding parts of various gods and goddesses (or even the divinities themselves).[26]

Most of the Coptic texts regarding Mary stress the notion of her purity and virginity – the virginity of her body – and body imagery is usually present. This was so important that it was incorporated into the liturgy, the body of Mary being pure and holy and inviolate. Indeed Mary's virginity itself is treated almost as if it were an independent part of her body. The insistence on the physicality of Mary's virginity left Coptic authors with a problem not unique to Egyptian Christianity: how did Mary conceive? The ingenious idea of conception through the ear (*conceptio per aurem*) allowed the conception of Christ but kept Mary's physical virginity intact, conception having been effected by a dove dropping a pearl into

Mary's ear. Though common throughout the Late Antique world, this doctrine had special popularity in Egypt, as evidenced not only from texts by Egyptian authors such as Athanasius and Clement of Alexandria, but also from its prevalence as an iconographic motif.[27] Again, as with the identifications of the body parts of the Virgin Mary, there may have been earlier Egyptian roots; there are Hieratic spells to prevent rape through the ears and, given the Egyptian perceptions of medicine, conception through any orifice was considered possible.[28]

Non-traditional methods of conception aside, Marian body-part imagery is commonly used to describe women (often legendary) of the Byzantine royal families, emphasising their piety and purity. Such women interact with their husbands or (more often) their fathers and brothers through the medium of body parts – the emperors are often described as greeting the women by touching and/or kissing a succession of body parts: the women's hair, eyes, cheeks, fingers and breasts. These body parts are sometimes further qualified by rich commodities: hair ornaments, necklaces, rings, shoes and various other coverings, described at times in more detail than the women's body parts themselves. Empresses such as Helena, mother of Constantine, and Constantine's mythical sister Eudoxia are celebrated thus.[29] In Coptic stories these women help find valuable relics, the holy cross and the holy tomb, and there is an emphasis on their hands as the doers of good and the instruments of God.

In general, however, women's bodies were a source of worry and concern to Coptic writers. Indeed, most of their writing about women is to some degree highly negative: criticism of women and attempts to regulate their behaviour. However, much of the documentary evidence shows women in a much more positive (or nonnegative) light through the documentation of their economic activities. The sermons, homilies and pastoral letters that disapprove of women's actions do so almost exclusively in terms of body parts. At times it seems as if they are disjoining or exploding the women's bodies into pieces to render them powerless.[30] A very typical example is found in a seventh-century sermon by Pisentius, Bishop of Coptos: he is writing and preaching to an audience of lay persons, both men and women, in a church somewhere near modern-day Luxor.[31]

Now, also, to you I write and beseech and to you I command

emphatically in a great instruction in order that no woman at all go outside of her house with her head uncovered, nor that she lift her eyes up to the face of any strange man at all. Rather, may you go about on every occasion, O women, with your eyes turned down to the ground, your covering on all sides (of your body) in all propriety. But also, as for your adornment of yourselves, may it become a true measure and a respectability, while you give your hearts at all times to the word of God obediently and you thirst for him at all times.

Notice the repeated reference to body–head covered, eyes turned down, sides covered. These are images that occur again and again in Coptic sermons and lectures.

The women he was preaching to, however, had different ideas about how to conduct themselves. Pisentius addresses them sternly:

Also, as for women who go about unabashedly, their eyes staring unashamedly into the faces of every man: do not go about with uncovered faces, not just here, but also in the streets of your town. For you know now that many times I have warned you, O women, concerning the commandments, but you did not pay attention and you were not ashamed and you did not stop your madness.

But, in an interesting corrective to Pisentius' sermon, we have an extensive corpus of Coptic non-literary texts relating to women from the same region where Pisentius was preaching. In these letters and business documents, women occupied an active and highly visible place in the society. Though they fulfilled traditional roles of mother, wife, homemaker, they were also active in business, trade, crafts, agriculture and particularly prominent in financial fields like banking and money lending. This is something that does not come through in the writings of religious authors like Pisentius, who were not particularly happy about women being active in the community outside the home. Instead we find the evidence in the personal papers of the women and their associates.[32] These documents of business activity are full of body imagery: money passes *through the hands*, a debt falls due *on the head* and so on, although such idioms are not inherently gender-specific. But in the eyes of Pisentius and other religious authorities it was these activities of women in terms of body parts – women with uncovered heads transacting business, passing money through their hands and having to look into the eyes of the men who were their business associates and customers – that constituted the dangerous active business body of women.

In the eyes of the religious writers, however, there were much more transgressive things that women's bodies could do; much of the literature is directed at keeping women from sexual activity outside marriage. In general, such texts are written for men, warning them of the misfortune that will come to them through women. Coptic authors in particular fastened on biblical accounts of men ruined by women to fashion what would ultimately become an actively misogynist literature. There is a whole series of songs written against what are called 'bad women', that take their language from the biblical books of Proverbs and Psalms, where the warnings are often couched in terms of transgressive female body parts:

> Women have sweet tongues,
> for they are like flowing honey.
> They talk with you so sweetly,
> But afterwards they lead you astray.[33]

In general, however, it was not the women's tongues that these writers were ultimately concerned with; but the specifics of women's sexual bodies tend not to be discussed in detail, perhaps for fear of inciting too much interest.

Even the bodies of women devoted to a religious life were objects of a concern expressed in terms of their parts. Egypt was one of the birthplaces of Christian monasticism and men's monastic activity was universally approved in Egypt, but when women became involved, the attitude of writers in Coptic was distinctly ambivalent. When convents began to form and women started becoming nuns in organised houses, almost immediately the male monastic authorities started regulating the convents and complaining about the nuns. The large communities of women seemed in some way threatening and there is much documentation about how the nuns were looked upon.[34] The nuns are described in these documents in a flurry of transgressive body parts: lying tongues, thieving hands, immodest eyes, uncovered heads – whole sermons are written to combat the nuns' perceived transgressions. Indeed, the monastic attitude toward these women is such as to imply that they were to be regulated and controlled at all times.

A sermon preached to the women's monastic community that was under the regulation of the abbot and author Shenoute in the fifth century makes clear that the regulation of the lives and bodies of female monastics in Egypt was not limited to mere written invective. This extraordinary document gives a vivid account of the punish ment of a group of women for a variety of named offences.[35] Shenoute cites the names of the individual women being punished and also the individual transgressions for which he is punishing them. Most of the actions that Shenoute considered as worthy of punishment are conveyed in terms of bodily actions of some sort: stealing with the hands, hitting a superior in the head, lying with the mouth. Two of the women are punished for reasons that Shenoute says that he knows very well, but does not describe. Two other women are punished individually for going into other women's cells 'in friendship and physical desire'. This is far from the only mention of lesbian activity in the writings of Shenoute and his successors, but it is a rare case in that the women are named.

The punishment meted out to the women was a number of 'blows with a stick', the number varying with the offence and proscribed by the abbot. The administration of this punishment took place in public, carried out by the abbot and with the help and complicity of important women in the community:

> As for all of these (beatings), the abbot shall administer them with his own hands to them (the women) on the bottoms of their feet while they are seated on the ground; the elder woman, Tahom, and other important women helping, holding them (the women) for him, and the other elder women who are there holding (them) down with rods over their feet until he stops beating them, as we have done to some others in the past.

The beating of the bottoms of the feet is a traditionally Egyptian form of corporal punishment, attested at least as far back as the late New Kingdom. Given the amount of walking required by the women's daily monastic duties, this punishment was intended to provide lasting pain, presumably as a warning to the nuns to control their bodily actions and desires. Women might even anticipate body-specific punishments after death. Egyptian wall-paintings[36] of the punishment of female sinners at the Last Judgement make clear how the torment would be made to fit the crime committed by the body (see Plates 7.1 and 7.2).

Since Shenoute is the source of this account, we have no record of the reactions of these women toward either being punished or participating in the punishment of others. But there were some bodily punishments willingly undergone by female monastics, and

Coptic literature is full of tales of the mortification of the bodies of ascetics. As in other areas of Coptic literature, there is a difference in the description of males' and females' physical modifications through ascetic practice. In both cases, the effects of ascetic activity are described with much attention to detail; but male ascetics are usually described in relation to their bodily endurance, while female ascetics are described in relation to the individual side-effects of their practices. Female ascetics in Coptic are most often described in terms of the stench and waste of the ascetic body, or else in terms of the effect of asceticism on the bodily characteristics of gender. Female ascetics in Coptic often enter into a state likened to that of eunuchs, a 'third gender' well known from Byzantine literature.[37] The classic example of a female ascetic's life in Coptic literature, and one of the most vivid compositions in Coptic, is the story of Hilaria.[38] Hilaria was a legendary daughter of the Byzantine emperor Zeno, who ran away to Egypt, dressed as a man, to become a monk. Upon arriving at the monastery of Apa Pambo, Hilaria is admitted to the monastery and lives with the monks as a man:

> After nine years, they saw that the young girl was beardless and they called her 'Hilarion the eunuch', since there were many such (eunuchs) wearing the habit. For her breasts, too, were not as those of all (other) women: above all, she was shrunken with ascetic practices and even her menstrual period had stopped because of the deprivation.

Her identity is eventually revealed to her superior in a dream, but he keeps her secret. Back in Constantinople, Hilaria's sister becomes possessed by demons and is eventually sent in order to be cured to the very monastery where Hilaria is living as Hilarion. Upon arrival, the sister has convulsions caused by her possession. Hilaria recognises her sister, but her sister does not recognise her: 'How could she know her since her flesh had withered through mortification and the beauty of her body had altered and her appearance, being nothing but skin and bone. Besides all of this, she was wearing men's clothing.'

None of Hilaria's brother monks feels that he can take charge of the girl overnight; one excuses himself saying: 'I have not reached such a point of perfection that I can take a woman into my room.' They decide to put her into Hilaria's room, saying: 'This is a thing for a person without passions,' describing her as a eunuch. So Hilaria takes charge of her sister overnight, kissing her face and body and

Plates 7.1 and 7.2 Wallpaintings from a church at Tebtunis, Fayum, Egypt, probably tenth century CE (now destroyed) shewing the physical punishment of sinners.

(Photographs reproduced by courtesy of the Egypt Exploration Society, London.)

Plate 7.1 In the bottom left-hand corner, a woman identified as 'she who lives with a pagan husband' has her breasts attack d by two serpents.

Plate 7.2 Two naked sinners, a man and a woman, are tormented by serpents who attack their sexual organs. The inscription identifies the man as 'he who fornicated with a woman', and the woman as 'she who gave her breasts for money'.

holding her and sleeping in her bed. The sister is healed overnight and is sent home. Emperor Zeno is overjoyed, but concerned when the girl tells him of the kind monk who kissed, held and slept with her. Zeno angrily sends for Hilaria to demand an explanation.[39] She reveals herself as his daughter and he reluctantly lets her go back to the monastery. Hilaria returns and lives unsuspected as a man; on her deathbed she begs to be buried in her habit so that none of her brother monks will know she was a woman. This condition is agreed to; Hilaria dies and is buried, but her superior eulogises her as a woman to her very surprised fellow monks.

The story of Hilaria is not unique and tales of 'transvestite' saints are not uncommon in the Near East, but the Hilaria story emphasises certain points: the modification of the body through ascetic practice (in effect, she becomes a man) and also the disjointed picture of the resulting body that emerges from the text. The translation of the female body into male is almost a trope of early Christian literature; in addition to the well-known story of Perpetua, there are several relevant cases in Gnostic literature.[40] The transmission of this tradition into Coptic allowed Egyptian authors to look for the very points which corresponded to their own ideas about the fragmentation of the female body.

Nowhere in Coptic literature is the body more fragmented, both literally and figuratively, than in the Coptic martyrdoms. In the preceding paper Gillian Clark has examined the human body in the general context of Christian martyrdoms. The present examination will concentrate on a distinctive feature of Coptic hagiography that seems to reverse the trend of the gender-based disjointedness: in Coptic martyr stories it is the bodies of men that are literally and metaphorically fragmented, while the female martyrs' bodies remain intact.

Coptic martyrdoms are part of the larger tradition of such literature in the Christian world, but develop in their own distinctive direction, especially after the Muslim conquest of Egypt. Traditionally, these martyrdoms are seen as a low point in Coptic literature: clichéd, repetitive and interminable, gratuitously gruesome and morbid. But to see them so is to judge them by modern standards and to ignore the context in which these works were written. Viewed against the sectarian divisiveness and persecution under the Byzantines, the conflicts for control of Egypt in the seventh century and the uneasy existence of Egyptian Christianity in the first few centuries of Muslim rule, the Coptic martyrdoms can be seen as distinctive and relevant productions for their times. In general, Coptic martyrdoms seem to be original Coptic compositions, with later versions translated into Arabic. Their development has been divided into a series of cycles by Copticist Tito Orlandi; recent studies have examined documents that seem to have served as the originals for such compositions.[41]

Some of the most lengthy and characteristic of the Coptic martyrdoms are attributed to one Julius of Aqfahs, who usually appears as a character in his own works; in spite of the suggestion of contemporaneity with the martyrs themselves, the Julius of Aqfahs martyrdoms probably date to a much later period. Though often with a cast of thousands, the principal players always consist of the martyr(s), the governor/official who persecutes them, and the biographer who records the story. A paradigmatic Coptic martyrdom containing all the stock elements, apparently reused in other martyrdoms,[42] is Julius of Aqfahs' account of the death of Shenoufe and his siblings. This text is accessible in both recent edition and English translation,[43] and is especially vivid relating to body part imagery, so it will be the focus in my discussion of the disjointed martyr's body.

The martyrdom is set up by scenes of Shenoufe and his family in their daily life as secret Christians, contrasted with scenes of the official crack-down on Christians. Eventually, Shenoufe and his brothers and sister are called before the governor Arianus, who orders them to sacrifice to the gods. When they refuse, he orders them to be stripped for punishment. While Arianus the governor is gazing at the defiant and naked Shenoufe we get an unusual (for Coptic) description of the male body in parts, and of the beauty of that male body:

> And the holy Apa Shenoufe was a fair person, more so than all the rest. He was ruddy with beautiful eyes and hair entwined like clusters of henna blossoms, of blushing complexion in his person like roses, being well-formed in his shape and body. He (Arianus) had him called and said to him: Shenoufe! Now I see the condition you are in.

Here the author of the story seems to be emphasising the beauty and perfection of Shenoufe's body, so that the ruin and destruction that will soon be wrought upon it seems more marked: and the attention to certain erotic bodily foci (hair, eyes) is noticeable. This is the most fully-realised such scene from a martyrdom, in which the governor makes what appears to be a sexual advance towards the martyr, but there are comparable examples of episodes where the governor admires the beauty of the male martyr.[14] The story afterwards is formulaic: the governor compliments the martyr on his physical beauty and his wisdom, and offers to do something (usually left unspecified) if only the martyr will sacrifice to the gods. The martyr refuses, often insulting the governor, whereupon the governor becomes angry and commences the tortures. After this, what might be termed proposition and rejection scene, we get the first cases of actual physical dismemberments: that is, the first time in which the saint's body is reduced to its constituent parts. Perhaps significantly, the initial target of the governor's wrath after the martyr's refusal to co-operate is often the martyr's sexual organs, usually referred to by the Greek term *anagkaion* (necessity) which are often cut off. Otherwise, the tortures are diverse: cutting, burning, and other mistreatment directed at specific body parts. Indeed, the Coptic text of Shenoufe's martyrdom records an otherwise unattested Greek word for a body-part-specific punishment: *sphincterazeue*, to disembowel through the anus with a hot poker. The editors of the text note the distinctiveness of this punishment, but do not pick up on the sexual implications: the governor penetrates at second hand the holy man who rejected him. The narratives of the martyrs are punctuated with such scenes, after each of which the martyr is miraculously healed or brought back to life to go through yet more.

While the male martyr is experiencing this literal bodily fragmentation, what is happening to the female martyrs? Again, the tale of Shenoufe and his siblings is instructive. While the brothers are undergoing their various dismemberments and rejoinings, their executions and miraculous healings, their sister Sophia does not escape the governor's notice. But his attentions to her do not take the same form as his attentions to her brother: there is a confrontation, but he makes no reference to her appearance and his dialogue with her is perfunctory, merely establishing the fact that she is indeed a Christian. She refuses to sacrifice to the gods and is tortured, but the torture is directed at her body as an entity: her body is split open, and mustard and vinegar poured into the wounds. She is revived, only to be roasted – whole. This is typical of the torments of the female martyrs in Coptic, punishments that keep the body whole, carried out with less repetition than those on their male counterparts. Thus we find Theopiste roasted with her children after her husband is killed; the episode is short and (for martyrdoms anyway) rather discreet. In these scenes of women's martyrdom, the ultimate objectifying of the female body hinted at by its textual fragmentation reaches its climax. There is no need to weaken the female body any more by dismantling it into a series of parts. It has become a totally passive object of consumption, like an animal prepared for the table: an impression that is reinforced in the roasting alive of Sophia by the employment of table condiments, vinegar and mustard, to exacerbate her sufferings.

In the end, it is not clear what to make of this characteristic treatment of male and female martyrs. Is the break-up into parts, the dis-joining, of the male martyr's body the governor's ultimate insult, the feminisation of the holy man? Or is the treatment of the female martyr's body as an integer similarly some sort of subtle masculinisation of contempt? It is significant in this context to note that finally, after the respective torments come to a close, both male and female martyrs are taken to the millstones and ground together into pieces, blood and skin sticking to stones, the whole becoming a highly-charged paste of martyrs eagerly sought after for its topical healing properties. After the faithful take what they need, the remnants are buried in secret, the active fragmented bodies of the martyrs finally restored, reconstituted and at rest.

In the course of this study, itself rather fragmented and disjointed, I hope to have at least provoked interest in the often underutilised Coptic evidence for the human body. This paper is really only a first effort at coming to terms with the evidence; further investigation may well bring about more exciting and better-documented results. The physical modification of the human body in the environment that produced the literature discussed above took on a variety of forms, some common to many neighbouring cultures, but others (especially the use of tattoos) highly distinctive. Similarly, the literary fragmentation of the female body is certainly not unique to Coptic sources,[45] but it does take on distinctive and specialised forms at the hands of Coptic authors and translators. Further exploration of the disjointed body in Coptic awaits a wider and more systematic identification and publication of relevant sources; hopefully the areas of research outlined above will provoke further inquiry.

ACKNOWLEDGEMENTS

I would like to thank Dominic Montserrat for inviting me to participate in the *Anthropometamorphosis* conference and to contribute a revision of my paper for the present volume; I have greatly benefited from his insight and great editorial patience. I have also benefited from discussion with Gillian Clark, Robert K. Ritner and Charles E. Jones, as well as from the input of the other conference participants.

NOTES

1 For the former, see Montserrat 1996a: 26–79, and for the latter, for example, Castelli 1991: 29–49.

2 In the following chapter, references to Coptic texts follow the abbreviations suggested in Schiller 1976: 99–123. All translations are my own unless otherwise acknowledged.

3 As such, two well-known groups of Coptic sources (the Coptic 'Gnostic' texts from Nag Hammadi and elsewhere and the Manichaean writings from Medinet Madi and Kellis) are largely excluded from the present study. Both sets of sources had a chronologically and geographically limited distribution and pose special problems to the researcher. They did not really represent or illustrate 'mainstream' Egyptian thought and are just beyond the chronological scope of this study.

4 For this and the following points, see Wilfong forthcoming a.

5 See Vivian 1993: 92.

6 See Precept 97 of the Rule of Pachomius (Veilleux 1981: 161), where even authorised hair-cutting or shaving is forbidden.

7 A number of the precepts of the Rule of Pachomius are devoted to prohibiting physical contact between the monks in any imaginable circumstance; see Precepts 93–7 and 109 especially (Veilleux 1981: 161–2).

8 Rutschowscaya (1990) *passim*.

9 Hölscher 1954 plate 39 A: 8–10, 20–2 for examples of earrings from the archaeological context of the predominantly Coptic-literate town of Jême. The piercings on the ceramic 'orant' figures from throughout Egypt (see, for example, the visible piercings in the orant figure illustrated in Hölscher 1954 plate 34D) may well represent ear piercings; the figures are so stylised that they do not have ears, but the holes are in the right position on the sides of the heads. Ear- and nose rings (the latter for animals) are found in textual sources: Crum: 1939 *s.v.* 'earring' and 'nose-(ring)'.

10 CLT 3.11–14; see the text in Schiller 1932: 36–7. For the semiotics of physical descriptions in the Greek papyri from Egypt, see Montserrat 1996a: 55–60.

11 Pseudo-Shenoute on Christian behaviour (Coptic text in Kuhn 1960: 24–5). Kuhn 1960: 22–3 translates this action as 'brand', but the Coptic word is *jakjek*, most commonly translated as 'to prick', which perfectly describes the action of tattooing.

12 Montserrat 1996b, with bibliography of older literature; see also Viaud 1979, which contains some useful information. Carswell 1956 is a useful corpus of tattoo designs taken directly from the blocks used to print the guidelines for the tattooist, but very hard to obtain.

13 For examples of such treatment of the dead, see Castel 1979, with plates 10–17; Buschhausen *et al.* 1995: 205–7, 219–22.
14 There is a somewhat inaccurate English translation in Budge 1913: 326–7. The various versions of the life of Pisentius are all in need of re-edition; for now, see Gabra 1984.
15 The standard reference is Till 1951, which includes German translations of all relevant texts known at the time.
16 See Till 1951: 112–13 for translations and references. All these treatments have much earlier Egyptian precedents.
17 Coptic magical texts are now conveniently available in the collected translation by Meyer and Smith 1994.
18 Text in Crum 1905: 505–6; see also Meyer and Smith 1994: 196.
19 For example, contrast the example quoted above, cursing a woman, with Meyer and Smith 1994: 188–90, cursing a man.
20 Concerning this genre, see the excellent introduction by David Frankfurter in Meyer and Smith 1994: 147–51.
21 Text in Meyer and Smith 1994: 167.
22 See especially Meyer and Smith 1994: 178–81, although the interpretation of the purpose of these spells is somewhat different from what the editors suggest. The spells are to cause impotence in a man and thereby prevent him from having sex with a specified woman, rather than to protect the woman from sexual advances as suggested. It is odd to see the continuing prudishness of the translation of the passages in a spell (Meyer and Smith: 178–9) referring to the potential sexual partners of the man being enchanted. As suggested by Robert Ritner in the note in Meyer and Smith 1994: 369, and earlier by the present author in his re-edition of this text (*BASP* 29 (1992): 93–5), the writer clearly does not want the man to be able to have sex with the named woman or 'any woman, man or beast' rather than the translator's nonsensical 'any woman, wild or tame', which reproduces verbatim from the bashful 1939 *editio princeps*.
23 In Meyer and Smith 1994: 178–9 it is almost certainly the penis and not the man being likened to a corpse; the example on p. 181 seems to equate the two.
24 Ryl 103 (= Meyer and Smith 1994: 231) provides a good example of this contrast: the spell includes conjuring by the breast of the Virgin Mary, by things upon the chest of God the Father (not by the body part itself) and by the sacrifice of Jesus Christ.
25 Text described but not fully edited in Crum 1905: 69.
26 Already in the *Pyramid Texts* §148–9, but continuing throughout the Egyptian religious tradition.
27 See, for instance, Clement of Alexandria, *Protrepticus* iv 61, where the ears are penetrated and violated by sexually explicit images. The iconography of this idea is studied in depth by Urbaniak-Walczak 1992.
28 For an extended discussion of this point and its implications within ancient Egyptian conception of the sexual body, see Wilfong forthcoming c.
29 See Wilfong forthcoming b for a discussion of depictions of Constantinian women.

30 Analogous to this, perhaps, is the Egyptian custom of drawing hiero-glyphs of dangerous beasts like snakes and crocodiles as physically dismembered in funerary contexts, such as in the Pyramid of Unas.

31 The text is taken from Crum 1915: 38–67, the analysis is developed in greater detail in Wilfong forthcoming a.

32 Wilfong 1990.

33 Junker 1911: 84–5; for the whole cycle see Junker 1911: 80–7.

34 The best documentation is from the women's community connected with Shenoute's White monastery near Sohag in Middle Egypt. Un-fortunately, the relevant texts are not fully published; indeed, Shenoute's writings to the nuns seem to be especially neglected in older editions. Most of the following discussion is based on material attributed to Shenoute's successor Besa published in Kuhn 1956. A number of these writings attributed to Besa are, in fact, by Shenoute himself; see Emmel 1993: 1274–5 for details.

35 The Coptic text with translation is published in Young 1993: 91–113; translations given below use Young's text. An in-depth analysis of this text and its implications for our understanding of Late Antique Egyptian constructions of homosexual activity ('"Friendship and Physical Desire": The Discourse of Same-Sex Erotic Relations in Fifth Century Egypt') is in preparation by the present author.

36 Full publication of these paintings in Walters 1989.

37 See Ringrose 1994: 85–109.

38 Coptic text and English translation in Drescher 1947: 1–13, 69–82.

39 This episode is also found in a Coptic song, published in Till 1941: 129–35. The relevant passage runs: 'My Father, Apa Hilarion / My daughter told me, my father / That on the very same bed with you, / on [her mouth] did you kiss her / From the evening until light ap[peared]. / I have heard concerning monks, / that they hate the likes of women. / So why then do you, Hilarion, / Love them more than anyone else?'

40 See Castelli 1991: 29–49.

41 See Van Minnen 1995. For martyrdoms in general, see Horn 1986–92, *passim*; Orlandi 1991.

42 There is a close relationship between the Shenoufe story and the martyrdom of Epima, noted in their introduction by Reymond and Barns 1974; Epima is published in Mina 1937.

43 Text edition by Reymond and Barns 1974.

44 See, for instance, the episodes in the martyrdom of Ptolemy (see Till 1936: 32) and in the martyrdom of Piroou and Athom (Hyvernat 1888: 136).

45 See, for example, the discussions in Bynum 1992, especially 11–26 and 181–238.

Part IV

THE ANCIENT BODY'S TRAJECTORY THROUGH TIME

8

THE IRRESISTIBLE BODY AND THE SEDUCTION OF ARCHAEOLOGY

Lynn Meskell

This chapter takes as its point of departure recent discussions in sociology, anthropology, queer theory, feminist studies and archaeology on the contextual constitution of sex and gender, with its surrounding debates. It also considers recent critique in the social sciences of Cartesian dualism and the more extreme formulations of social constructionism. The chapter then addresses a Foucauldian archaeology with its primary focus upon power, at the expense of the embodied individual and agency. It explores the adoption, and implications, of the body as a phenomenon in archaeology and, more specifically, as one central project for an engendered archaeology. To conclude, it offers one tentative option for divesting the discipline of rigid categorisations and prioritising specific discourses of difference, through the identification of constructions of self or identity.

AN INTRODUCTION TO THE BODY

Archaeologists interested in issues of gender would agree that it is no longer tenable to involve ourselves in gendered discourse simply as a vehicle for the identification and location of *women*, though it remains necessary to balance the scales in terms of writing histories. To be engaged in gender research is not tantamount to studying women in the past, as if they alone were synonymous with *gender* or somehow constituted a monolithic and unchanging entity. However, gender still remains peripheral in many minds as a topic of focus, perhaps because earlier archaeological theorising often sought to isolate gender as a single structuring principle, yet divorced it from other social factors. While such a radically political standpoint was entirely warranted at the outset, it should not be the case that *gender* is assigned primacy; otherwise the resultant field of speciality emerges as another privileged mode of discourse with its own bounds of exclusivity.[1] It is now axiomatic that gender is embedded within a more elaborated, sophisticated social matrix, yet this is rarely operative within archaeological inquiry as opposed to the social sciences.

One recent trend in archaeology and particularly engendered archaeology, directly borrowed from post-structuralist philosophy, sociology and anthropology,[2] is to elevate the body as a theoretical space. The body has become the site of mapped and inscribed social relations, specifically displays and negotiations of power and gender dynamics. This continuance of the western pre-occupation with exteriority has been amply critiqued and theorised in the social sciences, yet appears to have been adopted wholesale in archaeology with little cognisance of the inherent structures and trajectories that we have acquired. In essence, the body has become one central project of gender/feminist archaeologies and while not explicitly theoretical in orientation these studies form part of a larger phenomenon in recent archaeological literature which focuses on the body as a distinct, socially constructed sphere. This can be seen in recent general developments within Egyptian, Near Eastern, and Mediterranean archaeologies, where the adoption of engendered analyses has been construed as the identification of women, sexuality and feminisation of specific groups.[3] In archaeology, the data employed are generally visually evocative; wall paintings, iconography, motifs, jewellery and ornamentation. In these examples, scholars are preoccupied with posture, gesture, costume, sexuality and representation in preference to the construction of individual identities, bodily experience or 'lived bodies' in any corporeal sense. In the field of classics, Page duBois' 1988 work exemplifies the female body as the mythical body: unproblematised and certainly uninhabited. Valuable as her study proves, its focus upon sexuality, mythology, and psychoanalysis leaves the sexes *essentially* polarised, under-nuanced and unreal. While such interests are valid enterprises, those engaging in gender (plus feminist and masculinist) discourse should be aware of their intellectual inheritance and its implications. If the body is to be central it needs to be thought through carefully, so that what we regard as patriarchal logic is to be subverted and not compounded.[4] From a feminist standpoint, Thomas Laqueur[5] suggests it is dangerous to place the body as central in the search for female identity (I would also add *male*) – for reasons I intend to elaborate.

Archaeology has been seduced by Foucauldian notions of control, where power relations are mapped on the body as a surface which can be analysed as a forum for display. Despite the eager and enthusiastic adoption in archaeology of these ideas, replete with post-modern posturing and sanctioned by feminist practitioners, there is still the implicit adoption of binary, dichotomous and essentially Cartesian notions of rigid sex typing. Such a critique crystallised through specific readings of masculinist theory and its critique of the social construction of hegemonic masculinity through the ascendancy of the mind over bodily or emotional experience. From these readings, it could be argued that the current preoccupation with control and elaboration is a typically androcentric, externalised separation of mind, body and emotions. This preoccupation forms an essentialist duality through its own mode of discourse and retrodicts that perspective into the past as if temporal and cultural stasis was tenable. The 'on the body' discourse adopted by feminists and non-feminists alike still focuses attention on notions of control over – essentially – the dominant male paradigm. It remains a phallocentric way of seeing which fails to offer any radical departure or to advance any fresh alternatives. All this mapping and elaborated treatment of the body may reflect the post-modern predilection for surface, but it still represents a separation from our bodies and our identities as individuals.

THE TROUBLE WITH TERMINOLOGY

Part of our central dilemma in our discourse on the body must be seen as terminological. Few scholars specifically define their terms of reference and thus we cannot assume consensus on even basic designations. The terms 'sex', 'gender', 'sexuality', 'gender relations' and 'social relations' are wrongly assumed to have common meaning to all groups and in fact are used in a number of quite distinct and different ways.[6] Hence these terms can never refer to pure concepts. In archaeology there have been at least two strident reactions to the concepts of *sex* and *gender*, both fundamentally flawed. First, that the two entities are quite distinct, with *sex* representing the externalised manifestation of a biological given and *gender* as a socially constituted elaboration which overlays itself on the former.[7] This position should now be regarded as problematic and I would encourage readers to fight the urge to dismiss instantly the possibility that in many of our debates on sex and gender we have actually been arguing about the same things. I aim to show that these two fundamental concepts may in fact be similarly constituted,[8] if not one and the same. The second reaction has been to leave both terms untheorised with *gender* and *sex* collapsed in upon each other so that the resultant examinations simply analyse predetermined categories of *males* and *females* as broad, but dichotomous groupings. This suggests that a form of essentialism was operative in the past, and further implies that such a situation exists in contemporary contexts.

I take essentialism to have two definitions which are relevant for the examination of social dynamics in archaeology: first, that particular things have intrinsic essences which serve to identify them as particular; and second, that abstract entities or universals exist across time and space. Such a position regards *woman*, or *man* for that matter, as a 'given' which is transhistorical and transcultural and constant over the trajectories of age, status and/or ethnicity: whereas the contributions of recent feminist theory and more particularly, masculinist theory, challenge such a stance.

The problem of disembedding sex and gender remains. Thomas Laqueur's impressive study has shown that sex is also a contextual issue and that the notion of two distinct sexes depends very much on the site of knowledge production. The location of his discussion, and indeed mine for the entirety of this chapter, is restricted within the confines of western intellectualism. Prior to the Enlightenment a one-sex model held prominence, influenced largely by classical authors such as Plato, Aristotle and Galen, who proposed that female biology was merely a variation on the male. Even language marks this view: for example the ovary was left without a name of its own for two millennia. Galen simply referred to it by the word he used for the male testes, *orcheis*, exemplifying this female-as-male model.[9] In fact Laqueur pushes the issue further by suggesting that in pre-Enlightenment texts *sex* must be understood as the epiphenomenon, while *gender* (what we would take to be a cultural category) was primary or 'real'. Thus sex before the seventeenth century was still a sociological and not an ontological category.[10] It is important to note that by 1800 various writers were arguing for fundamental differences between the male and female sexes. This rewriting of the body could have been shaped by sociopolitical transformations as diverse as the rise of evangelical religion, the effects of the French Revolution, the factory system and the sexual division of labour, and the rise of the free market economy. Whatever the setting, the particular construction and understanding of *sex* cannot be isolated from its discursive milieu.[11]

As I will argue later, binary separations such as mind:body have

142

been prevailing preoccupations within western intellectualism. Ultimately sex:gender could be seen within this dualistic framework. As previously stated, theorists of the last few decades have argued that gender was socially constructed, with the underlying premise that although gender was not determined by biology, it was the social elaboration of the obvious facts of biological sex difference.[12] Even social constructionists like Foucault specify that sex is a category and the result of specific discursive practices: an effect rather than an origin, not a given at all.

Both Thomas Laqueur and Judith Butler adopt this position, arguing that perhaps there is no distinction at all between sex and gender. As a practitioner of queer theory, Butler[13] asserts it is no longer tenable to advocate the existence of prediscursive 'sex' which acts as the stable referent on top of which the cultural construction of gender proceeds. The category of sex is, from the outset, normative or, in Foucauldian terms, a regulatory ideal. Furthermore, we cannot assume that biological sex everywhere provides the universalist basis for the cultural categories *male* and *female*.[14] Sex, as far as we understand it within the terms of western discourse, is something which differentiates between bodies, while gender is the set of variable social constructions placed upon those differentiated bodies. It is precisely this formula which obscures rather than clarifies when it comes to cross-cultural analyses of sex, sexual difference and gender.[15] Perhaps we are now arguing the same cases for sex as gender and that both are constructed and neither are intransient. This is clearly illustrated if we look beyond western culture to other social constructions of sex. Perhaps we can argue the sex:gender scenario in our culture, yet can we legitimately project this model transhistorically?

THE CARTESIAN COG(N)ITO

The nature/culture bifurcation pervades the body literature and can be traced directly to Descartes and his essential separation of mind and body, the former being privileged over the latter. However, this reasoning was firmly established in classical antiquity, as witnessed by Plato's *Cratylus*, where the body imprisons the non-corporeal soul. Plato's *Timaeus* continues this notion with a twist, arguing that the male body imbued individual bodies, including non-human ones, with form, shape and specific features: 'for those who framed us knew that later on women and other animals would be produced from men, and that many creatures would need claws and hoofs for different purposes; so they provided the rudiments of them in men at their first creation'.[16] In the seventeenth century, this was to be challenged much by Spinoza (*Ethics* III Prop. 2), who opted for a more holistic treatment whereby a system of integration was preferable. The body, *being* and power were also at issue in the work of Nietzsche whose lineage was later extended in Foucault's work on genealogy and power.[17]

The body has continued as a focus in mainstream western philosophical thought and in contemporary feminist theory. However, one underlying concern is the way in which feminism has uncritically adopted many philosophical assumptions regarding the role of the body in social, political, cultural, psychical and sexual life which is similarly somehow complicit in much of the misogyny that characterises western reason. This Cartesian bifurcation does not represent a neutral division but is hierarchised and ranked, thus privileging one term and suppressing and subordinating the other. In such an equation *body* is simply what is not *mind*, what is distinct from and other than the privileged term. It is what the mind must expel in order to secure its 'integrity'. The body is depicted as disruptive and in need of ordered direction. It is merely incidental to the defining characteristics of mind and reason which are privileged within philosophical thought.[18] According to Grosz, mind:body is a critical metaphor for other binary motifs within a Cartesian paradigm:

self	other
inside	outside
depth	surface
reality	appearance
mechanism	vitality
transcendence	immanence
temporality	spatiality
psychology	physiology
form	matter

In essence, Cartesian dualism establishes an unbridgeable gulf between mind and matter. This false dichotomy has serious implications in our (re)construction of individuals in an archaeological past and more specifically, for feminist scholars who are attempting to challenge the inherently phallocentric modes of thinking within western intellectualism.

There are several issues at stake within archaeological interpretations involving the body. One might be termed the body as scene of display, in Mediterranean, Near Eastern and Egyptian contexts, which follows from the work of social constructionists like Michel Foucault – though this lineage is seldom acknowledged. Second, there exists, primarily in the literature of British and European prehistory,[19] a predilection for the body as artefact. This social body is described in relationship to its landscape or spatially experiencing the phenomenon of monuments,[20] again without any corporeal, lived or individual identity. The physical body is the object that describes the monument, just as a compass describes a circle in mathematical terms. Barrett's bodies are 'faceless blobs', to use Ruth Tringham's terminology, as one glance at the illustrations in Barrett's book will exemplify. Each set of bodies consists of social players, normative representatives of larger social entities fulfilling their negotiated roles circumscribed by powerful social forces. These formulations obviously provide interesting insights and alternative perspectives on antiquity. Yet they bypass the individual in favour of a body which is a passive reflector of large-scale social processes – or what I term the society in microcosm model. The corporeal phenomenology of Merleau-Ponty challenges the notion of body as object: only I can live my body, which is a phenomenon experienced by me and thus provides a perspectival point which places me in the world enabling relations between me and other subjects and objects.[21] Both trends are derivative of social constructionism which was once exceedingly popular and now heavily critiqued by sociologists, anthropologists and feminists alike. To map the historical landscape of the body and social constructionism in archaeology, we must acknowledge our substantive debt to Foucault (see below).

THE BODY AS THE CENTRAL PROJECT OF GENDER RESEARCH

Our return to the body has not been a straightforward matter. It now constitutes the site of further sociopolitical intrigue as can be seen by the various positions taken up by groups of feminists. Many now elevate and bestow primacy upon the body, specifically the female body, as the critical metaphor and motif exemplifying not only 'our' strengths but 'our' seemingly timeless struggles. The body offers feminists a voice, yet it would appear to be an ahistorical, essentialist, unitary voice which is in itself an elitist, ethnocentric and patriarchal concept. It assumes a commonality between women which is pre-cultural and transhistorical: at this juncture we need to critique all universalising theories, metanarratives and totalising typologies.

Consider the different types of female body – the differences between women on the bases of race, class and sexuality alone. There are inherent problems for feminists who uncritically adopt the body as an icon for their proactive political position. Some recent feminist epistemologists and ecofeminists (e.g. Shulamith Firestone, Mariga Gimbutas, Starhawk, Riane Eisler, Peg Streep) see the body as a unique means of access to knowledge and specific ways of living.[22] The bodies of women, past and present, are unified by archaeo-mythologists like Gimbutas and thus privileged over their male counterparts. This has obvious appeal for those presently engaged in ecofeminism, archaeofeminism, and New Age spirituality. Drawing on mythology, and bolstered by outdated interpretations stressing matriarchy, Gimbutas elevated the experience of the female through a reductionist and biologically determined narrative. The bodies of women enable unique insights and experiences to which men are denied access: they are more natural, more connected to the global rhythms. They embody the *Gaia* principle and constitute our only hope for salvation from the ecological holocaust the planet faces. These writers view binary sex divisions as 'given' and biologically determined and often fail to question or problematise the categories of *sex* and *gender*. They continue to accept the same arguments that delimit and define women in terms of their ability to give birth, and privilege this above all else. I for one do not want to reduce the female body to its sexual and reproductive functions – there is a female body which is not the maternal body.[23] Some of the more radical positions within feminism attempt to privilege the female body, which in itself relies on dangerous assumptions of biologism and naturalism, and it is these discourses from which we need to divorce ourselves. The status quo which positions the body as secondary and the female body subordinate to the male is the result of essentialism, naturalism and biologism. Women's corporeal specificity is used to explain and justify the different, and unequal, social positions and cognitive abilities of the two sexes. This universalist, overriding preoccupation does not represent the totality of all women's experience and continues to be a totalising, oppressive metanarrative.

Other feminist theorists who engage with the body are social constructionists (Juliet Mitchell, Michèle Barrett, Julia Kristeva, and Nancy Chodorow) or Marxist and psychoanalytic feminists who are committed to the notion of the social construction of subjectivity. They too see the body as biologically determined and fixed, adhere to ahistorical notions of the body and retain the mind:body dualism. Bodies provide the raw material base for the inculcation of and interpolation into ideology but are merely media of communication rather than the object or focus of ideological (re)production. Presuming that biology or sex is fixed, feminists have tended to focus on transformations at the level of gender and its corresponding cultural meanings and values. A third group situates itself in terms of sexual difference, which includes Luce Irigaray, Moira Gatens, Judith Butler, Hélène Cixous, Naomi Schor and Monique Wittig. For them the body is crucial to women's psychical and social existence though it is no longer understood as an ahistorical, biologically given, acultural object. They are concerned with the *lived body* so far as it is specifically represented and used in particular cultures. The body is not passively mapped, but is interwoven with, and constitutive of, systems of meaning, signification, and representation. On the one hand it is a signifying and signified body; on the other it is an object of systems of social coercion, legal inscription, and sexual and economic exchange. The body is thus regarded as the political, social and cultural object *par excellence*, not the raw, passive body which is overlaid and inscribed with culture. However, if we are to engage in the body dialogue surely we must regard it not only as a site of social, political, cultural and geographical mapping but as recursively engaged in production or constitution.

What underlies the body project quite insidiously is the antique belief that women are well situated within the flesh zone as designated by men. What is doubly disconcerting is that some feminists are actively pursuing and claiming this site as their own forum of expertise without recognising this undesirable heritage. Reclamation of *individual* bodies, rather than universalist collectives, may be our way out of the dilemma. Grosz argues[24] that if corporeality can no longer be linked with one sex, then women can no longer take on the function of being *the body* for men, who are left free to soar the heights of theoretical reflection and cultural production, just as people of colour, indigenous people, or slaves can no longer fulfil the role of the *working body* for white élites, who are free to create values, morality, knowledges. In view of this assertion, the central dilemma for gender studies within our field is that they have claimed the body as their own area of speciality and positioned themselves as privileged in these discourses. However, in retrospect, by claiming or reclaiming the body we have failed to produce any radical perspectives or alternatives, but have simply adhered to the dichotomous structures already established by élite western males since the time of Descartes and earlier. Some feminists have failed to see the lineage of their current position or to realise that they have simply subscribed to a subordinating and deterministic paradigm. This has serious implications for gender theorists in archaeology, whose project it has been to alter the discipline radically, to offer fresh insights and an altogether different framework through which to conduct archaeological interpretation. The above assertions would suggest that these objectives have been impeded and that the way forward does not lie with further analyses of the body in any naturalistic, biological or extreme social constructionist sense.

POWERFUL BODIES: SEX, POWER AND FOUCAULDIAN ARCHAEOLOGY

The body as a frame of discourse has become a central project of high modernity. It has become both a theoretical space and classificatory system for scholars such as Pierre Bourdieu, Jacques Lacan, Jean Baudrillard, Anthony Giddens, Bryan Turner, Richard Sennet and of course Foucault himself. Just as proactive women are seeking to reclaim their bodies in a very real sense within our own society, the body has been appropriated once again within the realm of academic conceptualisations and discourses of power. However, this upsurge in theorising has prompted a new desire for groundedness, whereby we regard the body as a material, physical and biological phenomenon which is irreducible to immediate social processes or classifications. Bodies cannot simply be explained away.[25] In contrast to social constructionists like Foucault, it is important to recognise that the body is not merely constrained by or invested with social relations, but also forms a basis for and contributes towards these relations. This has undoubtedly emerged as a reactionary tide against the profound influence of the Cartesian tradition which emphasises the dual status of the mind:body dichotomy discussed earlier. Another criticism which feminists have vigorously levelled at Foucault is his *gender blindness* whereby the general human subject is assumed to be male.[26] In general, Foucault does not consider Other voices, rather taking his departure from administrators, doctors, architects, penal reformers and male authorities in general. Hartsock takes this further by arguing that Foucault's world lacks people altogether – it is a world where the subject becomes obliterated or recreated into a passive object. In such a world passivity or refusal represent the only choices.[27]

It is always the body that is at issue within Foucault's work – the body and its forces, their utility and their docility, their distribution and their submission. This is where the notion of passivity appears to stem from; the body is like a surface waiting to be elaborated upon, a vehicle for the display of power relations. There seem to be at least two complimentary issues presented in Foucault's thesis. First, it is argued that the body is a forum upon which social dynamics are mapped, a means of visible and tangible display. Bodies are transformed into objects of knowledge. Second, Foucault suggests that there is a political investment of the body. It is essentially invested with relations of power and domination. Here the political economy of the body finds its ultimate expression. Moreover, in his hugely influential *History of Sexuality*, the body as a separate entity is central and is described as if it were a passive front which became imbued with a specific sexuality *via* an empowered dynamic. Sexuality was deployed from a hegemonic centre and eventually the entire social body was provided with a sexual body.[28] The body itself is invested with power relations, more specifically *power over*. His is the model of domination and resistance that archaeologists have found so seductive.

In essence, power is exercised rather than possessed by the dominant group and it situates and invests them as well as the oppressed class. It is also transmitted by, and through, the dominated just as they struggle against the grip in which it holds them. These relations permeate the depths of society and are not simply localised between the state and its citizens or at the boundaries of class groups; they do not merely reproduce at the level of individuals, gestures and behaviour, although there may be continuity.[29] From this perspective power is one of the conditions of knowledge; they are co-dependent. For Foucault, the body is not simply a focus for discourse, but provides the linkage between daily practices and the large-scale organisation of power.[30] To implant this image of the 'body politic' firmly in the mind of the reader Foucault employs biological language and metaphor almost as a continuous textual example of body, knowledge and power at play.

In the *History of Sexuality* Foucault is, not surprisingly, obsessed with power relations over the social body, although I would argue that he adopts a more moderate position than that expressed in *Discipline and Punish*. For Foucault the history of sexuality is analogous to the historical relationships of power and discourse on sex, which is ultimately a self-recursive process. However, he does not situate power as an institution, structure or a strength we are endowed with. Rather, it is the name given to a complex strategical situation in a particular society. Power is not an abstract which can be acquired or seized: it is exercised within a schema of asymmetrical relationships, which similarly include interactions of a social, economic, sexual or knowledge-based nature. He denies the binary power dynamic of ruler and ruled, in favour of a more complex matrix in which each group actively reinforces their placement within the social body. However, he adheres to the notion of domination and resistance, though neither can adopt a position of exteriority. There is a plurality of resistance which is irregular and dispersed temporally and spatially, and which may even cut across social stratifications and individual unities. Finally, he seeks to cast off the preoccupation with rationality within such processes, since power relations can be both intentional and non-discursive or nonsubjective.[31] Archaeology has readily adopted these canons, although major adherents of power-based Foucauldian constructionism such as Shanks and Tilley[32] give primacy to a more narrow and rigid concept of hegemonic power, exploitation, domination and resistance, etc. which presents a simplistic and formulaic binary equation that is in conflict with the original paradigm Foucault proposed. It is the former, rather than the latter, which has attracted and taken hold of a post-modern archaeology.[33]

For Foucault, power is an impersonal set of negotiations between practices, discourses and non-discursive events, a mode of management of a multiplicity of relations, a set of technologies linking the most massive cultural movements to the most minute day-to-day events in interpersonal life. His *power* has no specifiable or universal goal, no pregiven shape or form, no privileged manoeuvres, no preferred targets or representations.[34] This arbitrary nature of power, its general fluidity, has been downplayed by archaeological theorists like Shanks and Tilley in favour of a more extreme social constructionist position. Archaeology has been seduced by discourses of power and preoccupation with its strategies, which assume a labour-time intensive, constant and all-consuming energy directed toward maintaining that position within a highly developed, well articulated system. This would seem another potent example of an overarching phallocentric paradigm. Ever popular models of domination and resistance continue to posit issues of power and control as central. Somehow this sells short the life experiences of the individuals involved and its reductionist formula results in a self-fulfilling, over-simplified version of social dynamics. There is an inherent danger in dealing with issues such as class and gender inasmuch as the picture presented is one which highlights a model of the oppressor versus the oppressed, which in itself is a form of temporal/cultural chauvin-ism that reinforces those relations – whether or not they existed in reality. A feminist contribution to the discipline should ideally break with androcentric paradigms, not merely replace a male with a female focus within the same essentialist structures. This presents a real challenge to those engaged in feminist (and masculinist) discourse which should not be met, in my view, with gynocentric or female-centred narratives which similarly adhere to a model of Cartesian bifurcation.

BODIES OF RESISTANCE

Many social constructionists of the body have been influenced by the anthropology of Mary Douglas and her assertions that the body is, above all, a metaphor for society. More than anything, it is the symbol of social location and stratification. Again the corporeal nature of the body is depicted as a secondary, subdued surface which is constrained by the social body. Butler argues that the aspects of bodily existence lie outside the range of social construction, whether it be living, dying, sleeping, eating or experiencing pleasure, pain or violence. Thus the discourse of constructionism cannot be entirely adequate to the task at hand – and this is inclusive of feminist notions.[35] It might be suggested that the nature of social con-structionism itself could be viewed as tacitly androcentric since external forces impose themselves upon, if you like penetrate, the passive (female?) surface of the subject. However, there are possible exceptions or challenges to these central tenets of social con-structionism, the major example being Bourdieu who dislocates the body from bearer of symbolic value to the body as material phenom-enon which both constitutes, and is constituted by, society.[36] Bourdieu still focuses on the importance of taste, body management and the surfaces, textures and appearances of the body. But bodies bear the imprint of their social class because of three major factors:

social location; formation of their *habitus*; development of tastes. *Habitus* is defined as a socially constituted system of cognitive and motivating structures which provide individuals with class-dependent, predisposed ways of relating and categorising both familiar and novel situations. It inculcates people with a 'world view'.[37]

Though this appears to be a more reflexive model, Bourdieu's body is still perceived as physical capital which acts in a deterministic manner, rather than an arbitrary or individual one. For Bourdieu, the term *individual* refers to a generic ontological category which is in itself a nomothetic enterprise rather than an idiographic one. Even the concept of bodily *hexis*, which appears to be formulated at a highly personal and experiential level, seeks to generalise the construction of self in broad categorical and mechanistic terms: yet another example of rhetoric versus praxis. His project could be described as one of unity and corporate identity, rather than *difference*. In scalar terms, Bourdieu's formulations are insightful at a general societal level as the underlying strata upon which the individual is constituted. He identifies the site of production, through its underlying structures; however, I would argue that the specific responses, trajectories and the resultant discursive formulation of embodied individuals is largely omitted. This is by far the most interesting, and elusive, construction which operates at the micro level – whereas grand social theory opts for macro-scale analyses. In sum, a reconciliation between *society* and *self* still requires implementation (see below).

Much of the difficulty in analysing social domination, power and resistance stems yet again from a terminological uncertainty. Resistance implies a conscious strategy, yet how do we determine whether behaviours are discursive or non-discursive? Oppressed groups frequently develop their own discourses that operate in contradistinction to dominant ones,[38] though the question remains: can we actively recognise and choose the subject positions they take up, and to what degree are they able to resist the terms of dominant discourses? Further to this, in theory we assume the individual to be rational, autonomous and unitary, author of their own destiny – which is ultimately entrenched in post-Enlightenment philosophy. At this point it should also be acknowledged that the category of *individual* itself is a social construction, often construed in a dichotomy against *society*, yet they are not inherently mutually exclusive. In reality, anthropological analysis suggests individuals have a very complex relationship with everyday experiences and often fail to conceive of themselves as rational or autonomous. Individuals should be depicted as multiply-constituted subjects; they can and do take up multiple subject positions within a range of discourses and social practices – some will also be in conflict with each other. Herein lies one fundamental contribution that an engendered or feminist archaeology could offer the discipline more generally, that is, to identify the centrality of the individual rather than totalising and generalising locational categories of sex or class. Feminists in the 1990s have sought to address the notion of *difference* in all its complex manifestations, and such contemporary theorising should prompt us to recognise the construction of individual identities in the past rather than the microcosmic representatives of society that have previously characterised our analyses.

ARTICULATING AN ARCHAEOLOGY OF THE INDIVIDUAL

What belies the recent preoccupation with the social construction of the individual in the social sciences is undoubtedly a very western fascination with identity, self, and difference.[39] We must acknowledge the centrality of self-construction in the time of high modernity. At the close of the twentieth century it is more that we experience *becoming* one's body and it is unlikely that any other epoch was so centrally focused on that specific construction, embodiment and lived quality. However, accessing the individual in antiquity obviously presents archaeology with some major challenges given that the concept itself is a loaded, historically situated term which is neither transhistorical nor transcultural.[40] Ethnographic research has questioned these normative assumptions about the relationship of personhood, gender identity and embodiment. Such categories vary widely, both temporally and culturally. In the west we assume that the body is the source and locus of identity and that the interior self is always the source or locus of intention or agency. We might also consider that persons are divisible, partible and unbounded and that experience may not simply find its location in the interior self.

From the often-applied Lacanian perspective[41] the subject (read: individual) is decentred and displaced through linguistic and discursive measures within the social field. Thus there is no pure constitution of the self, since it is always situated relationally.

Basically a referent is a necessary prerequisite which serves as Other, and thus a situating device. This constitution is continually in a state of flux: a constellation which is constantly being defined, individuated and constructed.[42] In essence, this construction occurs within a preordained system and the individual is bound within that network in the production of self. However, in treating individuals explicitly, or by default, as simply socio-culturally driven, ignoring the *self-driven* aspects of behaviour, is to render them, at least partially, as fictitious ciphers of our own invention.[43] The myriad choices and possible trajectories an individual may follow and whether these actually constitute discursive or non-discursive behaviours are not elaborated upon. In such a system, particularly within the field of archaeology as opposed to anthropology, this measure of contingency is problematic as it tends to imply extreme relativism or at worst, nihilism. In post-processual archaeology great emphasis has been placed on the individual and human intentionality – this is the case in theory, although Johnson has argued that, in practice, most accompanying case studies still omit 'real people'.[44]

Whilst prominent theorists acknowledge a desire to locate self-identity in the past, rather than reduce the individual to a mere 'ghost in the machine', this is hardly ever explicitly demonstrated. For example, Thomas clearly wishes to reject the Cartesian tradition and explore the experiential levels of corporeal bodies, yet he still remains locked in Foucauldian constructionism whereby the body simply mediates the reading of spatial texts and is subject to constraints of domination and resistance. Like Barrett, he sees the importance of locating real bodies, yet their prime function still appears to be a clearer articulation of monuments rather than selves. In only a single sentence he refers to 'human actors moving about ... meeting, talking, exchanging goods and separating'.[45] Gosden's recent volume, *Social Being and Time* (1994) also holds promise of accessing states of *being* in a very personal and individual context, via vignettes of historical episodes punctuated by discussions of temporality. Whilst the aim represents a unique endeavour, the result is ultimately a synthetic overview of the major philosophical developments of the century, rather than an articulation of *being*. In this sense Johnson's initial criticism still stands.

In attempting to locate the individual I am referring to two quite different projects. The first is what Matthew Johnson refers to as a practical concern with 'specifically existing moments, present particularly in historical archaeology where one can identify "real people" and relate them to traces in the archaeological record'.[46] The second project, and one which is more generally attainable in archaeology, is a search for the construction of identity or self. Selfhood varies cross-culturally and I do not claim that we can access specific self-conscious individuals or empathise in any cognitive way, since we are inherently tangled in a hermeneutic construction. However, my own preliminary investigations into the villagers of Deir el Medina,[47] an Egyptian domestic settlement occupied during the New Kingdom (c. 1567–1085 BCE), suggest that it is possible to see reflections of individual selves in all their variability. This view does not discount constituting factors of age, status, class, gender, ethnicity or marital status, yet it does not prioritise these categories as opposed to individual or family choices. I am not advocating access to individual self-consciousness – anthropology has clearly illustrated the problematics of this position – but rather the formulation of identity. In this context, single burials of children, couples, family groups – often named individuals with written histories – may show how notions of identity or constructions of self were embodied. Individual selves were also presented to other members of the community during life (through individual houses, decoration and material culture) and to other individuals, family and members of the afterworld through death (by means of burials, tombs, chapels and monuments).

A compelling example from Deir el Medina comes from the Eastern Necropolis,[48] the poorest cemetery on the site with specific areas reserved for children and adolescents. Several of the small children here were placed in roughly hewn wooden boxes that were designed specifically for their funerary context. One individual merits particular attention – a young boy named Iryky. The family that lost this child must have suffered throughout his life and death – Iryky was so badly deformed that his survival beyond the first year of life must have been something of a miracle. His torso and head were abnormally large and his limbs stunted. He was not the only deformed child in the cemetery who had survived beyond birth; there is another unnamed boy in tomb 1373, some 80cm tall, who suffered from scoliosis. He was buried with jewellery, vases and plates full of bread, grain and dom nuts in an oval basket. However, Iryky's family also went to considerable effort to bury him in a decorated chest, painted yellow with black borders with two large lateral bands containing hieratic script in black ink, including his name. The archaeology suggests that these two young boys were supported through life and cared for in death, which tells us something of their individual lives, that of their families and the society in which they were situated. A personal point of contact with the families at Deir el Medina could be our own western desire for the souls of children to live again or have an afterlife of sorts, irrespective of the various religious beliefs we subscribe to. I am not arguing for a form of essentialism which binds 'people' across spatio-temporal boundaries, as if the total experience of death was somehow commensurate. However, some measure of empathy, which lies beyond the rigid framework of social constructionism, must be considered. The discourse of constructionism, whether it be power, prestige or social aggrandisement, cannot be entirely adequate to the task at hand. Not only does such a position evacuate agency and the individual, it undermines human intentionality as well as the emotive and experiential dimension.

The endeavour to locate individuals meaningfully is further evidenced in Sarah Tarlow's recent discussion of bereavement, emotional embodiment and selfhood in eighteenth- and nineteenth-century Orkney. This is possible not only through analysis of local material culture and mortuary practice, but also through the specific life/death experiences of named individuals within that geographical and temporal framework. In this manner she successfully addresses both Johnson's projects for locating conceptions of self. Tarlow sees major changes in personal and family relationships in the late eighteenth century, and this was reflected in changing attitudes to the dead. The Orkney graveyard survey, which forms the material background, indicates a great variety in style, shape and inscription of gravestones, suggesting that presentation was individualistic, rather than conventionalised. Such monuments reflect highly emotional responses to individualised relationships which accordingly demanded individualisation in commemoration. Similarly, they expressed the unique personality of the deceased and the special relationship between the deceased and the bereaved, whilst distinguishing each memorial from the mass of others. Indeed, absolute numbers of gravestones increase dramatically through the nineteenth century, an increase seemingly related to changing sensibilities, where the commemoration of individual relationships assumes greater significance. Tarlow's examination of metaphors of death and individual epitaphs goes beyond simply documenting this rise of affective individualism – it gives access to embodied 'real' people and their particular expressions of emotive experience.[49] Further, the study successfully challenges the notion that individual mortuary practice can be reductively viewed as status display and aggrandisement in any social constructionist sense and offers the much needed, and overlooked, human dimension.

THE INDIVIDUAL AS SOCIETY IN MICROCOSM: A VIEW FROM THE TOP

Archaeology has tended to ignore the relationship of the individual to society in favour of treating individuals simply as micro versions of larger social entities. This is achieved by extrapolating from the supposedly representative sample of *society* to the assumption that subjects are the normative constituents which aggregate to make the whole. Western social science proceeds from the top downwards, from society to the individual, deriving individuals from social structures to which they belong: class, nationality, state, gender, religion, generation and so on.[50] However, fields such as social psychology, interactionism and ethnomethodology could be seen as exceptions. Generally, we focus on collective structures and categories, leaving the individual sadly under-theorised. The corollary is that we have simply created fictions which need serious revision. The problem with theories such as Giddens' 'structuration theory', widely cited in the archaeological literature, is that they treat society as an ontology which is somehow independent of its members. There is a failing to see society as created by selves which thus fails to accord them their creative input. The agency he allows individuals gives them the power of reflexivity, but not of motivation: they are doomed to be perpetrators rather than architects of action.[51]

We must qualify these assumptions by recognising that the relationship between individual and society is far more complex and infinitely variable than can be explained by a simple, uni-dimensional deductive model. This view from the top does not easily facilitate an archaeology of *difference*, or individuality, or allow for an analysis of the construction of self. Archaeology's concern has always been with representativeness, aiming for generalising practices and behaviours rather than individual responses, the latter being positioned as an insurmountable task. We have always been interested in decoding cultural symbols, yet have only recently considered the processes of that symbolisation. However, if we attempt to tap into these unique structures, an historic milieu with multi-levelled data would prove most appropriate.

Archaeology has been quick to adopt social constructionism as a model predicated on this view from the top which situates the self as merely a reflex of superordinate determining forces – a reflexive entity which is inconstant and chameleon-like in its interactions with specific circumstances. Society cannot clone its members or determine the *selves* of its members. Cohen's metaphor is beautifully evocative: society and the self dance an improvised *pas de deux*, each tries to cover the moves of the other, sometimes they merge, at others they separate.[52] Perhaps this too is symptomatic of yet another form of dualistic essentialism between *society* and the *self*, though it is difficult to envisage an alternative construction. Somehow we have to resolve the general dichotomy between apprehending social phenomena as structures (i.e. as various mechanical, functional, structural articulations of social elements) and constituting them as meaningful constellations linked to complexes created and interpreted in various ways by individual or collective social subjects. In this sense the body represents the particular site of interface between several different irreducible domains: the biological and the social, the collective and the individual, structure and agent, cause and meaning, constraint and free will.[53]

AN EMBODIED CONCLUSION

> The body as a social being . . . the articulation of agency and structure, causality and meaning, rationality and imagination, physical determinations and symbolic resonances.[54]

If we give primacy to sexual difference or gendered difference we are excluding other significant forms of difference such as the discourses of race, class and ethnicity and sexuality, etc., and thus returning to the same binary modes of thinking and the same dogmatic structure we seek to critique. Neither can we assume that sexed difference is positioned first or is the immediate structuring principle from which all others disseminate. All the major axes of difference, race, class, ethnicity, sexuality and religion, intersect with gender in ways which proffer a multiplicity of subject positions within any discourse which need to be examined contextually. The above terms themselves are used within academic discourse as generalising categories with very specific assumptions and structures already in place. In some respects this may explain why feminist theory has seemed to many not only arcane, but élitist, racist and/or patriarchal.[55] Moreover, the *woman as victim* scenario oversimplifies the complexities and historical contingencies of specific subordinations. It overemphasises the universalist nature of oppression and the common, isomorphic enemy of *men*, pushing women back into modern formulations of passivity and silence.

Furthermore, there are inherent problems with the uncritical adoption of extreme forms of social constructionism which privilege impersonal forces such as culture or discourse or power; and there are problems about where these terms occupy the grammatical site of the subject after the 'human' has been dislodged from its place. In sum, most constructionist positions are essentially deterministic and simply evacuate or displace human agency.[56] Perhaps it would also prove expedient to review, if not dispense with, these constructed categories which serve to universalise the generalities of human experience, rather than (re)construct or (re)place individual persons.

From my own position, I believe that feminist discourse could provide the catalyst for an analysis of the individual. The potential exists for developing a feminist theory of embodied subjectivity which would take account of other forms of difference or individuality within a broader social framework. However, this project is likely to remain out of reach if sex, gender and sexual difference remain foundational in some sense, either as categories or sets of relations.[57] The way out of the current dilemma may be significantly impeded if emphasis is placed upon the body in an uncritical, untheorised milieu, at the expense of a more rounded, holistic notion of individuality. An embodied body represents, and is, a lived experience where the interplay of irreducible natural, social, cultural and psychical phenomena are brought to fruition through each individual's resolution of external structures, embodied experience and choice. In part, this may relate to Frank's trilateral composition of the body: institutions, discourses and corporeality.[58] Thus, subjective bodily experience is mitigated by factors such as social constraints, practicality, contingency and free will: this dialectical position potentially circumvents the determinism associated with extreme social constructionism, Cartesianism and essentialism.

Prioritising and elevating the body as a central project for engendered archaeology is problematic if we are claiming political awareness coupled with a desire to change the trajectory of the discipline. An indiscriminate adoption of the body phenomenon, variously critiqued in the social sciences, may not represent a radical departure or herald the way forward in terms of attaining equity or revolutionising our discipline. A more positive conclusion is that as a result of archaeology's increasing willingness to incorporate ideas from other social sciences we might benefit from their insights as to our western intellectual inheritance. We are now in a position to build on synchronic developments in anthropology and sociology which seek to identify the construction of self, thus offering new avenues to accessing individuals in the past.

ACKNOWLEDGEMENTS

More than anyone, I would like to thank Sarah Tarlow, not only for permission to cite her work, but for her ongoing inspiration and support. I am also indebted to Ian Hodder who has patiently listened to my subversive ideas – challenged many of them, provided references and motivated me to write. Other people have been incredibly helpful and interested: Kathryn Denning, Robin Boast, Bernard Knapp, Dominic Montserrat, Johnny Patrick, and Paul Treherne. My thanks to all those involved.

NOTES

1 See Bordo 1990: 133–56.
2 There is an extensive bibliography: see Braidotti 1989; Butler 1990a, 1990b; De Lauretis 1986 *passim*; Dutton 1995; Foucault 1977, 1978, 1985, 1986; Giddens 1984, 1992 *passim*; Grosz 1994; Laqueur 1990; Moore 1994; Seidler 1989; Shilling 1993.
3 See duBois 1988; Marcus 1993; Richlin 1992; Rousselle 1988; Wilfong and Jones forthcoming; see also Feher *et al.* 1989, vols 1–3; Winkler 1990 *passim*.
4 McNay 1992: 18.
5 Laqueur 1990: 12.
6 Moore 1994: 6.
7 See e.g. Gilchrist 1991: 497.
8 See Yates 1990; Yates and Nordbladh 1990.
9 Laqueur 1990: 4–5.
10 Laqueur 1990: 8.
11 Foucault 1972: 52, 157.
12 Butler 1990a; McNay 1992: 22; Moore 1994: 12–13; Yates 1990.
13 Butler 1990b: 6–9; Butler 1993: 1.
14 Perhaps the best example of this is the now widely published and theorised case of the Native American *berdache* or 'two-spirit': see Jacobs 1994, with references.
15 Moore 1994: 14.
16 *Tim.* 76: see also *Tim.* 91–92. For more on women as aberrant men, see Vlahogiannis above.

17 Gosden 1994: 142; Lash 1991: 256.
18 Gatens 1994: 99; Grosz 1994: 3.
19 See Barrett 1994; Shanks and Tilley 1982; Thomas and Tilley 1993; Yates 1990.
20 See Barrett 1994: 15, 18, 23; Thomas 1995.
21 On Merleau-Ponty and the body, see Grosz 1994: 86; Kus 1992.
22 Grosz 1994; McNay 1992: 18–24; Shilling 1993: 60; Turner 1991: 19.
23 Meskell 1995: 83.
24 Grosz 1994: 22.
25 Shilling 1993: 10.
26 See Braidotti 1991: 87; McNay 1992: 87.
27 Hartsock 1990: 167.
28 Foucault 1978: 127.
29 Foucault 1977: 27.
30 See further on this, Shilling 1993: 75.
31 See Foucault 1978: 90–96.
32 Shanks and Tilley 1987a: 70–73; 1987b: 129–30.
33 See contributions by Gosden 1994 *passim*; Miller *et al.* 1989; Miller and Tilley 1984; Shanks and Tilley 1987a, 1987b; Thomas 1989, 1993; Tilley 1990.
34 See further Grosz 1994: 147.
35 Butler 1993: xi.
36 Shilling 1993: 73–74.
37 See Bourdieu 1977: 85.
38 Moore 1994: 5.
39 Recent studies are Cohen 1994; Foucault 1972, 1977, 1978, 1985, 1986; Grosz 1994; Hodder 1991; Johnson 1989; Moore 1994; Shanks and Tilley 1987a; Thomas 1989, 1995.
40 Shanks and Tilley 1987a: 62.
41 For a summary, see Bowie above.
42 Shanks and Tilley 1987a: 64–65.
43 Cohen 1994: 7.
44 Johnson 1989: 189–90.
45 Thomas 1993: 92.
46 Johnson 1989: 190.
47 See Meskell 1994a and 1994b.
48 Bruyère 1937: 202.
49 See Tarlow 1992 and forthcoming.
50 Cohen 1994: 6.
51 Cohen 1994: 21.
52 Cohen 1994: 23, 71.
53 Berthelot 1991: 395–98.
54 Berthelot 1991: 400.
55 See Bordo 1990: 35.
56 See Butler 1993: 9.
57 Moore 1994: 23.
58 Frank 1991: 48–49.

9

UNIDENTIFIED HUMAN REMAINS

Mummies and the erotics of biography

Dominic Montserrat

The *idiot-savant* film director and pornographer Edward W. Wood Jr. (1924–78), who is now rapidly attaining cult status, had his finger as firmly on the pulse of popular ideas about Egyptian mummies as he did about so many other cultural phenomena, such as vampires and UFOs. The cover blurb of his lurid 1968 potboiler about necrophilia, *The Love of the Dead*, claimed that it: 'reveals the limitless depths to which man can sink in his sexual cravings. A REAL SHOCKER!' Unsurprisingly, mummies play a part in Wood's survey of 'the dark pages of history devoted to sex crimes':

> More so we might, for a moment take up the ancient Pharoahs (*sic*) of Egypt . . . the great temples built in their honour, their memorials, their tombs . . . their demand of the female mate or mates and Eunuchs to accompany them through the land of the dead. It is not above thought that the brides of the corpse (the Pharoah) have taken him on sexually even in death. Most men actually die with a hard-on and the instrument must be broken before he can be folded into his everlasting box.
>
> The ancients didn't bother to break the thing of the Pharoah. After a time the girls took care of that for the undertakers. Dead or alive, no man can keep a hard-on forever.[1]

Underlying this typically delirious example of Wood's prose are some widely-held ideas about mummies which are of more general relevance to the study of the ancient human body. My theme here is the construction of the mummy as a sexually charged entity – an entity whose sexuality is ambiguous and equivocal, and inextricably linked with the somatic status of the mummy itself. In western culture mummies are liminal bodies which are troublingly difficult to locate. They are dead at the same time as seeming eerily alive: do they inhabit a world of the living or the dead? The mummy defies the most significant physical transition that the human body makes, from a living person to a corpse, and the investment of the mummy with an erotic potential is an acknowledgement of that defiance: the mummy can be an object or agent of desire in the same way as a living person. The shifting sexualities ascribed to mummies by cultures subsequent to the one that originally produced them reflect this problematic bodily status. Mummies can threaten or titillate, penetrate or be penetrated, be naked or covered, consume or be consumed themselves. Note here that Wood's mummified 'pharoah' is not merely phallic but also bisexual: he maintains his erection after death, but requires a harem of both girls *and* eunuchs to satisfy him in the next world.

My focus in this essay is the different ways in which the Egyptian mummy, the ancient human body *par excellence*, has been utilised as an object of western 'pornography'; and what these reuses may have to say about reactions to the human body in other times and cultures – a theme that has already been developed from an archaeological perspective in the previous chapter. First, I will concentrate on the erotic re-embodiment of the ancient individual via the mummified body itself, and the way in which these erotic revivifications often depend on the construction of a fictitious 'biography', replete with orientalist tropes, around the anonymous dead person. Second, I will look at how mummies were used in public performances in the nineteenth century to investigate sexualities, especially for encoding 'deviant' sexuality.

Paradoxically, some of Wood's ideas about the mummy as a sexual, embodied being would not have been wholly incomprehensible to the Egyptians themselves. Their notions about the afterlife revolved around the preservation of the body, so that the deceased could be reborn in the most perfect and vital form. For élite men, this meant being reborn as a sexually potent office-holder, a scribe or bureaucrat; for women, as a fecund wife. The iconography of Egyptian tombs encrypts a complex web of visual/textual references incorporating erotic elements that help bring about this rebirth.[2] But the modifications wrought by the embalmers on the bodies themselves also emphasise these aspirations. For example, in the 21st Dynasty (*c*. 1000 BCE) the breasts and thighs of women, desiccated by the mummification process, were rounded out with subcutaneous packing to restore a lifelike fullness. The result gives the bodies an almost doll-like appearance. In later periods, women's nipples were gilded and vaginas covered with gold plates, or the entire body might be covered with gold leaf so that the dead person was reborn with the golden flesh of a divinity.[3] The erotic foci of men's bodies were also highlighted, with the penis being gilded or sometimes an artificial one included in the mummy wrappings, to act as a substitute should the original be lost or damaged. Similarly, the iconography used on the external coverings of the mummified bodies emphasises the sexuality of the deceased as a means for his or her optimal rebirth. This is perhaps best exemplified by some late Ptolemaic and Roman anthropomorphic female coffins. These are constructed around three-dimensional figures, on which the breasts of women are ornamented with rosettes or gilded nipples, the pelvic area is exaggeratedly broad, and the navel is disproportionately wide and raised with a deep indentation, so that it resembles a bagel. Rebirth in the perfect body is a standard theme of the funerary prayers sometimes found written on these coffins, which talk about the mummification process providing strong, vital limbs so that the deceased will live eternally.[4] Death, rebirth and sexuality were thus intertwined in the Egyptian mind, but this only made sense within the larger framework of their own belief system. Taken out of its social and religious context, the sexual vitality that imbued the mummy began to assume very different meanings, as I shall discuss.

CLASSICAL AND RENAISSANCE AUTHORS ON EGYPTIAN MUMMIFICATION

Before moving on to nineteenth-century and subsequent collocations of mummies and sexuality, it is necessary to examine the cultural antecedents for these ideas which, in some ways, provide a striking continuity. Herodotus, author of the earliest major ancient account of Egypt to have survived, provides the first unambiguous linking of sex with mummies. Appended to his long description of mummification practices is the following anecdote (ii 89):

They do not hand over to be embalmed immediately the wives of notable men, nor women celebrated for beauty or reputation, when they die; but only after they have been dead three or four days do they produce them for the embalmer. This is done so that the embalmers cannot copulate with the women; for it is said that an embalmer was found having intercourse with a woman newly dead, and was betrayed by his fellow workers.

In fact Herodotus' description may not have been very far from the truth. Papyrological sources and the evidence of the mummies themselves suggest that some corpses were kept unburied for a while before being delivered to the embalmers, to the extent that sometimes the bodies had partially decomposed and were disarticulated inside their wrappings.[5] This may have arisen from the custom of friends and family visiting the dead before their journey to the embalmers rather than from the motive Herodotus suggests. What is important here is not so much the historicity of his account, but of the ideas behind it. Egyptian bodies, he implies, are sexy, and the embalming house where they are treated is a possible location for deviant sexuality. In the section directly before this, Herodotus has gone into almost fetishistic detail about the plundering of the internal organs from the body, the anointing of its dead flesh with myrrh, cassia and other spices bruised to release their sweet scents.

One of the tropes of Herodotus' description of Egypt is that everything about it is other to Greece. In Egypt, Greek customs and ways of doing things are literally turned on their head, which Herodotus elaborates in a famous passage (ii 35) about the inversion of gender roles, where the normal activities of Greek men are performed by Egyptian women. The otherness of Egypt extends to the actions and symbols surrounding the dead body. In Greece the corpse is something miasmic, a pollutant which must be taken away and burned or disposed of outside the limits of human habitation. Herodotus and other Greek writers express amazement at the Egyptian habit of preserving the physical form of their dead and then staying in close contact with the remains, rather than banishing them. The best illustration of this is a passage in the novelist Xenophon of Ephesus (v 1.9). Aegialeus, a Spartan exile living in Syracuse and working as a fisherman, tells Habrocomes, the hero of the story, how he was unable to bear to part with his wife Thelxinoë after her death:

> 'Thelxinoë died here in Sicily not long ago; but I didn't bury her body and I have it here with me; I always have her company and adore her.' At this point he brought Habrocomes into the inner room and showed him Thelxinoë. She was now an old woman but still seemed beautiful to Aegialeus. Her body was embalmed in the Egyptian fashion, for the old fisherman had learned embalming as well. 'And so, Habrocomes my boy,' he

explained, 'I still talk to her as if she were alive, and lie down beside her and have my meals with her, and if I come home exhausted from fishing, the sight of her consoles me, for to me she looks different than she does to you: I think of her as she was in Sparta, and when we eloped.'

There is a great deal in this passage, not least of humour. Apart from the whole incongruity of the situation, there is a parody of a scene in Euripides' *Alcestis*, and perhaps more significantly a joke poking fun at the Egyptians and mummies. Aegialeus, the old fisherman, has learned how to mummify, and the verb usually used in Greek to describe this is *taricheuein*, literally 'to salt down a fish'. Aegialeus' skill with Thelxinoë's remains is perhaps a result of his job as fisherman, Xenophon seems to suggest. An element of Greek revulsion at the custom may also be read into this scene. Aegialeus himself is a marginal person, 'a poor stranger who just scraped a living from his work' as Xenophon says, and his personal practices are as marginal and aberrant as his social status within a Hellenic world. In Greek terms, the mummified Thelxinoë is not fully dead, and therefore can continue to function sexually like a living person, as indeed she does to Aegialeus. The mendacity of her mummified body is also clear. In reality Thelxinoë is an old, wrinkled corpse, but to Aegialeus she is still a beautiful young girl. The mummy's bodily duplicity is an important topos, to which I will return later.

The ideas of both Herodotus and Xenophon of Ephesus about the eroticism of the mummy and its accoutrements were taken up and developed by subsequent classical authors.[6] Two themes run through these accounts. The first is that there is an element of display involved in the keeping of the mummy – the preserved body is to some extent a contained spectacle in itself.[7] The second is that the mummies themselves are expensive, commodified objects. Covered in costly linen wrappings, impregnated with exotic perfumes and decorated with gold, mummies represent a conspicuous consumption and an aesthetic of surface that was part of the package of luxury that Romans especially associated with the east. Generally, Roman judgements on mummification are disapproving. Tacitus certainly expressed a low opinion of Nero's decision to have his wife Poppaea mummified, part of his whole litany of this emperor's paradigmatic 'badness' (Tacitus *Ann.* xvi 6):

> The body of Poppaea was not cremated, as was the custom of the Romans, but preserved according to the manner of foreign

kings, with various aromatic spices, and laid to rest in the imperial mausoleum. A public funeral was held, and the emperor at the rostrum eulogised her beauty.

Tacitus seems to see this act as an insult to honest Roman burial practices, especially when the aberrant body of Poppaea is interred in the Julio-Claudian family mausoleum. The mention of Nero eulogising the beauty of his dead wife is interesting: is Tacitus implying that the mummification is an aberrant means of preserving this beauty? Also prominent is the emphasis on the smell of the mummy as a result of the odoriferous substances used to preserve it. Herodotus' account of mummification dwelt on all the spices employed in the process; and later this is expanded in Corippus' poetic description of the numerous unguents used to preserve the body of the emperor Justinian (*De laudibus Justiniani* iii 22–5): 'They burned the Sabaean incense, and poured libations of perfumed honey and a balm with a fragrant juice. One hundred other types of marvellous aromatic herbs were brought to preserve the holy body through the eternity of time.' Other sources are less complimentary about the smell of the embalmed corpse. Herodotus, Tacitus and Corippus may be fascinated by the lavishing of expensive imported fragrances on the dead, but for others the smell of the mummy could be an unpleasant reminder of the pollution that comes with the death of the physical body. Here I quote in full a second-century CE funerary inscription from the cemetery at Hermopolis in Middle Egypt:

> Do not pass in silence by me, the son of Epimachus, as you go on your way. Stop: the disagreeable smell (*dusôdia*) of cedar-oil will not bother you near me. Stay, and hear a little about a fragrant (*euôdos*) corpse. My grandfather, who nobly carried out civic functions in his native town, had as a son Epimachus, who certainly did not belie his ancestry because, after his father, he carried out the duties of *agoranomus* well in the city. It is he who was my father. He also distinguished himself as a horse-trainer in numerous victories. When I was a boy and had only lived eleven years, suddenly Destiny ... carried me away, assisted by her servant Cough. Behold, do not cry, dearest friend. It is just because I hate tears that I have requested Philhermes not to bury me with a cortège of hired female mourners. Philhermes was a faithful and affectionate brother for me, not by birth (he was actually my cousin), but in his care

for me he fulfilled the role of a father. I requested him not to lament at all over me and not to bury me again having interred me for the first time,[8] but to bury me once only, without cedar oil or smelly exhalation (*apophora*) so that you do not flee away from me as one does with other corpses.[9]

This inscription is one of the first explicit statements about the perceived 'contagion' of the mummy, which is here used as a metaphor for social and cultural divisions between Greeks and Egyptians. The writer's revulsion at the bad smell of the mummy symbolises his dislike of Egyptian burial customs, which are a synecdoche for 'Egyptianness' as a whole. He is notably at pains to stress his impeccable Greek ancestry, and the civil functions his father and grandfather had performed in this Hellenised town in Egypt. It may be significant that this expression of disgust was produced in Egypt itself, where one might expect more knowledge of what mummies were really like – and anyone who has handled any mummified human remains knows that the grave inscription is nearer the truth than the fragrant rhetorical descriptions of the Latin authors.

Thus the classical (especially Latin) references to mummified bodies provide all the antecedents for subsequent reactions to them. First, there is the interest in mummies as *products*, particularly as products of an exotic eastern civilisation with all its attendant connotations of excess, luxury and degeneracy. Second, there is the ambivalence towards these products that reflects the problematic status of the mummy as a human body. The mummy lies at the nexus of a chiasmus of abjection – that 'vortex of summons and repulsion' which Kristeva identifies as the subject's desire *vis-à-vis* what the culture finds disgusting and loathsome:

ALIVE   ALLURING
X
DISGUSTING   DEAD

These kinds of ideas characterise attitudes towards the mummy in the European Renaissance, albeit in a totally different cultural and economic context. Here mummies were used primarily in powdered form as a medication, a practice which can be traced back to the use of bitumen in the pharmacopoeia of late antiquity. This was taken up by Arabic medical writers, who in fact coined the term *mumia*, from the Arabic for bitumen: the black, pitchy deposits found in ancient preserved bodies were equated with this substance, which became the designation for the body as a whole. Terminologically, then, a mummy is an object for consumption, a commodity which is traded and bought.

Sixteenth- and seventeenth-century English references to mummy or 'mummia' are united in how repellent are the by-products of 'these dead bodies ... the Mumie which the Phisitians and Apothecaries doe against our willes make us to swallow'.[10] In Webster's *The White Devil*, Gasparo says (Act I, Scene I, 15–18):

> Your followers
> Have swallowed you like mummia, and being sick
> With such unnatural and horrid physic
> Vomit you up i'th'kennel.

Other ideas underlie Falstaff's speech in *The Merry Wives of Windsor* (Act III, Scene V, 11–16): 'I had been drown'd ... a death that I abhor; for the water swells a man; and what a thing should I have been when I had swell'd! I should have been a mountain of mummy.' Here Webster and Shakespeare express different types of revulsion: distaste at swallowing the bitter medication, and horror at the sodden, desquamated flesh of a drowned man, so different texturally from the dry, powdered mumia. Falstaff's self-comparison with mummy is interesting in relation to his own, grotesque body, because elsewhere Shakespeare presents Falstaff as an unprincipled body of excess, an unbounded body which requires containment. But mummy is certainly something repugnant here, a grotesque comparison perhaps rendered comic by Falstaff's own enormous vanity.

Yet in spite of its repellent qualities, *mumia* was also an eastern commodity, and as such imbued with erotic potential. The handkerchief that causes such disastrous events in Shakespeare's *Othello* is a good example of this. The mummy here is one of a series of portentous ingredients that produce 'the magic in the web' of the handkerchief – the magic that will produce sexual attractiveness or repulsion in the owner or user (Act III, Scene IV, 55–75):

> ... that handkerchief
> Did an Egyptian to my mother give ...
> The worms were hallowed that did breed the silk,
> And it was dy'd in mummy, which the skilful
> Conserv'd of maidens' hearts.

Before the nineteenth century, then, mummies are essentially *passive* erotic objects. They are spectacles to be gazed at, commodities which are traded, consumed or ingested (though ingestion can bring about remarkable results). The Renaissance sources commodify the mummy through cultural association and physical fragmentation. The latter may explain the lack of Renaissance interest in bio-graphising the mummy, since the product made from them was only associated with real social bodies in the most vague and generic way. Compare Sir Thomas Browne's famous aphorism in *Urne-Burial*: 'Mummie is become Merchandise, Mizraim cures wounds, and Pharaoh is sold for Balsoms.' While the few Renaissance accounts of discovering whole mummified bodies do evince an interest in the preservation techniques used, the response to the body was to give it a Christian burial as soon as possible as a sort of redemption from paganism.[11] Conversely, the dislocated bodies that produce 'mummie' evoked a mirage of Egypt, but no personal histories, no lived realities anchored in the body or its basic experiences. This is striking when one looks at some of the ways that mummies are presented in the nineteenth century, to which I now turn.

NAMING THE MUMMY

Plate 9.1 is a photograph of a label concocted to describe a mummy in the Niagara Falls Museum, Canada, on the occasion of the state visit of Edward, Prince of Wales in 1860. Of course all this informa-tion is completely fictitious, on the same level of veracity as a carnival barker's patter.[12] Again it evokes a generic Egypt – linguistically other (the unpronounceable name with its cluster of consonants), royal, commodified, sexual. The heady concatenation of perfumes, poison and gold in this text is surely born out of contemporaneous ideas about Cleopatra, herself consummately sexual, evil and com-modified. Compare the way she is represented in paintings such as Jean-André Rixen's *The Death of Cleopatra* (1874: now in Toulouse, Musée des Augustins). Here the pallid body of the queen, naked except for her heavy jewellery, lies supine on an elaborate bed after taking poison. Similar ideas are at play in Alexandre Cabanel's *Cleopatra Testing Poisons on Condemned Prisoners* (1887: now in Antwerp, Koninklijk Museum voor Schone Kunst) where Cleopatra, partially clad in royal regalia that highlights her semi-nudity, watches the agonies of expiring prisoners with a detached air.

Yet this label is an early example of a trend which becomes more

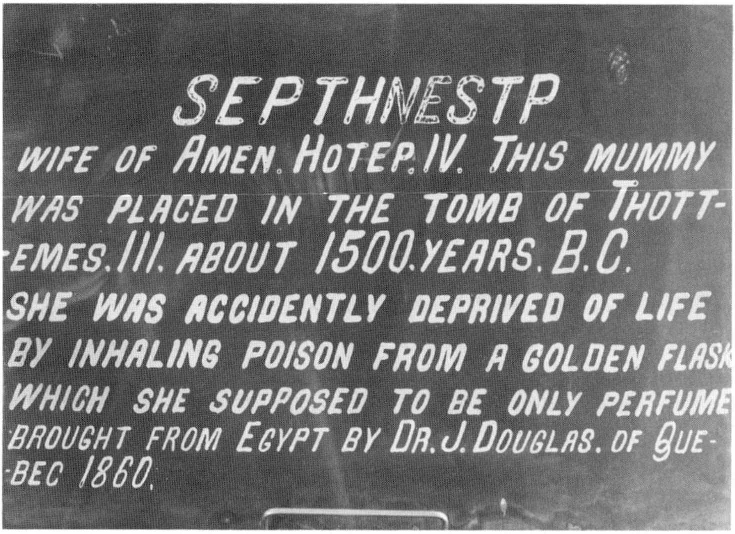

Plate 9.1 Mummy label from the Niagara Falls Museum, Canada, 1860.
(Photograph reproduced by courtesy of Sue Hogarth and Fred Farnham.)

and more important as the nineteenth century progresses: the desire to provide the mummified body with a name and a personal history, often a history which is implicitly or overtly sexual. My argument is based on the idea that biographising the ancient body is a sexual act because it is essentially scopophilic or voyeuristic: that is, it involves a pleasurable looking at an object unaware of the watcher, who in this case is separated by time. One could even go further and say that it is a pornographic act because it is based on a powerful viewer and a powerless viewed. Again and again we come across the mummy, often female, as a passive, objectified body under a gaze, often male and colonialist. Creating narratives and identities for anonymous mummies is, I would argue, part of the pornography of representation – such texts are crystallisations of this power relationship and are used to reproduce, translate and trade in such power.

The origins for this nineteenth-century desire to personalise are complex and difficult to disentangle. Maybe it is related to the general commodification of culture identifiable in early Victorian England, where objects are personified and people reified. Marx famously describes this process in the first volume of *Capital*, and it can be observed in such novels of Dickens as *The Old Curiosity Shop* (1841) or *Our Mutual Friend* (1863): in the latter, for instance, there is a *nouveau-riche* family called the Veneerings, who are essentially animated pieces of shiny new furniture. Mummies were an important part of this commodity culture, but where do they belong within it?[13] They have a problematic status, being both objects and people at the same time. The imperialist desire is to control the colonised body by creating an imposed taxonomy upon it, in this case, the museum: but mummies do not submit willingly to this control. Simultaneously people and objects, they can simultaneously be reified and personalised. It is relevant here to consider the development of the discipline of Egyptology in the latter part of the nineteenth century. With the deciphering of hieroglyphs and the concomitant growth of interest in Egyptian history and culture, the pool of possible identities for mummies began to expand. In fact, in the 1890s the mummy becomes a sort of mnemonic for Egyptian culture generally, as illustrated in E. A. Wallis Budge's famous and influential book *The Mummy: A Handbook of Egyptian Funerary Archaeology* (1893), still in print after more than a century. Although ostensibly about the mummy, the book was really a vade-mecum to Egyptian culture, with extensive sections on the geography of Egypt, the Nile flood, hieroglyphics and Egyptian history. As the grand narrative of Egyptian culture became less fragmentary, the fragments of that culture needed to be located and positioned. Mummies began to be seen as potential social bodies with recoverable histories. 'To live means to leave traces ... the detective story that follows these traces then comes into being', as Walter Benjamin put it.[14] The narratives reconstructed from these traces were as fictive as Benjamin's detective story, based on a set of associations that Egypt had for the western mind, especially carnality, ritual and death – as the Canadian mummy label illustrates.

This process of linking real bodies with archaeological and/or documentary evidence to produce fictive biographies is best illustrated by two almost contemporaneous sets of discoveries in Egypt at the end of the nineteenth century. The first was the large-scale discovery of Roman period mummy portraits in the Fayum, a district in the north-west of Egypt in the late 1880s. These portraits (see Plate 9.2) although 'classical' in appearance, were incorporated in typically Egyptian-looking wrappings, and fixed over the face of the deceased. A few years later, in the 1890s, came the first extensive finds of documentary papyri in the same area of Egypt. These papyri, with their vivid but fragmentary evocations of daily life in the towns of

Roman Egypt, made quite an impact at the time via extensive press coverage. Although the papyri and the portraits were unrelated historically, they came from the same geographical area and seemed at the time to complement each other perfectly: the papyri brought back to life the portraits (by extension, the mummified bodies inside as well), and vice versa. A comment from the unpublished excavation diary of David Hogarth, director of the first dig for papyri in the Fayum in 1895, made clear the inextricable link between these products of Egyptian culture: 'no papyrus and no portraits'.

The mummy portraits were first exhibited in London from 18 June to mid-July 1888. The exhibition was very well-publicised, at least in part because their excavator, Flinders Petrie, was anxious to sell as many of the pieces as possible to fund his next season of excavation. His publicity sense was unerring: tantalising previews of the exhibition appeared in the quality press, such as *The Academy* (9 June 1888) and *The Athenaeum* (7 July 1888). Subsequently, reviews of Petrie's exhibition appeared in all the major journals, including *The Academy* (7 July 1888), *The Saturday Review* (30 June 1888) and *The Illustrated London News* (30 June 1888), whose review is quoted below. Appropriately enough, it took place at the Egyptian Hall, Piccadilly, a delirious fantasy of ancient Egypt. The Egyptian Hall not only boasted extensive exhibition space but was also the venue for popular magico-mystic shows, and later became one of London's very first cinemas. Throughout the period that the exhibition of portraits was mounted at the Egyptian Hall, the front page of *The Times* advertised this gallery as 'England's home of mystery and arcana', where one could see 'expositions of automata-mental tele-graphy, so-called thought transference, and ventriloqual sketches'. I think it is relevant for the initial reception of the portraits that they were exhibited in this venue with its overtones of mysticism and magic, where things and voices were conjured up out of the darkness by 'automata-mental telegraphy' and spoke via 'ventril-oqual sketches': a venue that was also deemed suitable for the first displays of 'moving pictures' in the early days of cinema.

At all events, scholars, art historians and journalists were enorm-ously enthusiastic about the exhibits, and justifiably so: these Egyp-tian mummy portraits were a virtually unknown genre of ancient painting. But apart from this, what really seems to have excited late nineteenth-century viewers were the vivid portrayals of the subjects, which seemed to bring the people of the past back to life, embodied in living, breathing flesh. A typical response is that of the anonymous journalist sent by the *Illustrated London News* to cover Petrie's exhibition:

> With the thorough conviction of the soul's immortality, the Egyptians in all ages did their best to make death beautiful; but in the Ptolemaic and Antonine epochs Greek art, which is the presentment of Nature herself, was grafted on to Egyptian conventionality, and beauty was crowned with joy. 'Think not of the wan, sunken face within,' the artist seems to say to us; 'but remember your dear lost one as he lived, with the glow of life quivering on his cheek and the light of life beaming from his eye.'
>
> These heads are by various artists, some of them wielding a brush as vigorous as Velasquez, others a pencil as delicate and refined as that of Sir Frederick Leighton or Bouguereau. There is no mistaking the fact that they are all veritable portraits of men and women who have been coffined these seventeen centuries.

The comments of this and other reviewers provide the earliest examples of some recurrent themes of late nineteenth- and twentieth-century writing on mummy portraits. First, there is the insistence on these funerary images as evocations of living bodies – there is no debate about when in the life-cycle of the subject the portraits were produced. Second, there is the ability of the portraits to reanimate and evoke the people of the past in a quasi-psychic way. The *Illustrated London News* reporter has the artist talking to the present day as if through a medium, denying the fact that the subjects of his portraits are dead: they speak and live again, eternally, through his skill. Third, the portraits have an intrinsic sensuality: the reviewer saw similarities between them and the lush painting of the contemporary artists Lord Leighton and Bouguereau, the latter well-known for his sensuous classical nudes. But this sensuality is not truthful: the external aspect of the body may look beautiful, but there is a 'wan sunken face' within.

The subjects of the mummy portraits offered splendid opportunities for fictionalisation. Commentators used the apparent demeanour and facial irregularities of the sitters to build up a whole life for a 're-discovered' individual, like a pathologist reconstructing a lifestyle from the anonymous corpse of a murder victim.[15] For instance, the subject of one female portrait was described in the catalogue as:

a woman who has grown prematurely old with sickness; her suffering, care-worn expression of countenance is yet increased by an anomaly of the left cheek-bone. The bluish hue of the long lachrymal sac, and the sickly appearance of the whole complexion, plainly show that this woman was afflicted with both mental and bodily sufferings, probably dropsy.[16]

The veristic individuality of the mummy portraits gave a feeling of real lives lived in real inhabited bodies – an individuality given all the more pathos by their anonymity, because very few of the portraits are identified.[17]

But images were not enough to provide biographies: the texts needed to be employed as well, and what text could be more suitable for providing sensual information than the letter? Numerous papyrus letters were excavated and published in the first decade of the twentieth century. Paradoxically, papyrus letters, while being the remnants of a social exchange, lent themselves to a novelistic reading because there are no extant replies. Lacking any intertext, the letter stands alone as an isolated mini-narrative without a knowable addressee to intervene or moderate the content. Contemporary popular writing about the papyrus discoveries pays voyeuristic attention to the many private letters found:

But there are ... a large number of private letters which, like all true letters, are often of the most self-revealing char-acter, and throw the clearest light upon the whole domestic and social relationships of the people. Not, perhaps, that their actual contents are often of any special interest. Their authors ... are as a rule content to state the matter in hand as briefly and baldly as possible. At the same time it is impossible not to feel the arresting charm of these frail papyrus messages, written with no thought of any other public than those to whom they were originally addressed, and on that very account calling up before our minds, as more elaborate documents could never have done, the persons alike of their senders and recipients.[18]

I find the vocabulary of this passage significant: 'frail papyrus messages ... calling up before our minds ... the persons alike of their senders and recipients'. As with the viewer of the portrait, it invites to an almost psychic communion, where the reader is a medium who channels the epiphany of the dead person 'revealed' by the ancient letter. It also suggests that papyri can aid the modern reader to be an historical scopophile, to read hidden secrets. This tantalising evidence becomes even more exciting when collocated with visuals, so that human faces, perhaps the faces of the mummy portraits, apparently lurk behind 'these frail papyrus messages' like the indistinct images in a medium's ectoplasm. So to the Victorian mind, text and image could be taken in conjunction, to construct fictive mini-biographies of the portrait subjects.

The erotics of this kind of biographisation rear their heads most palpably in the first popular book on the mummy portraits, written by the German Egyptologist Georg Ebers and translated into English in 1893. Ebers was a friend of the painter Laurence Alma-Tadema, well known for his classically-themed paintings, and it is possible that Alma-Tadema's aesthetic may have influenced Ebers' interpretation of the mummy portraits. Ebers' book starts by highlighting the relevance of the portraits 'to our interest in the history of culture and in ethnographic research into what may be called the physiognomy of nations' and goes on to assign carefully-graded racial types to individuals in the Fayum portraits on pseudo-physiognomic principles.[19] Ebers was particularly captivated by the images of young males in the mummy portraits (see Plate 9.2). These are among the most distinctive of the iconographic types represented: athletic-looking, suntanned young men in their prime, bare-shouldered to imply the total nudity that was appropriate for exercise in the gymnasium. Sometimes they are garlanded, and they often have small, downy moustaches. Ebers interpreted such portraits of two young men from the Graf collection according to contemporary paradigms of youthful eroticism. He biographises them as 'two boys who, though scarcely past their school days, cherish, if in vain, the first downy promise of a moustache' as follows. One is:

> the dark-olive son of rich parents, of Egyptian race, and perhaps of princely birth, for gold foliage is twined with his black hair. Defiance and sensuality accentuate his full lips, self-reliance sparkles in his large dark eyes, and ... still enables us to look into the soul of a youth untroubled by any thought of death, who enjoyed all the pleasures of his age and was already satiated with some.

Another young male's portrait was described as having

> a face of light complexion, with hair cut straight over the forehead. Softer boyish features are hardly conceivable, and yet

176

Plate 9.2 Mummy portrait of a young man from er-Rubayat, Fayum,
Egypt, second century CE (Petrie Museum of Egyptian Archaeology,
University College London, inventory number UC 19613).
(Photograph reproduced by courtesy of the Petrie Museum of Egyptian Archaeology,
University College London.)

this youth was not easily led ... his tutor may have found
it hard to discipline this pupil, for a faint tinge of melancholy
shrouds this sweet, purely Greek countenance. It would be
easy to believe that this delicate blossom of manhood foresaw
its early end.[20]

So Ebers' physiognomic and racial preconceptions turn the adolescent boys of the portraits into either dissipated, hot-blooded sensualists (Orientals) or romantic, languid flowers who embrace death
(Greeks). These are both standard figures in the language of *fin-de-siècle* decadence, particularly for encrypting 'deviant' sexual desire.
Ebers also eroticises these subjects by the fact of their early deaths,
another preoccupation of decadence. This may well relate to the
1890s curiosity about the figure of Antinoüs, the handsome lover of
the Emperor Hadrian who was drowned in the Nile while accompanying the Emperor on a trip to Egypt in 130 CE. In the writings
of late nineteenth-century aesthetes such as Oscar Wilde, John
Addington Symonds, Walter Pater, Frederick Rolfe and others,
Antinoüs comes up repeatedly as the paradigm of doomed male
beauty, and also as a way of encoding male homosexual desire. In the
first chapter of Wilde's *The Picture of Dorian Gray*, for instance, the
artist Basil Hallward talks about the dangerous beauty of Dorian in
classical terms, invoking the historical Antinoüs along with figures
from Greek mythology: 'I had drawn you as Paris in dainty armour,
and as Adonis with huntsman's cloak and polished spear. Crowned
with heavy lotus-blossoms you had sat on the prow of Hadrian's
barge, gazing across the green turbid Nile.'

Wilde's interest in the ancient Greek world is well documented:
he graduated in classics from Oxford and maintained a lifelong
friendship with his former Professor at Dublin, J. P. Mahaffy, one of
the pioneers of Greek papyrology and a collaborator of Bernard
Grenfell. His interest in Egypt, however, is less well known. However, Wilde's father had travelled to Egypt and published a book
about the journey in 1840. His accounts of the voyage may even have
influenced Bram Stoker, a visitor to the Wildes' house in the 1860s,
to pursue Egyptological themes in his novels.[21] This interest communicated itself to his son, illustrated by the fact that among the
books Oscar Wilde requested from Reading Jail was one of Petrie's
works on ancient Egypt.[22] Indeed, a spectral Egypt flits in and out
of Wilde's writing as an exotic prop.[23] I would like to suggest that
Oscar Wilde saw or read about Petrie's exhibition of mummy

UNIDENTIFIED HUMAN REMAINS

portraits in the summer of 1888, and that this may, in some way, have influenced two of his then-current literary projects which had at their core dangerously beautiful portraits of young men: *The Picture of Dorian Gray*, of course, and the less well-known *Portrait of Mr W. H.*, about a death-bringing portrait supposedly representing the young addressee of Shakespeare's *Sonnets*. Although I have only circumstantial evidence for this suggestion, I consider it likely that Oscar Wilde visited Petrie's exhibition of the portraits; and even if he did not, he certainly would have known about it from the extensive newspaper coverage. Wilde was in London for the month of the exhibition, and I have already given a flavour of the reviews in the quality newspapers of the period, one of which was written by a close friend of Wilde, Johnson Forbes-Robertson.[24] An exhibition promising images of languid Greek youths with a glint in their eyes, suggested by the seductive write-up in the *Illustrated London News*, would have an obvious appeal for Wilde as classicist, aesthete and homosexual. In fact, there is in *The Picture of Dorian Gray* a reference to other exhibitions held at the Egyptian Hall, so Wilde was *au fait* with what was going on there. Wilde's personal and familial interest in Egypt also has to be taken into account. All in all, it seems highly probable that even if Wilde did not visit the exhibition himself, he would have read or heard about it.

Camille Paglia has suggested that it is instructive to reread *The Picture of Dorian Gray* bearing in mind the idea of a possible Egyptian influence on it.[25] She employs a typically confused set of data to support her argument, but it may be useful to apply her larger thesis to the theory that Wilde was acquainted somehow with eroticised interpretations of Romano-Egyptian mummy portraits. Dorian throughout is presented in terms of a languid Greek beauty, just as Ebers described the mummy portraits of young men. Then think of the ultimate fate of Dorian's portrait, ritually sequestered in a dusty hidden chamber, covered with a glittering purple shroud. Hanging up alone in the deserted room it is both iconic and decontextualised, like the mummy portraits – a 'curious memorial' hanging on a wall. The horrified discoverers who break into the chamber and find the hideously transmogrified Dorian, only recognisable by his rings, are like archaeologists finding a mummy thrown on the floor by grave robbers. Becoming a corpse, Dorian reaches his ultimate objectification: thus his beautiful but mendacious portrait is like the *ka* or double of the deceased in Egyptian funerary art, representing the dead in a perfect and vital form, so unlike 'the wan shrunken face' of the mummy inside the wrappings.

Beautiful, anonymous, silent and Greek: the young male subjects of the mummy portraits had found their cultural moment in the discourses surrounding male homosexuality that were emerging in England at the end of the nineteenth century.[26] They also looked comfortingly 'classical' for a world which found that the achievements of Egyptian culture often led in troubling directions. Yet the mummy portraits were often deprived of their original physical context, over the face of a wrapped and embalmed body. Decontextualisation of the portraits is another form of their commodification: divorced from intended and culturally specific circumstances of production and use, they became curiosities ripe for commodification and appropriation. I would argue that this process facilitates the erotics of biographising the mummy. I see the 'biographies' like that of 'SEPTHNESTP' as analogous to the 'biographies' that are created around models in contemporary porn magazines. Both employ fictitious names and identities to narrow the subjectivity of the individual to a purely sexual subjectivity, thus constructing the object as a totally sexual being.[27] The comparison may go further. Like nude models, mummies are also physically on display, divested of their coverings: and the erotics of the unwrapped mummy will be the subject of the next section. (See Figure 9.1.)

STRIPPING THE MUMMY

Here I am interested in examining how the mummy, the orientalist prop *par excellence*, has been used in public performances and how mutable sexualities are invented for it or grafted on to it. There is a growing body of work on how orientalism was used in nineteenth-century theatrical performances as a means of investigating socially problematic sexual identities.[28] Much of this takes as its springboard the notion of performativity in the work of Judith Butler, where parody, the body and sexuality are linked to explore mutable sexualities, body parts semiotically open to erotic opportunity, or sexed bodies recast as morphologically plastic and phantasmically unbound. There are some interesting examples of such offshoots of orientalism from France at the end of the nineteenth century and the beginning of the twentieth, but I would prefer to locate these performances within the wider context of the mummy as both

The Nobility and Gentry, Visiters and Inhabitants of **BATH** and its Vicinity, are respectfully informed, that

TWO EGYPTIAN

MUMMIES,

A MALE AND FEMALE,

In the highest State of Preservation, *with various other Relics,*

BROUGHT TO THIS COUNTRY BY

Mr. BELZONI,

The celebrated Traveller, are now open for Exhibition at

10, New Bond-Street.

The MUMMIES are of the first Class : the Inspection of them it is presumed must be highly satisfactory to every Person, as exhibiting two distinct Specimens; the Bandages of the Male having been entirely removed from the Body, which is perfect, while the mode of applying them is beautifully illustrated in the Envelope of the Female.

The CASES are covered with Hieroglyphics, enriched with Ornaments most elaborately executed ; the Interiors containing the Histories of the Lives of their very ancient Occupiers, in Egyptian Characters, as fresh as when inscribed by the Hand of the Artist, after a Lapse of probably

THREE THOUSAND YEARS.

" Perchance that very Hand, now pinioned flat,
" Has hob-a-nob'd with Pharaoh glass to glass,
" Or dropp'd a halfpenny in Homer's hat,
" Or doff'd its own to let Queen Dido pass,
" Or held, by Solomon's own invitation,
" A torch at the great Temple's dedication."

AMONG THE OTHER RELICS WILL BE FOUND

A MUMMY OF THE IBIS,

THE SACRED BIRD OF EGYPT;

An Urn with Intestines from Elei; an Inscription on the far-famed Paper of Egypt (the Papyrus); a massive Fragment of Granite with Hieroglyphics from Memphis; a variety of Idols in Stone, Clay, and Wood, from the Tombs of the Kings in the Valley of Beban-el-Malook, and the Ruins at Carnac; Urns, Vessels of Libation, Bronzes, Coins, &c. &c.

N.B. A few **EGYPTIAN** and other **ANTIQUITIES for SALE.**

Admittance, One Shilling each.

☞ PURCHASERS WILL BE ALWAYS RE-ADMISSIBLE.

A DESCRIPTIVE ACCOUNT of this COLLECTION will be published in a few Days.

WOOD and CO. Printers of the Bath and Cheltenham Gazette, UNION-STREET, BATH.

1842

Figure 9.1 Advertisement for the display of unwrapped mummies and other Egyptological finds in Bath, 1842.

theatrical and sexualised object. Mummies as objects of spectacle have a long history, as the references in the classical authors suggest, but the mummy as performer, whether active or passive, is a distinctly nineteenth-century phenomenon, produced from a complex genealogy of influences and associations. In these performances it is possible to see all the affecting factors that produced the myth of the sexual mummy, especially commodification and biographisation, culminating in an erotic apotheosis.

The theatrical performances I will discuss later of course used actors or dancers to imitate mummies. However, displays of the unrolling of actual mummified bodies enjoyed a vogue as a fashionable pastime for the English élite in the 1830s and 1840s.[29] In June 1850 Lord Londesborough (the grandfather of the Sitwells) invited guests to a mummy unrolling at his house, and public unrollings continued, albeit with a scientific gloss, well into the twentieth-century. Unwrapping mummies, whether literally or using non-invasive methods like CT scanning, still continues to fascinate, as a glance along the shelves of the British Museum bookshop will show.

The main instigator of the early nineteenth-century displays was the London physician Dr Thomas Pettigrew, who was well aware of the drawing potential of these ceremonial unwrappings. These were surrounded by all the paraphernalia of a theatrical opening night, such as the issuing of tickets and even the preparation of 'house full' notices. Pettigrew's advance arrangements for the unwrapping included writing

> large Notices against the meeting tomorrow, to obviate as much as may be the effects of disappointment on those who will not be able to gain admission:
>
> 'Gentlemen who may be disappointed in witnessing the Unrolling of the Mummy this day, will have an opportunity of viewing it in the Museum every Monday, Wednesday and Friday, from 12 till 4 o'clock.'[30]

The unrolling displays by Pettigrew and his followers, I think, illustrate the essential passivity of the mummy prior to the desire to revivify discernible in the biographising trend later in the century. As Pettigrew himself points out, the mummy is also on display in the regulated time of the museum, a world of exotic objects under a domesticating taxonomic regime.

Accounts and illustrations of mummy unwrappings are reminiscent of autopsies, which in a sense is what they are: but a major difference is the great emphasis placed on the gradual revealing of the mummy's body as its external wrappings are slowly removed. Instead of the quick drawing-back of the sheet covering the naked corpse at a post-mortem, the mummy's different bandages are intimately and fetishistically described as they are peeled off, like layers of alluring underwear. The mummies perform a passive striptease. Pettigrew again:

> The bandages are now removed as carefully as time and circumstances permitted. The outer smooth cloth being removed, exposed the circular hand-breadth rollers, which extended from head to foot several times in succession: – others oblique and diagonal very neatly but without much regularity or uniformity till we reached the very innermost layer or two which firmly adhered to the surface.[31]

There is an element of the same passivity traceable in some narratives of archaeologists and travellers about the unwrapping of mummies and their consequences. Later unwrapping stories, specifically those based around stripped mummies displayed in museums, espouse the biographical tradition of the mummy that had become well-established by the last decade of the nineteenth century. Good examples of this are two poems by the Rev. H. D. Rawnsley, a popular travel writer and Egyptophile, in his *Idylls and Lyrics of the Nile* (1894). The first rhapsodises about the public unwrapping of the mummy of Pharaoh Seqenenre Tao (Rawnsley's 'Tåå-Ken') which Rawnsley watched at the Cairo Museum on 9 June 1886. The Pharaoh's body seemed to show the marks of violent death, a death on which the actual human remains bestow a lived immediacy:

> When that dark face beneath the triple blow
> Lay battered, tongue bit thro', and mouth awry,
> And o'er Tåå-Ken's last death agony
> The Theban warriors felt their freedom grow
> They little thought far centuries would know
> Those cruel wounds had never ceased to cry. . . .[32]

The second is a poem called 'The Mummy of Sesostris', which concentrates fetishistically on the mummified Pharaoh's body parts as modified by the embalmers, rendering him more asleep than dead:

Among his perfumed wrappings Ramses lay,
Son of the sun, the conqueror without peers;
The jewel-holes were in his wounded ears,
His lips tight-closed above th'embalmer's clay;
Unguent had turned his white locks amber-grey,
And on his puissant chin fresh from the shears
The thin hair gleamed which full three thousand years
Of careless sleep could never disarray. . . .[33]

Yet this very passivity can itself become sexualised. With particular reference to the mummy fiction of Rider Haggard and Bram Stoker, Nicholas Daly has pointed out how the collector/consumer of the mummy tries to gain control of the object-world as personified by the mummy. This ascendancy can take the form of purchasing or possession by other means, such as romance. 'The fantasy of the collector is abandoned for a fantasy in which the Western consumer woos the object-world. In mummy fiction – as in advertising – mummies begin to behave as sex-objects.'[34] British authors like Rider Haggard, Arthur Conan Doyle and especially Bram Stoker replace the continental consumer with the figure of the Egyptologist as controller of the mummy as object of desire, but neither proves successful. In Bram Stoker's *The Jewel of Seven Stars* (1903) for example, the plot revolves around the voyeuristic unwrapping of the mummy of Queen Tera. The narrative build-up to this includes the journey into the desert valley, the entry into the cavern which hides the queen's tomb within a tomb. Stoker interestingly emphasises the personalisation of the queen's tomb in an episode where the archaeologist Trelawny reads the lapis lazuli inscription identifying its occupant: '"Tera, Queen of the Egypts, daughter of Antef. Monarch of the North and the South ... Queen of the Diadems." It then set out, in full record, the history of her life and reign.' So before the queen's mummy is even encountered by the archaeologists and revivified, it is provided with a full biography – as it turns out a transgressive one, mirroring the mutable and troubling status of her body. Tera was a magician, 'skilled in all the science of her time', who rules as Pharaoh in her own right, appropriating the accoutrements of male power. At the same moment as Trelawny discovers the body of Tera, his daughter Margaret is born, later to be the love interest in the novel. It is surely not coincidental that the ostensibly Egyptian name 'Tera' is the last two syllables of 'Margaret' inverted. Margaret/Tera are an enmeshed pair, almost like a good and evil twin, and

Margaret's fate is invested in Tera's body: when her mummy is destroyed, Margaret dies.[35]

Stoker's sexy mummy is developed from many sources including, I would suggest, knowledge of the early nineteenth-century mummy unrollings. But he was also clearly influenced by contemporary travelogues and popular presentations of archaeological discoveries[36] in which different kinds of physical encounters with mummies play an important part. As an example of the kind of writing that may have influenced Stoker to explore this theme, it is again worth looking at the work of David Hogarth (1862–1926), the adept and active archaeological populariser of the late nineteenth century and early twentieth century already referred to. He wrote not only journalistic pieces describing his experiences in Egypt, but also two highly successful popular books, *A Wandering Scholar in the Levant* (1895) and *Accidents of An Antiquary's Life*, published in 1910 but utilising some of his earlier articles.[37] *Accidents of An Antiquary's Life* contains an interesting set of episodes of physical contact with mummies, presented as a reply to an uncomprehending female dinner companion's questions about hardships out in the field.

Here, once again, the stripping of the mummy appears as public entertainment, albeit enacted within the controlling domestic environment. In Hogarth's narrative, going into an ancient tomb seems almost to be an act of defloration, a bridegroom penetrating a virgin bride. Yet the bride is a mummy, the mendacious mummy who turns out not to be a virgin at all, but already despoiled. She awaits the archaeologist/rapist with her body tantalisingly bared from the waist up:

> I have dug for 20 years and set next foot after the sexton's in very many ancient sepulchres; but I still feel, as at first, the flutter of poignant hope that the tomb may be virgin ... I know well that, in Egypt at least, one hardly ever opens a perfectly virgin sepulchre. Someone robbed it on the night of burial ere the door was sealed. Some malign intruder has rumpled those grave clothes down to the waist in quest of the jewels on neck and breast.[38]

This anecdote offers itself to an obvious colonialist reading: the tomb/body are colonised by the occupying imperial power. Hogarth is also repelled by the mummies he encounters in the course of his fossicking, and uses the now familiar appeal to the sense of smell to express his revulsion (156–7):

Crawling on all fours in the dark, one often found the passage barred by a heap of dim swaddled mummies turned out of their coffins by some earlier snatcher of bodies; and over these one had to go, feeling their breast-bones crack under one's knees and their swathed heads shift horribly this way or that under one's hands. And having found nothing to loot in a thrice-plundered charnel-house, one crawled back by the same grisly path to the sunlight, choked with mummy dust and redolent of more rotten grave-clothes than the balms of Arabia could sweeten. Partner of the scented dinner-table, is that the trade you desire?

Later in Hogarth's dinner-party story, the mummy is symbolically consumed as its coffins are burned to provide wood for the archaeologists' camp-fire. But here again the mummy insinuates itself as a subtle (and uncontrollable) instrument of contagion: 'The dead wood, seasoned by four thousand years of drought, threw off an ancient and corpse-like smell, which left its faint savour on the toast which we scorched at the embers.' The literary accounts of archaeological popularisers like Hogarth and Rawnsley illustrate the polyvalency of the mummy as body; and fiction was to develop its sexy mummies from a complex inter-relationship of such popular narratives, travelogues and other genres of writing about Egypt. But the most interesting manifestations of the mummy as sexual spectacle come in early twentieth-century France, when biographies, fiction and theatricality become melded into an undifferentiated 'rêve d'Égypte' – the title of the most scandalous of these shows. Before looking at two of these, it is worth considering the sexual status of some characters associated with ancient Egypt in *fin-de-siècle* France:

> The enactment of objectification can be seen at work quite self-consciously in the way in which French feminism mobilized Orientalist stereotypes to fashion 'new' sexual identities that functioned as props on which to hang a pose. 'Monstrous superhuman figures' to borrow Mario Praz's terms, were excavated from cultural history: women such as ... Thaïs and Cleopatra, whose erotic appetites were legendarily matched to their thirst for political authority.[39]

Notice here the importance of Thaïs, the heroine of Anatole France's enormously successful 1890 novel about a courtesan in Alexandria who is converted to Christianity by a hermit. France's novel provided the libretto for an opera by Jules Massenet in 1894, which featured Thaïs as a seductive bejewelled actress and courtesan who ruins her lovers: like the mummy, she is an object at the same time consumed and consuming, 'fetishized and mobilized in conceptual and visual space'.[40] Both of these sources in turn influenced the archaeologist Albert Gayet, who had a particular interest in the art of early Christian Egypt, the period when the 'historical' Thaïs was supposed to have lived. In 1896 Gayet was sponsored by the collector, amateur Egyptologist and keen theatre-goer Émile Étienne Guimet to go and dig in Egypt at the Roman site of Antinoöpolis – a site in itself perhaps sexualised by association with Antinous. Gayet found an extensive Late Antique necropolis with a large number of well-preserved mummies, many still equipped with splendid textiles and funerary wreaths. His publication of the season is illustrated with 'before and after' engravings of the mummies (see Figures 9.2 and 9.3). In the first, the wrapped mummies taken from their tombs lie exposed in the desert, separated into neat rows facing each other. In the second, after unwrapping, all is confusion. Torn cloths are flung everywhere and the individual bodies are mostly undifferentiable: only two mummies in the middle of the picture rear up from the mess around them, perhaps symbolising the potentially chaotic, uncategorisable body of the mummy once it is stripped of its restricting bandages.

At all events, this collocation of material culture, mummies and fiction was too much for Gayet, who claimed to have found the actual body of France's heroine Thaïs.[41] In the same publication, Gayet published several images of the supposed mummy of Thaïs, including two elaborate watercolours: one of the dead Thaïs, her body tightly bound in its graveclothes, the other of the revivified Thaïs, freed from the strictures of the mummy bindings and about to break into ecstatic movement (Plates 9.3 and 9.4). The mummy, partially unwrapped, was exhibited at Guimet's museum in Paris with an elaborate constellation of associated finds – perhaps the most unequivocal example of a wholly fictional sexual biography being inscribed upon an actual mummified body (Plate 9.5).

But Gayet and Guimet took the implicit theatricality of their museum display a step further, again perhaps influenced by Massenet's opera. At a private all-male party at Guimet's house, probably in 1904, an extraordinary after-dinner entertainment took place. The lights were lowered and a real Egyptian anthropoid coffin was brought into the drawing-room where the gentlemen were enjoying

LES CORPS APRÈS LE DÉFOUILLEMENT. — Fouilles du cimetière byzantin.

Figures 9.2 and 9.3 Mummies at Antinoöpolis, Egypt, as found (top) and after unwrapping (bottom). (From A. Gayet, *Antinoë et les Sépultures de Thaïs et Sérapion,* Paris 1902.)

Plates 9.3 and 9.4 The mummy of 'Thaïs' wrapped (left), and her revivified mummy (right): anonymous aquatint from A. Gayet, *Antinoë et les Sépultures de Thaïs et Sérapion*, Paris 1902.

Plate 9.5 The mummies of 'Thaïs' and 'Sarapion', excavated by Albert Gayet at Antinoöpolis, 1900, as exhibited in the Musée Guimet (contemporary photograph).

post-prandial brandy and cigars. To the sound of eastern pipe music, the lid of the coffin slowly opened and a figure rose up, swathed in garments directly imitating those found on the body from Antin-öopolis supposed to be that of Thaïs. The reanimated Thaïs, impersonated by a dancer, performed a sinuous ballet, gradually shedding her heavy swathings until she was almost naked. As the music climaxed, the dancer sank back into the coffin, the lid fell shut and she was conveyed out of the drawing-room.[42]

A stripping mummy was also the centrepiece of a performance which took place about three years later in a considerably more public space, the Moulin Rouge. This was *Rêve d'Égypte*, a pantomime or 'mimodrame' written by the writer Colette's lover, Marie de Morny, Marquise de Belbeuf (known as 'Missy') and performed on 3 January 1907. Colette and Missy played the principal parts in the show. The whole connection of names and biographies with mummies comes into prominence here. Much has been written about the symbolism of Colette's experiments with naming and re-naming herself.[43] Born Sidonie-Gabrielle Colette, she was performing on the stage at this time under the pseudonym Colette Willy, her surname fabricated from the nickname of her then husband, Henri Gauthier-Villars. The posters for *Rêve d'Égypte* played around with the assumed names of the actors even more. They advertised them as:

Yssim?

et

Colette Willy

dans

Rêve d'Égypte

Pantomime de Madame la Marquise de Morny

The question-mark after 'Yssim' was a playful touch, since it was not difficult to recognise the pseudo-Arabic name as la Marquise de Morny's nickname inverted – especially when the posters were also decorated with the Morny family crest.[44]

One scene in *Rêve d'Égypte* caused a scandal. This was where 'Yssim' in drag as a male archaeologist, encountered the mummy of Colette, swathed in gauzy bandages. Colette arose and performed an erotic dance enacting her loves of old, meanwhile gradually shedding

193

her wrappings until, almost nude, she and 'Yssim' closed the scene in a passionate embrace.

The house was full of thugs hired by outraged relatives of the Marquise, who shouted the performers down. Further performances were forbidden and the theatre temporarily closed (though the show was revived at Nice later the same year). A furore ensued, much of it generated by the press. The critic Félicien Pascal wrote in *L'Eclair de Montpellier* four days later:

> It is almost impossible to explain to readers one respects how the exhibition of Mme la Marquise de Belbeuf, in drag, and Mme Colette Willy, in the presence of her husband, constitutes a scandal so repulsive that the audience wanted to put an end to it ... the pantomime could just as well have been a re-enactment of only too real scenes from the private lives of these three individuals, and it was a spectacle of such audacious shamelessness that the entire audience gathered into a mob against them.[45]

Why did Missy choose an Egyptian mummy as the *tabula rasa* on which to project her own sexuality and relationship with Colette? The scandal surrounding *Rêve d'Égypte* was concerned with the way it dissolved sexual and social boundaries: a transvestite lesbian aristocrat disporting herself on the stage with her lover in the compliant presence of the lover's husband. Colette's and Missy's tinkering with their names and pseudonyms mirrors this fluidity, since when a name is altered, so are a whole set of signifiers about identity and social location. Colette herself was as unfixed in the symbolic as the mummy she was impersonating. Yet Colette's mummy was not anonymous because, as Pascal pointed out, everyone knew what it represented: her and the sexual mores of her ménage. The whole joke behind the theatre posters depended on familiarity with the identity of the performers. All this was very different from Guimet's Thaïs, an untroublingly heterosexual mummy who danced before an audience of men at the bidding of the man who, quite literally, owned her body. Also, Thaïs considerately got back in her box and was removed before the time came to put her troubling corporeality to the test. Colette's mummy was far more transgressive. She did not disappear like Thaïs, but held the embrace with Missy in the collective face of an outraged audience. The erotics of biographising the mummy have come full circle in *Rêve d'Égypte*.

ACKNOWLEDGEMENTS

This is a much revised version of a paper read to the Lesbian and Gay Studies Research Group at Warwick University in January 1996. Special thanks go to Mike Davis, who made many invaluable comments on an early draft and put up with me while I was revising it. I am also most grateful to Kate Chedgzoy for pointing me to the Colette story; to Julia Schottlander for suggesting that the Victorian reception of mummy portraits might be a fruitful line of research; to Terry Wilfong for supplying the Gayet and other references; and to Bridget Bennett, Sue Hogarth, Lynn Meskell, Liz Prettejohn and Sue Wiseman for much-needed help and encouragement.

NOTES

1 Wood quoted in Grey 1994: 188.
2 For a succinct account, see Robins 1988.
3 See Zimmer 1993.
4 Good examples of this type of coffin are EA 29585 and 29586, on display in the Egyptian galleries of the British Museum. For the prayers, see Smith 1993, who also illustrates EA 29585.
5 See Dawson and Gray 1968: 31 on the bodies: Montserrat 1997 on the papyrological evidence.
6 There is a useful listing in Dawson 1928 (add the passage from Xenophon of Ephesus quoted above).
7 E.g. Pomponius Mela i 9.27; Cicero, *Tusc. Disp.* i; Silius Italicus, *Punica* iii 474–6.
8 This is a reference to the Egyptian burial custom of 'second internment' (Greek *deutera taphê*) after the body had been mummified and displayed. Processions of hired female mourners were also important features of Egyptian funerals: for both of these customs see Montserrat 1997.
9 Text in Bernand 1969: 377ff. (n.97).
10 Hakluyt quoted in Harris 1971: 134.
11 The fullest Renaissance account is of finding a female mummy in April 1485 during building work on the Via Appia, and preserved in a Latin letter from the humanist Bartolommeo Fonte to Francesco Sassetti. Fonte marvels at the superb state of the body's preservation, and records the body being exhibited publicly. Shortly after, it was secretly interred on the orders of Pope Innocent VIII: see Ceram 1958: 2–4, with contemporary illustration of the unwrapped body.
12 Labels identifying other mummies in the same collection were composed according to comparable concatenations of Egyptianising ideas and props. I quote another:

> General Ossinumphneferu. The general in chief of Thotmes.III.
> The ablest sovereign of old Egypt. He was a man of great military

skill also a famous magician. He was 60 years old when he died. The scar on his forehead was caused by an enraged elephant while defending the king from his onslaughts. A palace was erected for the general near that of the king. He was entombed with royal honors by the king and placed in his tomb.

13 The ideas in this section owe much to the stimulating work of Daly 1994: however, I think he underestimates the problematic status of the mummy as a human body.

14 Benjamin 1969: 29.

15 Petrie made some even more explicit articulations of this idea: see Montserrat 1996a: 26–7.

16 Richter 1922: 16, no. 43: portrait now in the Antikensammlung, Staatliche Museen zu Berlin, Inv. 31 161, 9.

17 This linking of the documentary, the visual and the archaeological permeates other Victorian ways of talking about artistic productions intimately linked with ancient human bodies: see Elizabeth Prettejohn's discussion of Edward Poynter's *Faithful Unto Death*, representing a Roman sentry remaining at his post during the eruption of Vesuvius (Prettejohn 1996: 126–8).

18 Milligan 1910: xvii–xviii.

19 Ebers 1893: 3–12.

20 This and the preceding quote are from Ebers 1893: 90.

21 See David Glover's introduction to the Oxford Popular Fiction edition of Stoker's *The Jewel of Seven Stars*.

22 Letter to Robbie Ross of 6 April 1897.

23 Dr Bridget Bennett of Warwick University's English Department and the present author are preparing an article on this aspect of Egypt in the work of Oscar Wilde.

24 Forbes-Robertson 1889: I am indebted to Elizabeth Prettejohn for this reference.

25 Paglia 1990: 529.

26 On these, with special relevance to Wilde's use of the portrait, see Chedgzoy 1996: 135–76.

27 Using a different line of argument, Kus 1992 also critiques the implicit pornography of modern museum displays of mummies.

28 Discussed in Apter 1996.

29 Dawson 1934.

30 Quoted in Dawson 1934: 173.

31 Account of an unwrapping performed by Thomas Pettigrew on 16 January 1834, quoted in Dawson 1934: 174.

32 Rawnsley 1894: 51.

33 Rawnsley 1894: 50.

34 Daly 1994: 38.

35 There is an interesting discussion of Tera in Hopkins forthcoming.

36 Stoker mentions by name the flamboyant Egyptological pioneers Flinders Petrie and E. A. Wallis Budge in *The Jewel of Seven Stars*.

37 *A Wandering Scholar in the Levant* went into a second printing in 1896 and there was a second edition in 1925. *The Times* chose it as 'book of the week' in early February 1896.

38 Hogarth 1910: 158.
39 Apter 1996: 19.
40 Apter 1996: 19.
41 Gayet 1902: 33–56.
42 This story is related in Ceram 1958: 113–14, who sadly does not state his source. Another play which included stripping female mummies was Alan Campbell's *The Dust of Egypt*, performed at the Gaiety Theatre, London, in 1910, but apparently unpublished: see Miller 1962: 50.
43 A good summary in Ward Jouve 1987: 36–51, 62–9; Sarde 1978 is subtitled 'histoire d'une femme sans nom'.
44 Sarde 1978: 210.
45 My translation of the quotation from Pascal in Sarde 1978: 210–11.

10

NACKTLEBEN

Jane Stevenson

Many a classics conference ends with a paper on *Nachleben*: the survival and reinterpretation of some aspect of the classical tradition. As its title indicates, this chapter falls within the general definition of *Nachleben*, but its particular focus is *Nacktheit* – nudity. Despite the pun, this is not as frivolous as it might seem. Nudity (or rather, male nudity) was an important feature of Greek society; a cultural manifestation which the Greeks themselves perceived as an important distinction between themselves and *barbaroi*. What I am proposing to address here is the encoding of 'Greekness' in late Victorian and Edwardian England via the Greek (nude, male) body. This period is one in which the concept of 'Hellenism' was bandied about by great numbers of self-appointed legislators in all shades from true-blue to aesthetic mauve.[1] The appeal to 'Hellenism' as a cultural value can mean many things; notably paganism, in contrast with Christianity, as it did to Matthew Arnold.[2] It can also be used as an encoding of 'deviant' sexuality, as here, for instance, in Ronald Firbank's *Concerning the Eccentricities of Cardinal Pirelli*: 'chafing also in the same loose captivity would be the roguish *niñas* of the pleasure-loving duchess of Sarmento, girls whose Hellenic ethics had given the good abbess more than one attack of fullness'.[3]

In some very specific ways, the associations of 'Greek' were to a great extent with nudity. Before the period under discussion here, Byron described Don Juan frisking with girls on the seashore as follows:

> And thus they formed a group that's quite antique,
> half-naked, loving, natural, and Greek.[4]

But it is the Victorian focus on the Greek body, rather than the Greek mind, which makes Victorian Hellenism an appropriate subject to pursue in this context. 'The Greeks' were lined up on both sides of a significant Victorian divide; between actions, states, and literature perceived as 'wholesome', 'sound', and 'healthy', and their mirror-images, the 'morbid', 'unwholesome' and 'diseased'. All these terms were freely applied both to works of literature, and to ways of life.[5] They have reference to the familiar Victorian belief in *mens sana in corpore sano*; a belief which was strongly associated with 'the Greeks'. Matthew Arnold posed the question of why Greek free-dom, and Greek gymnastics, drew the admiration of all subsequent civilisations: 'surely because the Greeks pursued freedom and pursued gymnastics not mechanically, but with constant reference to some ideal of complete human perfection and happiness'.[6]

A decade or so earlier, John Ruskin had struck a similar note in his essay 'Of Classical Landscape' in *Modern Painters*. The Greeks neither fasted nor overate, and spent most of their time out of doors: 'full of animal spirit and physical power, they became incapable of every morbid condition of mental emotion'.[7] This is to enlist the Greeks on the side of wholesomeness. Nudity and athleticism produce rationality, democracy and general 'soundness'.[8] As we shall see later, Greek nudity could be, and was, also enlisted by the apostles of morbidity and unwholesomeness. It is of no concern to me in this context whether either of these positions helps to make sense of the ancient Greeks. My subject here is what was *believed* to be true in nineteenth-century England, and on this, there is a remarkable degree of consensus from writers approaching the idea of Greekness from a wide variety of angles that naked athleticism, balance of mind and body, and the rational cultivation of the intellect were necessarily combined in Greek culture and, as a corollary, that in order to match the glory that was Greece, modern education would have to combine the same elements. Here, for example, is an old Harrovian, invoking the Greeks to explain the virtual idolatry offered to the captain of the first XI:

> No thinking man will blame us for idolising the athlete. The cricketer in his flannels was our hero, not the student immersed in his books. Can there ever be the question as to which is the more picturesque figure? Was there ever a race more intel-lectual than the ancient Greeks, and did they not worship the human form divine?[9]

This appears to imply that the cultivation of athleticism (or indeed, salivating over athletes) will cause 'culture', in the intellectual sense, as a quasi-inevitable by-product; a remarkable failure of logic. The association of the flannelled youth of England with the Greek ideal is similarly made by no less a figure than Walter Pater, who suggested that Myron, the sculptor of the *Discobolos*, 'were he here, might have given us the cricketer, the passing generations of cricketers, *sub specie eternitatis*, under the eternal form of art'.[10] Sir Neville Cardus also drew on this potent emotional nexus: 'The cricket field has seen no sight more Grecian than the one presented by C. B. Fry in the pride and handsomeness of his young manhood.'[11] Fry was, of course, a type of the philosopher-athlete, but what is Grecian about a cricket field?[12]

Nudity *à la grecque* had a hard fight of it in late nineteenth-century England. In 1867, the Athletic Society of Great Britain required athletes to compete in 'a shirt or guernsey, and trousers or knicker-bockers', and commented severely in the *Athletic Review* that, 'it is by no means an edifying sight to see competitors come to the scratch in tights or fleshings or scanty drawers'.[13] The pursuit of the 'noble, nude and antique' was swimming against the tide of late Victorian moral consensus. The curious result of this is that a propensity to take one's clothes off in public became a curious but significant marker of social class. Rupert Brooke and his friends swam naked in the Cam at Grantchester: their coevals of other social classes tended to associate nudity either with sin or with poverty (in either case, a lack of respectability, and thus a loss of caste). The way that social class influenced perceptions of nudity is illuminated by an incident reported by Frank Harris, who came across Oscar Wilde in the Café Royale talking brilliantly about the Olympic games to two Cockney youths of dubious aspect:

'Did you sy they was niked?'
'Of course', Oscar replied, 'nude, clothed only in sunshine and beauty.'[14]

Gilbert and Sullivan's *The Grand Duke* (1896) speaks both for the association of Greekness with nudity, and for its unacceptability in the eyes of Middle England:

Yes, on reconsideration, there are customs of that nation
Which are not in strict accordance with the habits of our day,
And when I come to codify, their rules I mean to modify,
Or Mrs Grundy, p'r'aps, may have a word or two to say . . .
They wore little underclothing – scarcely anything – or
    no-thing –

And their dress of Coan silk was quite transparent in design –
Well, in fact, in summer weather, something like the
  'altogether' –
And it's *there*, I rather fancy, I shall have to draw the line.[15]

The concatenation of nudity with political idealism led to a curious phenomenon of the late eighteenth and nineteenth century: the portrayal of the public figure as, literally, a public figure, a nude. This was a highly self-conscious Greekness which was far from commanding wide public acceptability. In the eighteenth century, Voltaire's status as a philosopher to rival the figures of the great age of Athens was underlined when Diderot and his circle commissioned a *nude* portrait of him from the sculptor Jean-Baptiste Pigalle in 1770;[16] a commission which may be connected with J. J. Winckelmann's publication of his *Thoughts on the Imitation of Greek Works of Art in Painting and Sculpture* (1755).[17] Voltaire himself was greatly amused by this statue: the French public were not.[18] Somewhat later, Antonio Canova, probably the greatest of all neoclassical sculptors of idealised nudes in a very high state of finish, succeeded in persuading Napoleon that a fifteen-foot-high nude statue was the most appropriate expression of his new imperial status, but the statue, once completed, was rejected by the Emperor.[19] As we shall see, the ambivalence over the appropriateness of representing modern statesmen as nude heroes which is expressed by commissioning, then rejecting, such images continued into the next century.

In the nineteenth century, sculptors continued to experiment with an heroic nudity which represents a continued, obstinate association of nakedness with political glory: examples include Eugenio Baroni's nude statue of Garibaldi.[20] In England, it is the eighteen-foot-high nude statue of Achilles by Richard Westmacott, which was paid for by subscription from the ladies of England and erected in Hyde Park in 1822 as a tribute to the Duke of Wellington, which is the most important public nude of the period.[21] This was at least a representation of the idea of the hero, rather than a portrait of the Iron Duke himself, but even so, it scandalised contemporaries – it is interesting, however, that a nude hero was fixed on as appropriate for a statue funded by women's subscriptions. Another statue which is important for what it tells us about contemporary attitudes, in America this time, is that of George Washington as the Father of his Country commissioned from Horatio Greenough (1820) which was intended to be placed beneath the vaulted arch of the Capitol. Washington is depicted nude except for a sort of neoclassical bath-towel which drapes over his legs and lap, with the end thrown over his left arm. The nation erupted, and not in laughter. As Greenough complained at the time, 'purblind squeemishness [*sic*] awoke with a roar at the colossal nakedness of Washington's manly breast'. As a result, the embarrassing commission was relegated to the park grounds, and hidden in a shrubbery. It is now in the Smithsonian.[22]

The viewpoint of 'purblind squeemishness' is expressed by Nathaniel Hawthorne. In *The Marble Faun* (1859), his novel about 'the white marmoreal horde' (as Henry James later termed them – the American sculptors working in Rome), an artistic young lady called Miriam objects to the modern nude (Chapter XIV):

> Nowadays people are as good as born in their clothes, and there is practically not a nude human being in existence. An artist, therefore ... cannot sculpture nudity with a pure heart, if only because he is compelled to steal guilty glimpses at hired models. The marble inevitably loses its chastity under such circumstances. An old Greek sculptor, no doubt, found his models in the open sunshine, and among pure and princely maidens, and thus the nude statues of antiquity are as modest as violets and sufficiently draped in their own beauty.

It bespeaks a certain lack of historical sense even for 1859 to imagine that upper-class Athenian virgins sat as nude models to sculptors, but the entrenched notion that nudity is a feature of upper-class Greek life (for both sexes) can be pursued far beyond Nathaniel Hawthorne.

This sequence of attempts to revive the nude in the context of the most serious, public and political art is a direct product of an underlying connection of nudity with the defence of liberty. Thus, in terms of the paradigm with which I started, the heroic representation of nude men could be, and was, seen as chaste, pure, and wholesome.

Inevitably, however, the squeaky-clean nudes of Greenough, Westmacott and their successors provided an alibi for a variety of representations to which none of these words would apply. The appeal to a chaste and noble Greek gymnastic tradition could also, inevitably, provide cover for a representation of Greek love.[23] The slipperiness of the distinction between the athletic and the erotic nude (a distinction which is, in fact, very much in the eye of the beholder: a fact exploited for many years by, for example, the magazine *Health and Efficiency*) is illustrated by three late nine-teenth-century photographic studies of naked men in Margaret Walters' book, *The Nude Male*. One is of the body-builder Bernarr McFadden wearing nothing but a pair of sandals and posed before a vaguely Mycenaean doorcase. This image is clearly intended as the embodiment of chaste virility, as is also the case with other con-temporaneous photographs of nude body-builders like Eugen Sandow in 'classical' poses which are often based directly on ancient statues.[24] The second photograph is of a young man standing with all his weight on one leg (thus lending an 'unmanly' sinuosity to his torso), and blowing into a double-flute (*aulos*) photographed by Thomas Eakins and labelled 'Nude study for Arcadia'. The third is of a pair of Sicilian youths of the 1880s sprawled knees akimbo on a marble bench with a *pithos* and some oak-leaves to set the scene, photographed by Baron von Gloeden. In the last picture, and many like it, the use of Greek props is a gloss providing a publicly acceptable context over overtly homoerotic representation.[25] The picture of McFadden lies at one pole, the Baron's boys at the other: Eakins is somewhere in the middle. One can point to specific differences of approach: do the models make eye-contact? Do their poses emphasise, or de-emphasise, their genitalia? But these are subtle points. The use of vaguely Greek trappings in these images means that it would have been possible for an Oxford aesthete of the 1890s to adorn his college set with photographs by Baron von Gloeden or Frederick Rolfe, and to claim that their value and interest was 'Greek'; a revival of the pure and manly world of Plato and the palaestra.

The case of Henry Scott Tuke (1858–1929) is an instructive one. He was a Member of the Royal Academy and an eminently respect-able figure.[26] He was able to spend most of his career painting (and selling) images of nude, adolescent boys without falling into the inferno which engulfed Oscar Wilde because he and his many customers were well able to avoid analysing the quality of their own enjoyment by appealing to this carefully articulated belief in the essential chastity of the nude, male body. As a painter, I find him extraordinary. Compositionally, and in terms of taste, he is roughly on a level with Norman Rockwell, but his sheer ability to handle paint (especially when representing nude human flesh) is more like that of Rubens: his portrait of his beloved Johnny Jackett (1899)[27] seems to me one of the most compelling portraits of the late

Plate 10.1 Henry Scott Tuke, *Perseus and Andromeda* (1889): present whereabouts unknown.

nineteenth century. He began painting nudes in the mid-1880s, and his first experiments are in the Greek mode. These have titles like *Endymion* and *Hermes at the Pool*: they received poor critical reception and Tuke eventually destroyed them, finding the painting of a nude female figure in the former picture 'the great obstacle'. *Perseus and Andromeda*, his large painting of 1889 (Plate 10.1) is a melancholy example of this impediment: Andromeda is strangely long-backed and square about the hips, and one is not surprised to learn that she was posed for by a Falmouth fisher-boy called Willy Rowling. According to Tuke's biographer, *Perseus and Andromeda* met a mixed reception (which England being what it is, probably means that two or three people made nasty remarks and a dozen or so asked for his address). One aesthete whose reaction was certainly positive was the homosexual John Addington Symonds, who wrote saying: 'I want to tell you how much I admire . . . your *Perseus*. . . . The feeling for the nude in it seems to me as delicate as it is vigorous. I wish you would . . . send me some photographs of your various pictures and studies.' Symonds went on to advise Tuke to give up kitting out his fisher-boys in rose-garlands and sandals: 'you ought to develop studies in the nude without pretending to make them "subject pictures" . . . your own inspiration is derived from nature's beauty. Classical or Romantic mythologies are not your starting point.'[28]

This advice was taken: Tuke spent the rest of a long and meritorious career painting boys, boats and water for what is now a recognisably homosexual clientèle of aesthetic bachelors, which included Symonds, Lord Ronald Gower (who was generally believed to be the model for Lord Henry Wootton in Wilde's *The Picture of Dorian Gray*), Laurence Housman, and later, T. E. Lawrence.[29] Yet he was able to maintain his position through the Wilde scandal, and the subsequent witch-hunt, apparently because of the association of his naked adolescents with the concept of Hellenic wholesomeness, and also because of his reluctance to depict his young subjects' genitalia, which he avoided by careful posing, shadows, or strategically-placed arms, knees, and drapery.[30] (See Plate 10.1.) The implications of Tuke's art are paralleled by the writing of his close friend Charles Kains Jackson, who edited a little magazine called *The Artist and Journal of Home Culture*. In 1894 (two years before the fall of Wilde), he published an editorial on 'The New Chivalry', contrasting 'The Old Chivalry, or the exaltation of the youthful feminine ideal . . . [with] the New Chivalry, or the exaltation of the youthful masculine ideal.'[31] This appeals to 'the joys of palaestra, of the river, of the hunt and the moor, the evening tent-pitching of campers-out, and the exhilaration of the early morning swim'.[32] Kains Jackson, Tuke, and a good many others were able to maintain this position of sentimental, etherealised homosexuality by thinking of this posture as 'Greek': note the word *palaestra* in the emotionally-loaded list above. Indeed Tuke himself referred (in Greek) to one of his favourite models, Bert White, as *kalos* 'handsome' – the word used for the (passive) beloved by the (active) lover in the discourse of male–male relations in classical Athens.[33]

The idea of the Greek body is thus the subject of a tug-of-war in late Victorian and Edwardian England. Pederasts of all persuasions from sentimental to sensual appealed to the concept of the nude boy as no mere boy, but a *kouros*; a representation of the imperishable glory of the human spirit, something far more than an object of homosexual lust. In some cases, this was a hypocritical, or overtly cynical, gloss on simple sexual interest, a way of dressing up the unacceptable in a cloudy glory of euphemism. In others, such as Henry Scott Tuke himself, the simple fact that his favourite models have confirmed in interview that his relationships with them were emotionally charged, but entirely chaste, suggests that he really believed it. As an indication of the homosocial context in which Tuke's work makes sense, I cannot resist quoting here a poem by the Rev. E. E. Bradford, called 'The Call', which is, as it were, a verse Tuke:

> Eros is up and away, away!
> Eros is up and away! . . .
> Strong, self-controlled, erect and free,
> He is marching along today!
>
> He is calling aloud to the men, the men!
> He is calling aloud to the men –
> 'Turn away from the wench, with her powder and paint,
> And follow the Boy who is fair as a Saint.'[34]

This poem is interesting from various perspectives; not merely because its latent content is off the top of the scale, but because of its identification of boys and boy-love with nature, and women with culture. At first sight this polarity (well entrenched in classical sources, as Richard Hawley has pointed out above) appears to reverse other strands of late nineteenth-century thought. Charles Baudelaire, for instance, declared, 'la femme est le contraire du *Dandy* ... la femme est *naturelle*, c'est-à-dire abominable'.[35] It suggests that a choice of two paradigms was made available by late nineteenth-century romanticism:

	NATURE		CULTURE
MAN	pure nude chaste	WOMAN	decadent clothed sexual
WOMAN	instinctual sexual uncontrolled	MAN	intellectual chaste disciplined

The first of these, which identifies Nature as positive and therefore associable with men, is implicitly or explicitly homosexual, and its intellectual basis is 'Greek', as the *fin de siècle* understood Greekness. The implication of Bradford's 'The Call' is that boys' beauty is nude, undecorated, whereas the beauty of women is clothed, ornamented, and artificial. Somewhere at the base of the Rev. Bradford's instinctive prejudice is a Greek contrast: the archaic, smiling *kouros*, always nude, one foot slightly advanced before the other, and the parallel *kore*, always represented in a heavily pleated floor-length tunic.[36]

The other team in this tug-of-war for the Greek body were Hellenists of a very different stamp, such as Matthew Arnold and Charles Kingsley, and the horde of educationalists actually concerned with the modification of the body who made the late nineteenth-century public school what it was: that is to say, games-mad. For these, the Greek ideal of 'the elevation of the powers of mind and soul to a beautiful harmony of the inner and outer man', 'intellectual development, and the unchangeable nobility of virile beauty',[37] was practically addressed by physical culture, in the hope that the glorious young athletes thus achieved would acquire the Greek civic virtues as a by-product of extensive cricket-practice.[38] The ephebe-worshipping Tuke, Kains Jackson, Housman and the rest seem to imply that beautiful boys just *are* (this may have something to do with the way that their characteristic objects of desire, fisher-boys, gondoliers, ploughboys and so forth, were members of the 'lower orders' who took a great deal of exercise in the course of their daily work). The muscular Hellenists, if one may so term them, are far more aware that for men of their own social class, a deliberate effort of self-modification is needed to achieve ephebe status.[39] And this effort was not only applicable to males. In 1873 Charles Kingsley published an essay called 'Nausicäa in London', which suggested that, 'if educators would develop in girls an admiration for such exemplary types, instead of making them read more books, they might witness the growth of a whole race of Nausicäas'.[40]

Rudyard Kipling's reaction to games, as to much else about true-blue Englishry, is more complex than those who do not read him imagine. In *Stalky & Co.* he offers a portrait of a boarding-school (the United Services College) which consciously stands aloof from the public school as such. However, this institution is infested by muscularly Christian teachers, who offer this simple paradigm to a recent recruit: 'King and Macrea, fellow house-masters, had borne it in upon him that by games, and games alone, was salvation wrought. Boys neglected were boys lost.'[41]

The assumptions of Kipling's King and Macrea are clarified in the most famous of the school poems. Look, for example, at Henry Newbolt's *Vitæ Lampada*: 'There's a breathless hush in the close tonight,' with its notorious refrain line, 'Play up! play up! and play the game!' The first stanza, of course, is the big match, with 'ten to make and the match to win'. But the second begins, 'The sand of the desert is sodden red.' The juxtaposition has a straightforward message; the modification of the soul by means of the body.[42] The captain of the First XI, that schoolboy hero, has become a man whose early training with bat and ball has endowed him with a permanent capacity for glorious action. Then there is *Forty Years On* (anonymous), which directly poses the question, 'Forty years on, growing older and older . . . what will it help you that once you were strong?' The answer comes straight from the shoulder:

> God gives us bases to guard or beleaguer,
> Games to play out, whether earnest or fun;
> Fights for the fearless! and goals for the eager,
> Twenty, and thirty, and forty years on![43]

E. B. Osborn's *Anthology of Sporting Verse* (1930), from which I have drawn these products of terminally muddled thinking, contains in its introduction the remarkable statement that 'the devotion of the ancient Greeks to open-air athletic exercises produced a standard physique of rounded elastic muscles which is really the crowning masterpiece of Greek art'.[44] The subtext of these poems (and others like them) is that the modification of the body in youth produces a modification of mind for life. Creating a beautiful body will *cause* a noble soul. Few, perhaps, would have gone as far as Winckelmann, who stated that even the capacity to understand beauty 'is more easily to be found in well-formed young men than in those who are not so', and who 'maintains that not merely a feeling for beauty, but also its expression, is the monopoly of beautiful youths'.[45] But in less extreme forms, nobility of body, and the *askesis* required to produce it, was widely understood to demonstrate more permanent qualities. The main point of *The Picture of Dorian Gray*, published in 1891, is that it shows up this belief for the fallacy that it is – one reason why this rather sophisticated fable caused so much annoyance.

NOTES

1 For a general survey, see Turner 1981. Dowling 1994 treats a specific, and very important, group of thinkers about Hellenism.
2 The principal statement of Arnold's famous contrast of Hebraism and Hellenism is in Arnold [1869] 1965: 163–75. See further DeLaura 1969.
3 Firbank [1926] 1961: 648.
4 *Don Juan*, canto cxciv.
5 Haley 1978: 46.
6 Arnold [1869] 1965: 178.
7 Ruskin [1856] 1904: 233.
8 See for example Turner 1981: 58 and 172–3.
9 Cotton Minchin 1898: 150. This passage recalls the 1860s. See also Haley 1978: 164: 'as early as 1864, when the Public Schools Commission looked into this matter among others, it found that at Eton the captain of boats was the greatest man in the school, the next in precedence being the captain of the XI'.
10 Pater 1910: 290.
11 Ross 1977: 153.
12 This question was inadvertently answered (in the negative) by Frederick Lord Leighton's painting of 1859, *Greek Girls Playing at Ball*. This misleadingly titled picture appears to represent a fast bowler insecurely wrapped in crêpe paper whanging a high ball the length of an invisible pitch (illustrated in Jenkyns 1991: 215).
13 *Athletic Review*, July 2 1867: 9.
14 Quoted in Dowling 1994: 145. The gap between this vision and the reality of Victorian London is illustrated in the most grisly fashion by an optimistic remark of Wilde's in a more public context: 'Over a substratum of pure wool, such as is supplied by Dr Jaeger under the modern German system, some modification of Greek costume is perfectly applicable to our climate, our country and our century.' Quoted in Jenkyns 1991: 295.
15 Quoted in Jenkyns 1991: 134.

16 Illustrated in Honour 1977: 120.
17 Revived by Pater 1867. See now Potts 1994.
18 Honour 1977: 202.
19 Walters 1978: 205. Canova's arguments in defence of his statue are in Goldwater and Treves 1976: 196. The statue has ended up in the stairwell of Apsley House, London, having been presented to the Duke of Wellington by the Prince Regent: what Wellington felt about confronting this colossal representation of his ancient enemy on a daily basis has not been recorded.
20 Honour 1977: 122. Other heroically conceived nude statues (of artists rather than statesmen) include Max Klinger's *Beethoven*, and Auguste Rodin's *Balzac* and *Victor Hugo*.
21 See Walters 1978: 205, illustrated on 223.
22 Rudofsky 1972: 269, illustration in Walters 1978: 223.
23 As, for example, in Symonds 1883: 78–9, with its defence of a manly, martial and chivalrous 'comrade-love'.
24 See Dutton 1995: 119–29, 138, 199–205 and plates 4.2–4.4, 7.3–7.5. On Sandow and the relationship between the visual presentation of body-builders and the classical world in the late nineteenth century, see Wyke 1997.
25 Walters 1978: 307. [Joseph William] Gleeson White, editor of *The Studio* and a man with many friends among aesthetic homosexuals, printed an illustrated article on 'The Male Nude in Photography' in the first issue of *The Studio* (1890), with examples by Baron Wilhelm von Gloeden and Frederick Rolfe (Baron Corvo), among others.
26 The acceptability of Tuke's work is demonstrated by the fact that one of his paintings of naked boys, *August Blue*, was bought for the nation by the Chantrey Bequest in 1894, for £525. The Chantrey Bequest had earlier bought one of the fully-clothed genre pieces with which he inaugurated his professional career, *All Hands to the Pump* (for £420, in 1889).
27 Illustrated in Wainwright and Dunn 1989, Plate 40.
28 Quoted in Wainwright and Dunn 1989: 49, 52.
29 And Lt.-Col. Sydney Lomer, who took his most attractive batman with him when he left the service (the boy, Leo Marshall, was painted nude by Tuke) and published translations from the *Anthologia Palatina*. See Wainwright and Dunn 1989: 124.
30 See Cooper 1987: 35–6. Tuke's own attitude was chaster than that of his patrons. In one painting, *The Diving Place*, a buyer (possibly Sydney Lomer) asked for the genitals to be defined more clearly: in another case, one Leonard Duke (another of Tuke's patrons) asked for a 'no trousers' version of *Noonday Heat*, in which the central figure lies sprawled on his back (Cooper 1987: 34–7).
31 Jackson was not alone. Another important apology for romantic pederasty is that of Johnson 1858. We may also note the existence of an Oxford pamphlet of the 1860s simply entitled *Boy-Worship*, which makes a serious defence of pederasty as a form of male romantic attachment, for which see Dowling 1994: 111.

32 Wainwright and Dunn 1989: 74–5: 'The article caused outrage, and at least one sermon was preached against it.'

33 Cooper 1987: 33.

34 Quoted in Gathorne-Hardy 1977: 214. E. E. Bradford's collection *Passing the Love of Women* was noticed in the *Westminster Review*, without distaste: 'the friendship between man and youth form[s] the theme of many of Dr Bradford's poems. He is as alive to the beauty of unsullied youth as was Plato.'

35 *Mon coeur mis à nu*, in Baudelaire [1863] 1975: 677.

36 See the cover illustration for the present volume, where the corseted, frilled and bedizened Victorian women look on the naked classical Venus in the gallery with amazement. For the Greek parallels, see Boardman 1973: 65–73.

37 Phrases quoted in Matthew Arnold's notebooks, the latter in French (the Sophoclean model of the ideal man: 'la plénitude et l'élévation du développement intellectuel, la noblesse inaltérable de la beauté virile'): see DeLaura 1969: 188.

38 C. Day-Lewis commented on his own school, Sherborne:

> Theoretically, of course, we were based on *mens sana in corpore sano*. But in practice there was a conflict in which *mens* lost hands down every time . . . Sherborne, as I have said, was a games-mad school. The "bloods", the boys with the highest prestige, were almost invariably athletes: if they had brains too nobody objected, but it was the blue-and-gold ties of the First XV or the First XI which made them demi-gods.

Quoted in Quigly 1982: 50, who also gives similar comments from survivors of Marlborough, Wellington and even St Paul's (a day-school).

39 It is only fair to note a certain degree of overlap between schoolmasters and ephebe–worshippers. Charles Vaughan (headmaster of Harrow), G. H. Shorting of Rugby, and Oscar Browning and William Johnson at Eton were all notorious for combining pedagogy with pederasty (see Pearsall 1969: 85–6 and 453–6; Gathorne-Hardy 1977: 79–84). There is also the curious figure of John Gambril Nicholson, himself a pupil of Frederick Rolfe's, and a highly respected schoolmaster, who was also notorious for his cult of personal favourites, all strappingly healthy types, and his publication of books of verse with titles which included *A Garland of Ladslove* and *The Romance of a Choirboy* (see Weeks 1971: 317).

40 Quoted in Haley 1978: 181. It is worth noting that this is a late nineteenth-century development: see Gathorne-Hardy 1977: 53. When this paper was given at Warwick, a fascinating discussion developed subsequently on the relevance (or otherwise) of these ideas to *girls'* education. The complete lack of consensus on what girls' education was intended to achieve (either in the nineteenth or twentieth centuries) means that the questions raised there, though worthy of a full discussion in themselves, cannot be addressed in a paper of this modest scope.

41 Kipling [1899] 1982: 66.

42 Osborn 1930: 206–7. A very similar number, called *School Football*, by

Eric Wilkinson (quoted in Osborn 1930: 251–2) makes the same point in the context of Ilkley footballers.

43 Osborn 1930: 211–12
44 Osborn 1930: 25.
45 Praz 1969: 44.

BIBLIOGRAPHY

Anderson, B. (1983) *Imagined Communities: reflections on the origin and spread of nationalism*, London.

Apter, E. (1996) 'Acting Out Orientalism: Sapphic theatricality in turn-of-the-century Paris', in E. Diamond (ed.) *Performance and Cultural Politics*, London: 15–34.

Arafat, K. W. (1990) *Classical Zeus: a study in art and literature*, Oxford.

Archer, L., Fischler, S. and Wyke, M. (eds) (1994) *Women in Ancient Societies: an illusion of the night*, London.

Arnold, M. [1869] (1965) *Culture and Anarchy*, ed. R. H. Super, Ann Arbor, MI.

Auguet, R. (1972) *Cruelty and Civilisation: the Roman games*, London.

Austin, R. G. (1955) *P. Vergili Maronis Aeneidos Liber Quartus*, Oxford.

—— (1971) *P. Vergili Maronis Aeneidos Liber Primus*, Oxford.

Bapty, I. and Yates, T. (eds) (1990) *Archaeology after Structuralism*, London.

Barkan, L. (1986) *Gods Made Flesh*, New Haven, CT.

Barnett, R. D. (1990) 'Six Fingers and Toes: polydactylism in the ancient world', *BAR* 16: 46–54.

Barrett, J. C. (1994) *Fragments from Antiquity: an archaeology of social life in Britain, 2900–1200 BC*, Oxford.

Barthes, R. (1973a) *Mythologies*, trans. A. Lavers, London.

—— (1973b) *S/Z*, trans. R. Miller, Oxford.

Barton, C. (1993) *The Sorrows of the Ancient Romans*, Princeton.

Baudelaire, C. [1863] (1975) *Œuvres complètes*, ed. C. Pichois, 3 vols, Paris: vol. 1.

Benjamin, W. (1969) *Illuminations*, trans. H. Arendt, New York.

Benner, A. R. and Fobes, F. H. (eds) (1949) *Alciphron, Aelian, Philostratus: The Letters*, Harvard, MA.

Benvenuto, B. and Kennedy, R. (1986) *The Works of Jacques Lacan*, London.

Bernand, E. (1969) *Inscriptions métriques de l'Égypte gréco-romaine* (Annales Littéraires de l'Université de Besançon 98) Besançon.

Berthelot, J. M. (1991) 'Sociological discourse and the body', in M. Featherstone, M. Hepworth and B. S. Turner (eds) *The Body: social process and cultural theory*, London: 390–404.

Boardman, J. (1973) *Greek Art*, London.

Bogdan, R. (1988) *Freak Shows: presenting human oddities for amusement and profit*, Chicago.

Bordu, 3. (1990) 'Teminism, postmodernism and gender scepticism', in L. J. Nicholson (ed.) *Feminism/Postmodernism*, New York: 133–56.

Bourdieu, P. (1977) *Outline of a Theory of Practice*, trans. R. Nice, Cambridge.

Bowie, M. (1979) 'Jacques Lacan', in J. Sturrock (ed.) *Structuralism and Since: from Lévi Strauss to Derrida*, Oxford: 116–53.

—— (1987) *Freud, Proust and Lacan: theory as fiction*, Cambridge.

Bradley, A. C. (1991) 'Aristotle's Conception of the State', in D. Keyt and F. D. Miller (eds) *A Companion to Aristotle's 'Politics'*, Oxford: 29–37.

Braidotti, R. (1989) 'The politics of ontological difference', in T. Brennan (ed.) *Between Feminism and Psychoanalysis*, London: 89–105.

—— (1991) *Patterns of Dissonance: a study of women in contemporary philosophy*, Cambridge.

Brain, R. (1979) *The Decorated Body*, London.

Bremmer, J. (1983) 'Scapegoat rituals in Ancient Greece', *HSCP* 87: 299–320.

Brock, R. (1994) 'The Labour of Women in Classical Athens', *CQ* 44: 336–46.

Brock, S. and Harvey, S.A. (1987) *Holy Women of the Syrian Orient*, Berkeley.

Brooks, P. (1993) *Body Work: objects of desire in modern narrative*, Cambridge, MA.

Brothwell, D. and Sandison, A. T. (eds) (1967) *Diseases in Antiquity: a survey of the diseases, injuries and surgery of early populations*, Springfield, IL.

Brown, P. (1981) *The Cult of the Saints: its rise and function in Latin Christianity*, Chicago.

—— (1988) *The Body and Society: men, women and sexual renunciation in early Christianity*, London.

Brown, S. (1992) 'Death as decoration: scenes from the arena in Roman domestic mosaics', in A. Richlin (ed.) *Pornography and Representation in Greece and Rome*, New York: 180–211.

Bruyère, B. (1937) *Rapport sur les fouilles de Deir el-Médineh (1934–1935)*, Cairo.

Budge, E. A. W. (1893) *The Mummy: a handbook of Egyptian funerary archaeology*, London.

—— (1913) *Coptic Apocrypha in the Dialect of Upper Egypt*, London.

Burn, L. (1987) *The Meidias Painter*, Oxford.

Burrus, V. (1995) 'Reading Agnes: the rhetoric of gender in Ambrose and Prudentius', *JECS* 3: 25–46.

Buschhausen, H., Horak, U. and Harrauer, H. (1995) *Der Lebenskreis der Kopten: Dokumente, Textilien, Funde, Ausgrabungen*, Vienna.

Butler, J. (1990a) 'Gender trouble, feminist theory, and psychoanalytic discourse', in L. J. Nicholson (ed.) *Feminism/Postmodernism*, New York: 324–40.

—— (1990b) *Gender Trouble: feminism and the subversion of identity*, New York.

—— (1993) *Bodies that Matter: on the discursive limits of sex*, New York.

Buxton, R. (1980) 'Blindness and Limits: Sophokles and the logic of myth', *JHS* 100: 22–37.

Bynum, C. W. (1992) *Fragmentation and Redemption: essays on gender and the human body in medieval religion*, New York.

—— (1995) *The Resurrection of the Body in Western Christianity, 200–1336*, New York.

Cameron, A. (1991) *Christianity and the Rhetoric of Empire*, Berkeley, CA.

Carswell, J. (1956) *Coptic Tattoo Designs*, Beirut.

Cartledge, P. (1987) *Agesilaos and the Crisis of Sparta*, London.

Castel, G. (1979) 'Etude d'une momie copte', in *Hommages à la mémoire de Serge Sauneron 1927–1976: II. Égypte Post-Pharaonique*, Cairo: 122–143.

Castelli, E. (1991) '"I Will Make Mary Male": pieties of body and gender transformation of Christian women in Late Antiquity', in J. Epstein and K. Straub, *Body Guards: the cultural politics of gender ambiguity*, New York: 29–49.

—— (1992) 'Vision and voyeurism', Berkeley Center for Hermeneutical Studies, CA.

Ceram, W. C. (1958) *The March of Archaeology*, trans. R. and C. Winston, New York.

Chambry, E. (1967) *Ésope Fables*, Budé, Paris.

Chedgzoy, K. (1996) *Shakespeare's Queer Children*, Manchester.

Clark, G. (1995) 'Women and asceticism in late antiquity: the refusal of status and gender', in V. L. Wimbush and R. Valantasis (eds) *Asceticism*, Oxford: 33–48.

—— (1996) 'The bright frontier of friendship', in R. Mathisen and H. Sivan (eds) *Shifting Frontiers in Late Antiquity*, Aldershot: 217–29.

Clark, S. (1983) *Aristotle's Man: speculations upon Aristotelian anthropology*, Oxford.

Cohen, A. P. (1994) *Self Consciousness: an alternative anthropology of identity*, London.

Cohen, S. (1991) 'Menstruants and the Sacred in Judaism and Christianity', in S. B. Pomeroy (ed.) *Women's History and Ancient History*, Chapel Hill, NC: 273–95.

Coleman, K. (1990) 'Fatal charades: Roman executions staged as mythological enactments', *JRS* 80: 44–73.

Cooper, E. (1987) *The Life and Work of Henry Scott Tuke*, London.

Coren, S. (1992) *The Left-hander Syndrome: the causes and consequences of left-handedness*, New York.

Cotton Minchin, J. G. (1898) *Old Harrow Days*, London.

Crum, W. E. (1905) *Catalogue of the Coptic Manuscripts in the British Museum*, London.

—— (1915) 'Discours de Pisenthius sur Saint Onnophrius', *ROC* 20: 38–67.

—— (1939) *A Coptic Dictionary*, Oxford.

Daly, N. (1994) 'That Obscure Object of Desire: Victorian commodity culture and fictions of the mummy', *Novel* 28: 24–51.

Dasen, V. (1993) *Dwarfs in Ancient Egypt and Greece*, Oxford.

Dassmann, E. (1975) 'Ambrosius und die Martyrer', *JAC* 18: 49–68.

David, E. (1984) *Aristophanes and the Athenian Society of the Early Fourth Century BC*, Leiden.

David, R. (1980) *The Macclesfield Collection of Egyptian Antiquities*, Warminster.

Davie, D. (1992) 'Baroque in the hymn-book', in D. Wood (ed.) *The Church and the Arts (Studies in Church History* 28) Oxford: 329–42.

Davies, S. L. (1980) *The Revolt of the Widows: the social world of the apocryphal Acts*, Carbondale, IL.

Dawson, W. (1928) 'References to Mummification by Greek and Latin Authors', *Aegyptus* 9: 106–112.

—— (1934) 'Pettigrew's Demonstrations upon Mummies. A Chapter in the History of Egyptology', *JEA* 20: 170–82.

Dawson, W. and Gray, P. H. K. (1968) *Catalogue of Egyptian Antiquities in the British Museum I: mummies and human remains*, London.

Dean-Jones, L. (1994) *Women's Bodies in Classical Greek Science*, Oxford.

DeLaura, D. J. (1969) *Hebrew and Hellene in Victorian England: Newman, Arnold, and Pater*, Austin, Texas and London.

De Lauretis, T. (ed.) (1986) *Feminist Studies/Critical Studies*, London.

Delehaye, H. (1966) *Les passions des martyrs et les genres littéraires (Subsidia Hagiographica* 13b) Brussels.

Detienne, M. (1981) 'Between Beasts and Gods', in R. L. Gordon (ed.) *Myth, Religion and Society: structuralist essays by M. Detienne, J.-P. Vernant and P. Vidal-Naquet*, Cambridge and Paris: 215–28.

Detienne, M. and Vernant, J.-P. (1978) *Cunning Intelligence in Greek Culture and Society*, trans. J. Lloyd, Cambridge.

Devereux, G. (1973) 'The Self-blinding of Oidipous in Sophokles' Oidipous Tyrannous', *JHS* 93: 36–49.

Dolbeau, F. (1992) 'Sermons inédits de saint Augustin préchés en 397: sermo de honorandis vel contemnendis parentibus', *RB* 102: 282–97.

Douglas, M. (1966) *Purity and Danger*, London.

Dowling, L. (1994) *Hellenism and Homosexuality in Victorian Oxford*, Ithaca, NY and London.

Doyal, L. (1983) 'The Crippling Effects of Underdevelopment', in O. Shirley (ed.) *A Cry for Health: poverty and disability in the Third World*, Frome: 7–14.

Drescher, J. (1947) *Three Coptic Legends: Hilaria, Archellites, the Seven Sleepers*, Cairo.

duBois, P. (1988) *Sowing the Body: psychoanalysis and ancient representations of women*, Chicago.

—— (1991) *Torture and Truth*, New York.

Dudley, D. R. (1967) *Urbs Roma: a source book of classical texts on the city and its monuments*, London.

Dudley, L. (1911) *The Egyptian Elements in the Legend of the Body and the Soul*, Baltimore, MD.

Dutton, K. R. (1995) *The Perfectible Body*, London.

Ebers, G. M. (1893) *The Hellenic Portraits from the Fayum at present in the Collection of Herr Graf*, New York.

Edelstein, L. [1967] (1987) *Ancient Medicine: selected papers of Ludwig Edelstein*, trans. O. Temkin, Baltimore, MD.

Eitrem, S. (1933) 'Das Ende Didos in Vergils *Aeneis*', *Festskrift til Halvdan Koht*, Oslo: 29–41.

Emmel, S. (1993) *Shenoute's Literary Corpus*, unpublished PhD thesis, University of Yale.

Featherstone, M., Hepworth, M. and Turner, B. S. (eds) (1991) *The Body: social process and cultural theory*, London.

Feeney, D. C. (1990) 'The Taciturnity of Aeneas', in S. J. Harrison (ed.) *Oxford Readings in Vergil's Aeneid*, Oxford: 167–90.

—— (1991) *The Gods in Epic*, Oxford.

Feher, M., Naddaff, R. and Tazi, N. (eds) (1989) *Fragments for a History of the Human Body*, 3 vols, New York.

Fiedler, L. [1978] (1993) *Freaks: myths and images of the secret self*, New York.

Firbank, R. [1926] (1961) 'Concerning the Eccentricities of Cardinal Pirelli', in *The Complete Firbank*, London.

Forbes-Irving, P. (1990) *Metamorphosis in Greek Myths*, Oxford.

Forbes-Robertson, J. (1889) 'Græco-Roman Portraiture in Egypt. A Recovered Page in the History of Painting', *The Magazine of Art* 12: 177–80.

Fortenbaugh, W. W. (1984) *Quellen zur Ethik Theophrasts*, Amsterdam.

Fortenbaugh, W. W. *et al.* (eds) (1992) *Theophrastus of Eresus – Sources for his Life, Writings, Thought and Influence*, Leiden.

Foucault, M. (1972) *The Archaeology of Knowledge*, trans. A. Sheridan, London.

—— (1973) *The Order of Things: an archaeology of the human sciences*, London.

—— (1977) *Discipline and Punish: the birth of the prison*, trans. A. Sheridan, London.

—— (1978) *The History of Sexuality; an introduction*, trans. R. Hurley, London.

—— (1985) *The History of Sexuality: the use of pleasure*, trans. R. Hurley, London.

—— (1986) *The History of Sexuality: the care of the self*, trans. R. Hurley, London.

Fowler, D. P. (1987) 'Vergil on killing virgins', in M. Whitby, P. Hardie and M. Whitby (eds) *Homo viator: classical essays for John Bramble*, Bristol: 185–94.

—— (1990) 'Deviant Focalisation in Virgil's Aeneid', *PCPhS* 36: 42–63.

Frank, A. W. (1991) 'For a sociology of the body: an analytical review', in M. Featherstone, M. Hepworth and B. S. Turner (eds) *The Body: social process and cultural theory*, London: 36–102.

Fränkel, H. (1969) *Ovid: a poet between two worlds*, Berkeley, CA.

Gabra, G. (1984) *Untersuchungen zu den Texten über Pesyntheus, Bischof von Coptos (569–632)*, Bonn.

Gagliardi, D. (1985) *Enciclopedia Virgiliana*, 4 vols, Rome: vol. 2.

Galinsky, G. K. (1975) *Ovid's Metamorphoses: an introduction to the basic aspects*, Oxford.

Gardner, J. (1994) *Being a Roman Citizen*, London.

Garland, R. (1995) *The Eye of the Beholder: deformity and disability in the Graeco-Roman world*, London.

Garnsey, P. D. (1970) *Social Status and Legal Privilege in the Roman Empire*, Oxford.

Gatens, M. (1994) 'The Dangers of a Woman-centred Philosophy', in *The Polity Reader in Gender Studies*, Cambridge: 93–107.

Gathorne-Hardy, J. (1977) *The Public School Phenomenon*, London.

Gayet, A. (1902) *Antinoë et les sépultures de Thaïs et Sérapion*, Paris.

Gero, J. M. and Conkey, M. W. (1991) *Engendering Archaeology: women and prehistory*, Oxford.

Giddens, A. (1984) *The Constitution of Society: outline of a theory of structuration*, Cambridge.

—— (1992) *The Transformation of Intimacy: sexuality, love and eroticism in modern societies*, Cambridge.

Gilchrist, R. (1991) 'Women's archaeology? Political feminism, gender theory and historical revision', *Antiquity* 65: 495–501.

Girard, R. (1983) *The Scapegoat*, trans. Y. Freccero, Baltimore, MD.

Goffman, E. (1963) *Stigma: notes on the management of spoiled identity*, Englewood Cliffs, NJ.

Goldhill, S. (1995) *Foucault's Virginity: ancient erotic fiction and the history of sexuality*, Cambridge.

Goldwater, R. and Treves, M. (1976) *Artists on Art*, London.

Gosden, C. (1994) *Social Being and Time*, Oxford.

Gow, A. S. F. (1952) *Theocritus, edited with a translation and commentary: commentary, appendix, indices and plates*, 2nd edition, 2 vols, Cambridge: vol. 2.

Grabar, A. (1945–6) *Martyrium: recherches sur le culte des reliques et l'art chrétien antique*, 2 vols, Paris.

Graeser, A. (1978) 'The Stoic theory of meaning', in J. M. Rist (ed.) *The Stoics*, Berkeley, CA and London: 77–100.

Grey, R. (1994) *Nightmare of Ecstasy: the life and art of Edward D. Wood, Jr.*, London.

Grmek, M. D. (1989) *Diseases in the Ancient Greek World*, trans. M. and L. Mueller, Baltimore, MD.

Grodszynski, D. (1984) 'Tortures mortelles et catégories sociales. Les summa supplicia dans le droit romain aux IIIe et IVe siècles', in *Du châtiment dans la cité: supplices corporels et peine de mort dans le monde antique* (*Collections de l'école française de Rome* 79) 361–403.

Grosz, E. (1994) *Volatile Bodies: toward a corporeal feminism*, Bloomington, IN.

Hahn, C. (1991) 'Speaking without tongues: the martyr Romanus and Augustine's theory of language in illustrations of Bern Burgerbibliothek Codex 264', in R. Blumenfeld-Kosinski and T. Szell (eds) *Images of Sainthood in Mediaeval Europe*, Cornell: 161–80.

Haley, B. (1978) *The Healthy Body in Victorian Culture*, Cambridge, MA.

Hall, E. (1989) *Inventing the Barbarian: Greek self-definition through tragedy*, Oxford.

Hardie, P. (1986) *Virgil's Aeneid: cosmos and imperium*, Oxford.

Harries, J. (1992) 'Death and the dead in the late Roman West', in S. Bassett (ed.) *Death in Towns: urban responses to the dying and the dead*, Leicester: 56–67.

Harris, J. R. (1971) 'Medicine', in J. R. Harris (ed.) *The Legacy of Egypt*, 2nd edition, Oxford: 112–37.

Harris, W. V. (1994) 'Child-Exposure in the Roman Empire', *JRS* 84: 1–22.

Harrison, A. (1968) *The Laws of Athens*, 2 vols, Oxford: vol. 1.

Hartsock, N. (1990) 'Foucault on power: a theory for women?', in L. J. Nicholson (ed.) *Feminism/Postmodernism*, New York: 157–175.

Hawley, R. (forthcoming) 'The Male Body as Spectacle in Attic Drama', in L. Foxhall and J. Salmon (eds) *Making Men*, London.

Hawley, R. and Levick, B. (eds) (1995) *Women in Antiquity: new assessments*, London.

Hawthorne, N. (1859) *The Marble Farm*, New York.

Henry, M. M. (1985) *Menander's Courtesans and the Greek Comic Tradition*, Frankfurt am Main.

Heuzé, P. (1985) *L'image du corps dans l'oeuvre de Virgile*, Paris.

Hodder, I. (1991) *Reading the Past*, Cambridge.

Hogarth, D. G. (1895) *A Wandering Scholar in the Levant*, London.

—— (1910) *Accidents of an Antiquary's Life*, London.

Holden, H. A. (1885) *Xenophon's Oeconomicus*, Cambridge.

Hölscher, U. (1954) *The Excavation of Medinet Habu V: post-Ramessid remains*, Chicago.

Honour, H. (1977) *Neoclassicism*, Harmondsworth.

Hopkins, K. (1983) *Death and Renewal*, Cambridge.

Hopkins, L. (forthcoming) 'Crowning the King, Mourning his Mother: *The Jewel of Seven Stars* and *The Lady of the Shroud*', in A. Smith and W. Hughes (eds) *Bram Stoker: History, Psychoanalysis, and the Gothic*, London.

Horn, J. (1986–92) *Studien zu den Märtyrern des nördlichen Oberägypten* (*Göttinger Orientforschungen* IV:15:1–2), Wiesbaden.

Humphreys, S. C. and King, H. (1980) *Mortality and Immortality: the anthropology and archaeology of death*, London.

Hutton, P. (1981) 'The History of Mentalities: the new map of cultural history', *History and Theory* 20: 237–59.

Hyvernat, H. (1888) *Les actes des martyres d'Égypte*, Paris.

Jacobs, S.-E. (1994) 'Native American Two-Spirits', *American Anthropological Association, Anthropology Newsletter* (November): 7.

Jax, K. (1933) *Die weibliche Schönheit in der griechischen Dichtung*, Innsbruck.

Jenkyns, R. (1991) *Dignity and Decadence: Victorian art and the Classical inheritance*, London.

Johnson, M. H. (1989) 'Conceptions of agency in archaeological interpretation', *JAA* 8: 189–211.

Johnson, W. (1858) *Ionica*, London.

Jones, A. H. (1990) 'Literature and Medicine: tradition and innovation', in B. Clarke and W. Aycock (eds) *The Body and the Text: comparative essays in literature and medicine*, Texas.

Jones, C. (1993) 'Women, death and the law during the Christian persecutions', in D. Wood (ed.) *Martyrs and Martyrologies* (*Studies in Church History* 30, Oxford) 23–34.

Jones, C. P. (1987) '*Stigma*: tattooing and branding in Graeco-Roman antiquity', *JRS* 77: 139–55.

Junker, H. (1911) *Koptische Poesie des 10. Jahrhunderts*, 2 vols, Berlin: vol. 2.

Kassel, R. and Austin, C. (eds) (1991) *Poetae Comici Graeci*, ongoing series, Berlin and New York: vol. 2.

Kenney, E. J. (1967) 'Discordia Semina Rerum', *CR* 17: 51–3.

King, H. (1995) 'Self-help, self-knowledge: in search of the patient in Hippocratic gynaecology', in R. Hawley and B. Levick (eds) *Women in Antiquity: new assessments*, London: 135–48.

Kipling, R. [1899] (1982) *Stalky & Co.*, London.

Kleiner, E. D. (1992) *Roman Sculpture*, New Haven, CT.

Körte, A. (1953) *Menandri quae supersunt*, Leipzig.

Kristeva, J. (1982) *Powers of Horror: an essay on abjection*, trans. L. S. Roudiez, New York.

Kuhn, K. H. (1956) *The Letters and Sermons of Besa* (*CSCO* 157–8) Louvain.

—— (1960) *Pseudo-Shenoute on Christian Behavior* (*CSCO* 206–7) Louvain.

Kundera, M. (1991) *Immortality*, trans. P. Kussi, London.

Kus, S. (1992) 'Toward an archaeology of body and soul', in J.-C. Gardin and C. Peebles (eds) *Representations in Archaeology*, Bloomington, IN: 168–177.

Lane Fox, R. (1986) *Pagans and Christians*, Harmondsworth.

Laqueur, T. (1990) *Making Sex: body and gender from the Greeks to Freud*, Cambridge, MA.

Lash, S. (1991) 'Genealogy and the body: Foucault/Deleuze/Nietzsche', in M. Featherstone, M. Hepworth and B. S. Turner (eds) *The Body: social process and cultural theory*, London: 256–80.

Le Goff, J. (1986) 'Mentalities: a history of ambiguities', in J. Le Goff and P. Nora (eds) *Constructing the Past: essays on historical methodology*, 2nd edition, New York 1986: 166–80.

—— (1992) *History and Memory*, trans. S. Rendall and E. Claman, New York.

Lefkowitz, M. R. and Fant, M. B. (1982) *Women's Life in Greece and Rome*, London.

Leftwich, G. (1987) *Ancient Conceptions of the Body and the Canon of Polykleitos*, unpublished PhD thesis, University of Princeton.

Leigh, M. (1995) 'Wounding and Popular Rhetoric at Rome', *BICS* 40: 195–212.

Leppmann, W. (1968) *Pompeii in Fact and Fiction*, London.

Levick, B. (1990) *Claudius*, London.

Lincoln, B. (1991) *Death, War, and Sacrifice: studies in ideology and practice*, Chicago.

Llewellyn, N. (1988) 'Illustrating Ovid', in C. Martindale (ed.) *Ovid Renewed: Ovidian influences on literature and art from the middle ages to the twentieth century*, Cambridge: 151–66.

Lloyd, G. E. R. (1966) *Polarity and Analogy*, Cambridge.

—— (1979) *Magic, Reason and Experience*, Cambridge.

—— (1983) *Science, Folklore and Ideology: studies in the life sciences in ancient Greece*, Cambridge.

Long, A. A. and Sedley, D. N. (1987) *The Hellenistic Philosophers*, 2 vols, Cambridge: vol. 1.

Loraux, N. (1989) 'Therefore, Socrates is Immortal' in M. Feher, R. Naddaf and N. Tazi (eds) *Fragments for a History of the Human Body*, 3 vols, New York: vol. 2: 13–45.

McLynn, N. (1994) *Ambrose of Milan: church and court in a Christian capital*, Berkeley, CA.

McNay, L. (1992) *Foucault and Feminism*, Cambridge.

McNeill, W. H. (1979) *Plagues and Peoples*, Harmondsworth.

Marcus, M. I. (1993) 'Incorporating the body: adornment, gender, and social identity in ancient Iran', *CAJ* 3(2): 157–78.

Markus, R. A. (1988) *Saeculum: history and theology in the thought of St Augustine*, revised edition, Cambridge.

Martindale, C. (1993) *Redeeming the Text*, Cambridge.

Mascia-Lees, F. E. and Sharpe, P. (eds) (1992) *Tattoo, Torture, Mutilation and Adornment: the denaturalization of the body in culture and text*, Albany, NY.

Merleau-Ponty, M. (1962) *The Phenomenology of Perception*, trans. C. Smith, London.

Meskell, L. M. (1994a) 'Deir el Medina in Hyperreality: seeking the people of Pharaonic Egypt', *JMA* 7(2): 193–216.

—— (1994b) 'Dying Young: the experience of death at Deir el Medina', *ARC* 13(2): 35–45.

—— (1995) 'Goddesses, Gimbutas and New Age archaeology', *Antiquity* 69: 74–86.

Meyer, M and Smith, R. (1994) *Ancient Christian Magic: Coptic texts of ritual power*, San Francisco, CA.

Miller, D. and Tilley, C. (eds) (1984) *Ideology, Power and Prehistory*, Cambridge.

Miller, D., Rowlands, M. and Tilley, C. (eds) (1989) *Domination and Resistance*, London.

Miller, P. (1993) 'The blazing body: ascetic desire in Jerome's letter to Eustochium', *JECS* 1: 21–45.

Miller, R. (1962) *Champagne from my Slipper*, London.

Milligan, G. (1910) *Selections from the Greek Papyri*, Cambridge.

Mina, T. (1937) *Le martyre d'Apa Epima*, Cairo.

Minow, M. (1990) *Making all the Difference: inclusion, exclusion and American law*, Ithaca, NY.

Moi, T. (1985) *Sexual/Textual Politics*, London.

Montserrat, D. (1996a) *Sex and Society in Graeco-Roman Egypt*, London.

—— (1996b) 'Coptic Art, Personal', in *The Macmillan Dictionary of Art*, London: 34 vols: vol. 7: 829–30.

—— (1997) 'Death and Funerals in the Roman Fayum', in M. L. Bierbrier (ed.) *Portraits and Masks*, London: 33–44.

Moon, W. G. (ed) (1995) *Polykleitos, the Doryphoros and Tradition*, Madison, WI.

Moore, H. L. (1994) *A Passion for Difference*, Cambridge.

Moriarty, M. (1991) *Roland Barthes*, Cambridge.

Morris, I. (1992) *Death Rituals and Social Structure in Classical Antiquity*, Cambridge.

Most, G. (1992) 'Disiecti membra poetae: the rhetoric of dismemberment in Neronian poetry', in R. Hexter and D. Selden, (eds) *Innovations of Antiquity*, London: 391–419.

Musurillo, H. (1972) *Acts of the Christian Martyrs*, Oxford.

Nauck, A. (ed.) (1889) *Tragicorum Graecorum Fragmenta*, 2nd edition, Leipzig.

Nicholson, L. J. (ed.) *Feminism/Postmodernism*, New York.

Orlandi, T. (1991) 'Literature, Coptic,' in A. S. Atiya, *Coptic Encyclopedia*, 12 vols, New York: vol. 5: 1450–60.

Osborn, E. B. (1930) *Anthology of Sporting Verse*, London.

Ostwald, M. (1986) *From Popular Sovereignty to the Sovereignty of Law: law, society, and politics in fifth-century Athens*, Berkeley, CA.

Page, D. (1978) *The Epigrams of Rufinus*, Cambridge.

Page, D. L. (ed.) (1938) *Euripides' Medea*, Oxford.

—— (1955) *Sappho and Alcaeus: an introduction to the study of ancient Lesbian poetry*, Oxford.

Paglia, C. (1990) *Sexual Personae: art and decadence from Nefertiti to Emily Dickinson*, London and New Haven, CT.

Palmer, A.-M. (1988) *Prudentius on the Martyrs*, Oxford.

Pater, W. (1867) *The Renaissance*, London.

—— (1910) *Greek Studies*, London.

Pearsall, R. (1969) *The Worm in the Bud: the world of Victorian sexuality*, London.

Pease, A. S. (ed.) (1935) *P. Vergili Maronis Aeneidos Liber Quartus*, Cambridge, MA.

Pellegrin, P. (1986) *Aristotle's Classification of Animals*, trans. A. Preuss, Berkeley.

Perry, B. E. (1965) *Babrius and Phaedrus*, Harvard.

Pomeroy, S. B. (1994) *Xenophon, Oeconomicus: a social and historical commentary*, Oxford.

Potts, A. (1994) *Flesh and the Ideal: Winckelmann and the origins of art history*, New Haven, CT and London.

Praz, M. (1969) *On Neoclassicism*, London.

Prettejohn, E. (1996) 'Recreating Rome', in M. Liversidge and C. Edwards (eds) *Imagining Rome: British artists and Rome in the nineteenth century*, Bristol: 125–70.

Quigly, I. (1982) *The Heirs of Tom Brown*, London.

Radt, S. (ed.) (1977) *Tragicorum Graecorum Fragmenta*, 4 vols, Göttingen.

Raglan-Sullivan, E. (1986) *Jacques Lacan and the Philosophy of Psycho-analysis*, London.

Rawnsley, H. D. (1894) *Idylls and Lyrics of the Nile*, London.

Reymond, E. A. E. and Barns, J. W. B. (1974) *Four Martyrdoms from the Pierpont Morgan Coptic Codices*, Oxford.

Riccobono, S. *et al.* (1940) *Fontes Iuris Romani Antejustiniani*, 2nd edition, Florence.

Richlin, A. (ed.) (1992) *Pornography and Representation in Greece and Rome*, Oxford.

Richter, F. H. von (1922) *Catalogue of the Theodor Graf Collection of Unique Ancient Greek Portraits, 2000 Years Old*, Vienna.

Riddehough, G. (1959) 'Man into beast changes in Ovid', *Phoenix* 13: 201–9.

Ringrose, K. M. (1994) 'Living in the Shadows: eunuchs and gender in Byzantium', in G. Herdt (ed.), *Third Sex, Third Gender: beyond sexual dimorphism in culture and history*, New York: 85–109.

Rist, J. (1994) *Augustine: ancient thought baptised*, Cambridge.

Roberts, M. (1993) *Poetry and the Cult of the Martyrs*, Ann Arbor, MI.

Robins, G. (1988) 'Ancient Egyptian Sexuality', *DE* 11: 61–72.

Ross, G. (1977) 'Breathless Hush in the Close' in G. M. Fraser (ed.) *The World of the Public School*, London: 151–63.

Rousselle, A. (1988) *Porneia: on desire and the body in antiquity*, Oxford.

Rudofsky, B. (1972) *The Unfashionable Human Body*, London.

Ruskin, J. [1856] (1904) *The Works of Ruskin: Library edition*, E. T. Cook and A. Wedderburn (eds), 39 vols: London: vol. 5 (*Modern Painters* III).

Rutschowscaya, M.-H. (1990) *Coptic Fabrics*, Paris.

Rydén, L. (1985) 'The Bride-shows of the Byzantine court – History or Fiction?' *Eranos* 83: 175–91.

Sanders, C. R. (1989) *Customizing the Body: the art and culture of tattooing*, Philadelphia.

Sarde, M. (1978) *Colette: libre et entravée*, Paris.

Satapati, P. R. (1988) *Rehabilitation of the Disabled in Developing Countries*, Frankfurt.

Saunders, T. J. (1991) *Plato's Penal Code: tradition, controversy, and reform in Greek penology*, Oxford.

Saxer, V. (1980) *Morts, martyrs, réliques en Afrique chrétienne aux premiers siècles*, Paris.

Schiller, A. A. (1932) *Ten Coptic Legal Texts*, New York.

—— (1976) 'A Checklist of Coptic Documents and Letters', *BASP* 13: 99–123.

Segal, C. (1969a) 'Myth and Philosophy in the Metamorphoses: Ovid's Augustanism and the Augustan conclusion of Book XV', *AJP* 90: 257–92.

—— (1969b) *Landscape in Ovid's* Metamorphoses: *a study in the transformation of a literary symbol (Hermes Einzelschriften* 23), Wiesbaden.

—— (1977) *The Theme of the Mutilation of the Corpse*, Leiden.

—— (1994) *Singers, Heroes and Gods in the 'Odyssey'*, Ithaca, NY.

Seidler, V. J. (1989) *Rediscovering Masculinity: reason, language and sexuality*, London.

Sennett, R. (1994) *Flesh and Stone: the human body and the city in western civilization*, London.

Shanks, M. and Tilley, C. (1982) 'Ideology, symbolic power and ritual communication: a reinterpretation of Neolithic mortuary practices', in I. Hodder (ed.) *The Archaeology of Contextual Meanings*, Cambridge: 129–54.

—— (1987a) *Social Theory and Archaeology*, Cambridge.

—— (1987b) *Reconstructing Archaeology: theory and practice*, London.

Sharrock, A. R. (1996) 'Representing Metamorphosis', in J. Elsner (ed.) *Art and Text in Roman Culture*, Cambridge: 103–30.

Shaw, D. D. (1993) 'The passion of Perpetua', *PP* 139. 3–45.

Shilling, C. (1993) *The Body and Social Theory*, London.

Skulsky, H. (1981) *The Mind in Exile*, Cambridge, MA.

Smith, M. (1993) 'A Demotica Formula of Intercession for the Dead', *Enchoria* 20: 131–53.

Smith, N. J. and Smith, H. C. (1991) *Physical Disability and Handicap: a social work approach*, Melbourne.

Solodow, J. B. (1988) *The World of Ovid's* Metamorphoses, Chapel Hill, NC.

Staden, H. von (1989) *Herophilus: the art of medicine in early Alexandria*, Cambridge.

Stinton, T. C. W. (1990) *Collected Papers on Greek Tragedy*, Oxford.

Stoker, B. (1903) *The Jewel of Seven Stars*, London.

Sturrock, J. (ed.) (1979) *Structuralism and since, from Lévi Strauss to Derrida*, Oxford.

Symonds, J. A. (1883) *A Problem in Greek Ethics*, London.

Tarlow, S. A. (1992) 'Each slow dusk a drawing-down of blinds', *ARC* 11(1): 125–140.

—— (forthcoming) *Remember and Be Sad: an archaeology of bereavement and commemoration*, Oxford.

Temkin, O. (1971) *The Falling Sickness: a history of epilepsy from the Greeks to the beginning of modern neurology*, 2nd edition, Baltimore, MD.

Thomas, J. (1989) 'Technologies of the self and the constitution of the subject', *ARC* 8(1): 101–7.

—— (1993) 'The hermeneutics of megalithic space', in C. Tilley (ed.) *Interpretive Archaeology*, Oxford: 73–97.

—— (1995) 'Reconciling symbolic significance with being-in-the-world', in I. Hodder *et al.* (eds) *Interpreting Archaeology: finding meaning in the past*, London: 210–11.

Thomas, J. and Tilley, C. (1993) 'The axe and the torso: symbolic structures', in C. Tilley (ed.) *Interpretive Archaeology*, Oxford: 225–324.

Thomas, K. (1984) *Man and the Natural World*, Harmondsworth.

Till, W. C. (1936) *Koptische Heiligen- und Märtyrerlegenden*, Rome.

—— (1941) 'Ein koptisches Lied', *MDIA* 10: 129–35.

—— (1951) *Die Arzneikunde der Kopter*, Berlin.

Tilley, C. (1990) 'Foucault: towards an archaeology of archaeology', in C. Tilley (ed.) *Reading Material Culture*, London: 281–347.

Töchterle, K. (1994) *Lucius Annaeus Seneca: Oedipus*, Heidelberg.

Tod, M. N. (1946) *A Selection of Greek Historical Inscriptions to the End of the Fifth Century B.C.*, 2 vols: Oxford: vol. 2.

Treadgold, W. T. (1979) 'The Bride-shows of the Byzantine Emperors', *Byzantion* 49: 395–413.

Treggiari, S. (1991) *Roman Marriage: iusti coniuges from the time of Cicero to the time of Ulpian*, Oxford.

Tringham, R. E. (1991) 'Households with Faces: the challenge of gender in prehistoric architectural remains', in J. M. Gero and M. W. Conkey (eds) *Engendering Archaeology: women and prehistory*, Oxford: 93–131.

Trout, D. (1994) 'Re-textualising Lucretia: cultural subversion in the City of God', *JECS* 2: 53–70.

Turner, B. S. (1984) *The Body and Society: explorations in social theory*, Oxford.

—— (1991) 'Recent developments in the theory of the body', in M. Featherstone, M. Hepworth and B. S. Turner (eds) *The Body: social process and cultural theory*, London: 1–35.

Turner, F. M. (1981) *The Greek Heritage in Victorian Britain*, New Haven, CT and London.

Urbaniak-Walczak, K. (1992) *Die 'conceptio per aurem': Untersuchungen zum Marienbild in Ägypten unter besonderer Berücksichtigung der Malereien in El-Bagawat*, Altenberghe.

Van Dam, R. (1993) *Saints and their Miracles in late antique Gaul*, Princeton, NJ.

Van Minnen, P. (1995) 'The Earliest account of a Martyrdom in Coptic', *AB* 113: 13–38.

Van Eijk, T. (1972) 'Marriage and Virginity, Death and Immortality', in C. Kannengiesser (ed.) *Epektasis: Mélanges J. Daniélou*, Paris: 209–35.

Veilleux, A. (1981) *Pachomian Koinona*, 3 vols, Kalamazoo, MI: vol. 2.

Vernant, J.-P. (1982) 'From Oedipus to Periander: lameness, tyranny, incest in legend and history', *Arethusa* 15: 19–38.

—— (1989) 'Dim body, Dazzling body', in M. Feher, R. Naddaff and N. Tazi (eds) *Fragments for a History of the Human Body*, 3 vols, New York: vol. 1: 18–47.

Viaud, G. (1979) *Les pèlerinages coptes en Égypte*, Cairo.

Vivian, T. (1993) *Histories of the Monks of Upper Egypt and the Life of Onnophrius*, Kalamazoo, MI.

Voigt, E. (ed.) (1971) *Sappho et Alcaeus*, Amsterdam.

Wainwright, D. and Dunn, C. (1989) *Henry Scott Tuke 1858–1929: under canvas*, London.

Walbank, F. W. (1957) *A Historical Commentary on Polybius, Books I–VI*, 3 vols: Oxford: vol. 1.

Walters, C. C. (1989) 'Christian Paintings from Tebtunis', *JEA* 75: 191–208.

Walters, M. (1978) *The Nude Male: a new perspective*, Harmondsworth.

Ward Jouve, N. (1987) *Colette*, Brighton.

Watson, A. (1991) *Roman Law and Comparative Law*, Athens, GA.

Weeks, D. (1971) *Corvo*, London.

Welch, K. (1994) 'The Roman arena in late-Republican Italy: a new interpretation', *JRA* 7: 59–80.

Wiedemann, T. (1992) *Emperors and Gladiators*, London.

Wiles, D. (1991) *The Masks of Menander*, Cambridge.

Wilfong, T. G. (1990) 'The Archive of a Family of Money-Lenders from Jême', *BASP* 27: 169–82.

—— (forthcoming a) *Gender at Jême: women's lives in a Coptic town in early Islamic Egypt*, Ann Arbor, MI.

—— (forthcoming b) 'Constantine in Coptic: Coptic constructions of Constantine the Great and his family' in S. N. C. Lieu and D. Montserrat (eds) *Constantine: History, Historiography and Legend*, London.

—— (forthcoming c) 'Aural Sex, Queered Pairs and Ambiguous Twins: the human body and *Sexual Life in Ancient Egypt*', in T. G. Wilfong and C. E. Jones (eds) *The Human body in the Ancient Near East*, Groeningen.

Wilfong, T. G. and Jones, C. E. (forthcoming) *The Human Body in the Ancient Near East*, Groeningen.

Wimbush, V. and Valantasis, R. (eds) (1995) *Asceticism*, New York.

Winckelmann, J. J. (1755) *Thoughts on the Imitation of Greek Works of Art in Painting and Sculpture*, London.

Winkler, J. J. (1990) *The Constraints of Desire: the anthropology of sex and gender in ancient Greece*, New York.

Wood, D. (ed.) (1993) *Martyrs and Martyrologies (Studies in Church History 30)*, Oxford.

Wyke, M. (1994) 'Woman in the Mirror: the rhetoric of adornment in the Roman world', in L. Archer, S. Fischler and M. Wyke (eds) *Women in Ancient Societies: an illusion of the night*, London: 134–51.

—— (1997) 'Herculean Muscle!: the classicizing rhetoric of bodybuilding', *Arion* 4(3).

Yates, T. (1990) 'Frameworks for an archaeology of the body', in C. Tilley (ed.) *Interpretive Archaeology*, Oxford: 31–72.

Yates, T. and Nordbladh, J. (1990) 'This perfect body, this virgin text: between sex and gender in archaeology' in I. Bapty and T. Yates (eds) *Archaeology after Structuralism*, London: 222–37.

Young, D. W. (1993) *Coptic Manuscripts from the White Monastery: Works of Shenute*, Vienna.

Zimmer, T. (1993) 'Momies Dorées: materiaux pour servir à l'établissement d'un corpus', *AAASH* 34: 1–38.

GENERAL INDEX

INDEX OF ANCIENT
SOURCES CITED OR
DISCUSSED

Note Abbreviations of the works of ancient authors in the text and footnotes generally follow those used in *A Greek–English Lexicon*, ed. H. G. Liddell and R. Scott (9th edition, revised by H. S. Jones, Oxford 1940) and *The Oxford Latin Dictionary*, ed. P. G. W. Glare (Oxford 1982). References to Greek papyri follow the abbreviations of J. F. Oates *et al.* in *Checklist of Editions of Greek and Latin Papyri, Ostraca and Tablets* (4th edition, Atlanta, 1992), and to Coptic papyri the abbreviations of A. A. Schiller (1976) 'A Checklist of Coptic Documents and Letters', *BASP* 13: 99–123.

231